DATE			

THE DIFFUSION OF PROCESS INNOVATIONS

THE DIFFUSION OF PROCESS INNOVATIONS

STEPHEN DAVIES

Lecturer in Economics, University of Sheffield

CAMBRIDGE UNIVERSITY PRESS

CAMBRIDGE

LONDON · NEW YORK · MELBOURNE

Published by the Syndics of the Cambridge University Press
The Pitt Building, Trumpington Street, Cambridge CB2 1RP
Bentley House, 200 Euston Road, London NW1 2DB
32 East 57th Street, New York, NY 10022, USA
296 Beaconsfield Parade, Middle Park, Melbourne 3206, Australia

First published 1979

Photoset and printed in Malta
by Interprint Limited

Library of Congress Cataloguing in Publication Data
Davies, Stephen, 1948–
The diffusion of process innovations.
A revision of the author's thesis, University
of Warwick, 1976.
Bibliography: p.
Includes index
1. Technological innovations. 2. Diffusion of innovations.
3. Technological innovations – Great Britain. 4. Diffusion
of innovations – Great Britain. I. Title.
HC79. T4 D38 1979 301.24′3   78–15143
ISBN 0 521 22193 5

Contents

List of tables

List of figures

To C, F and C and AFC

Preface

This monograph is presented as a contribution to the study of the Economics of Technical Change; more specifically, it investigates the forces influencing the diffusion, or spread, of new production processes within industry. It is a somewhat modified and shortened version of my Ph.D. thesis, presented to the University of Warwick in 1976.

Whilst working on that thesis, I received help and encouragement from very many people and to all of them I offer sincere thanks. My main debt of gratitude must be to my supervisor at Warwick, Graham Pyatt: his guidance and support were of incalculable value to me and are very much appreciated. More generally, I thank the Department of Economics at Warwick, as a whole, for providing me with such a stimulating environment in which to conduct my research – at various times I have benefited from advice and helpful discussions with P. Stoneman, K. Cowling, J. R. Sargent, F. el Sheikh and many others.

The onerous task of data collection has been eased substantially by the kind co-operation of a number of people but, in particular, G. D. N. Worswick, the Director of the National Institute of Economic and Social Research, who generously made available to me large quantities of the Institute's data on the diffusion of various innovations. Moreover, it is to Mr Worswick and G. F. Ray at the Institute that I owe thanks for first stimulating my interest in this subject.

The other acknowledgements I would like to make are to the S.S.R.C. for funding my research at Warwick; to my examiners at Warwick; to members of the Economics Department at Sheffield, for advice on how best to revise and shorten the presentation of the thesis into its present form, and to the Knoop Research Fund for financial help with the costs involved in that revision.

To my wife, I offer special thanks for her moral support, patience and encouragement throughout the duration of my research. Without her help there is no doubt that my dissertation and this monograph would not have been written.

Needless to say, all opinions, interpretations and errors are my responsibility alone.

Definitions and notation

Some of the more important definitions and notations used in chapters 4–8:

Symbol	Definition	Page of first mention
ER_{it}	Firm i's expectation of the payoff period associated with adoption at time t (inversely related to the profitability of adoption).	67
R^*_{it}	A yardstick or target pay-off which i views as the maximum period if adoption is to be acceptable at t. (Thus low values indicate stringent yardsticks, perhaps reflecting a view that the innovation is risky.)	68
S_{it}	The size of firm i at time t (measured, perhaps, by output or size of work force employed).	68
β	$= \beta(2) - \beta(1)$. A scale parameter reflecting the net influence of firm size on R^*/ER_{it}. $\beta > 0$ would indicate that large firm size tends to increase the chances of ownership (i.e. having adopted) at t.	72
ϵ_{it}	$= \epsilon_{2it}/\epsilon_{1it}$. An error term reflecting all the non-size-related influences (X_{ijt} where $j = 1, \ldots, r$ and Y_{ijt} where $j = 1, \ldots, u$) on i's expectations and yardstick at t. Assumed to be log-normally distributed across i at t with geometric mean of 1 and variance σ_t^2, i.e. $\log \epsilon_t \sim N(0, \sigma_t^2)$ Thus σ_t^2 reflects the variance across potential adopters in the actual profitability of adoption, the quality of information possessed concerning the innovation, and in the target rates used to assess adoption.	72
θ_t	$= \theta_{2t}/\theta_{1t}$. Some function of time representing those factors, common to	72

all firms, which change over time and lead to revisions in the expectations of the pay-off from adoption and in the targets used to assess adoption. For all innovations, it is hypothesized that θ_t will, typically, increase over time as expectations become more favourable and the targets required less stringent. However, the functional form of θ_t is assumed to be different between group A and group B innovations. Moreover, where ER and R^* vary over the business cycle, θ_t will also include a cyclical component.

group A	An innovation which is relatively cheap to install and technologically simple. Learning by manufacturers may be initially substantial in this case, but fairly short lived.	50
group B	An innovation which requires a large initial outlay by the adopter, and which is technologically complex usually implying a lengthy installation period. Learning is assumed to be more sustained in this case.	50
α	Initial value of θ_t (at $t = 0$ for group B, at $t = 1$ for group A).	77
ψ	The growth parameter in θ_t reflecting the strength of the learning effect, improvements in information and competitive pressures on non-adopters.	77
Ω	The cyclical parameter in θ_t. For instance $\Omega > 0$ would indicate that adoption tends to be more profitable in times of boom.	85
S_{cit}	Critical size of firm i at time $t = (\theta_t \epsilon_{it})^{-1/\beta}$	72
$-(\log\theta_t)/\beta$	Logarithm of geometric mean critical size.	74
$(\sigma_t/\beta)^2$	Variance of log critical firm size. Also referred to as reflecting 'inter-firm differences' and a constituent of aggregate diffusion speed. Other things being equal, inversely related to diffusion speed.	74
P_{it}	The probability that firm i will have adopted by time t, given that the firm is of size S_t	73

See also pages 74–5 for the notation employed when referring to lognormal and normal distributions.

1

Introduction

1.1 *Introductory remarks*

Technological change in the industrial context is often conceived of by economists as comprizing three more or less distinct stages. The process is set in motion by an *invention* (or inventions), which may be based on new scientific knowledge or which, more commonly, uses well known scientific principles. The *innovation* stage occurs when, and if, the invention is first commercially introduced by a firm, often called the innovator.[1] Then, as the new process or product is recognized as superior to competing existing technologies, this results in its further application within the innovating firm and its introduction by other firms in the industry: that is, *imitation* or *diffusion* of the innovation occurs.

Whilst this three way distinction can sometimes be misleading (it is not always possible, for instance, to ascertain where one stage ends and the next starts), it does provide a conceptually useful framework in which the present and previous studies in the economics of technical progress can operate. Here, the main concern is to provide a theoretical and empirical analysis of the diffusion of new industrial processes and only rarely will that analysis touch on matters such as the sources and determinants of invention and innovation.[2] However, even this fairly narrowly defined subject area should be of some interest to policy makers and theorists concerned mainly with other, perhaps more mainstream, areas of economics.

For instance, considering now only new processes,[3] it can be seen that whilst inventive and innovative activity may influence the 'best practice' productivity levels within an economy, diffusion is necessary if these are to be translated into actual achieved productivity levels. With this in mind, it is interesting to note that the duration of the diffusion stage is often fairly lengthy, and appears to vary widely between innovations and industries. For instance, from his pioneering study of the diffusion of twelve major innovations amongst the larger firms in four U.S. industries, Edwin Mansfield (1961) notes that 'it took about fifteen years for half of the major pig-iron producers to use the by-product coke oven, but only about three years for half of the major coal producers to use the continuous mining machine. The number of years elapsing before half the firms had introduced an innovation varied from 0.9 to fifteen, the average being 7.8.' A similar picture emerges for the twenty-two innovations to be considered in the present U.K. study: for four of the innovations, 50% diffusion was attained in seven or fewer years but for seven others, over half of all potential adopters had still not adopted fourteen years after the first appearance of the new innovation. Now if these figures are at all representative, differences in the speed at which new processes are diffused may go a long way to explaining inter-industry differences in productivity and performance and, in a wider context, the 'technology gap' which is often said to exist between the U.K. and the U.S. (and perhaps other developed countries). It is possible, for instance, that an industry or country with an impressive inventive and innovative record may still only attain a lowly place in the 'productivity league table' if its performance in diffusing innovations is relatively sluggish.[4]

In the same vein, an understanding of the mechanics of diffusion is potentially relevant to the study of industrial economics and, in particular, to the long-running debate concerning the implications for technical progressiveness of high concentration and large firm size. In this connection it must be important to ascertain whether the competitive structure of adopting industries has any influence on the speed with which they adopt new processes and whether, within industries, there is evidence to suggest that larger firms are quicker or slower in adopting than are small firms. Unfortunately, as is apparent from reading any of the standard survey articles on the economics of technical progress, very little attention has been paid in the past to the theoretical and empirical relationship between concentration and speed of diffusion.[5] Whatever the reasons are for this neglect, it is in stark contrast to the relative glut of research in recent years concerning concentration, innovation and invention.

Another dimension of diffusion which merits some investigation concerns its close connection with investment behaviour. In general, for diffusion to take place, the adopting firms must make certain capital outlays (and, if the evidence of chapter 3 in the present study is at all representative, these outlays often run into thousands or sometimes millions of pounds). More generally, Stoneman (1978) has recently shown that the introduction of new processes and products typically forms a quantitatively important motive for new investment. He goes on to argue, convincingly, that information concerning the typical time pattern of diffusion, and the influences to which it is subject, may help to provide a far richer theoretical and empirical explanation of aggregate investment behaviour than has been possible to date.

Turning to the supply side of the diffusion phenomenon, it is apparent in most cases that what constitutes, for the adopting industry, a new process innovation is for another, capital goods, industry a new product innovation. Within the sample of innovations to be considered below, the capital goods industries can nearly always be identified as having played a far from passive role in each of the invention, innovation and diffusion stages. As such, a study of diffusion might usefully draw on (and, in turn, have implications for) the existing literatures on the marketing of new industrial products, learning by doing by the manufacturers of new industrial products and, less obviously, the spread of new consumer durables.

Finally, and on a more overtly academic level, much of the interest value of diffusion derives from the fact that it concerns a state of affairs which lies outside the scope of much standard text book economic theory. By definition, any attempt to model the diffusion process must constitute an analysis of an industry or economy in the throes of change. More specifically, diffusion can be seen to be the transition from one potential state of equilibrium (in which all firms employ the 'old technology' machinery) to another (in which all output is produced using the 'new process'). Thus one is concerned with an industry or economy in a state of disequilibrium and the determinants and specification of the transition path must form the centre of the analysis.

In addition, so long as diffusion is non-instantaneous, it follows that firms are reacting differently to basically the same stimulus. (If different firms were all to adopt simultaneously, there would be no non-trivial diffusion period of course.) In consequence, much of the conventional theoretical framework of micro economics is somewhat irrelevant, being based on an analysis of the behaviour of the 'representative firm'. For instance, in order to explain the differences which appear between industries in the speed with which they diffuse innovations, the analysis must be concerned with, as much as anything, explaining differences between industries in the variability of behaviour of the firms within those industries. Any model which rules out, or has nothing to say on, heterogeneity *within* an industry can at best offer only a partial explanation.

1.2 Main objectives

The methodology of the present study is straightforward and reflects three broad objectives.

As a first step, data was collected on the diffusion of twenty-two process innovations, diffusing in various U.K. industries since the war. For some of these innovations the data was already available in published form in various case studies by previous researchers.

This data, much of which is of a fairly technological nature, provides the raw materials for the later empirical chapters of the monograph and is used in support of various technological assumptions required in the middle theoretical chapter. In addition, however, the collection of this data was viewed as an end in its own right. To date, with only two known exceptions (Mansfield's study mentioned above and Nabseth and Ray's (1974) international study of eight innovations) empirical research on diffusion has concentrated on case studies of individual innovations. This means that, particularly for the U.K. (but also other countries), surprisingly little is known concerning such questions as the *typical* duration of the diffusion period and whether or not most new processes share any common characteristics which may have consequences for the time pattern of diffusion. By basing the present study on such a relatively large number of innovations, it is hoped to provide more general information than has so far been available.

A second major objective was to provide a theoretical model of diffusion employing quite explicit assumptions concerning the technological nature of new innovations and based on specific hypotheses concerning the nature of the adoption decision at the individual firm level. Predictions were required of this model at both a very micro level, i.e. why, within industries, some firms adopt a given innovation more quickly than other firms, and at a more aggregate level, i.e. concerning the shape of the diffusion growth curve and why some industries adopt innovations quicker than other industiries. Each of these issues has been addressed *separately* by previous models but, as far as is known, the present model is the first to provide predictions at both the firm and industry level.

In more general terms, this model therefore attempts to meet the often voiced (and probably justified) criticism that the development of theory in industrial economics too frequently concentrates on the behaviour of firms in aggregate, with little attention being given to the micro-foundations of the theory. In other words, it is intended that the model faces, head on, the aggregation problem which must nearly always exist in industrial economics.

Finally, and turning now to the specific empirical objectives of the monograph, three broad themes will recur frequently in the later chapters. First, what is the nature of the relationship, if any, between industry structure and the speed of diffusion? This, in turn, can be decomposed into two related questions: are concentrated industries more or less prone to diffuse innovations quickly, and, within industries, are larger firms quicker or slower than small firms in adopting? As stated above, similar questions have featured in past empirical work on invention and innovation and the potential implications for government competition policy may be important.

Second, does the economic environment in which the adopting industries find themselves influence the speed with which they adopt new innovations? For example, does an environment of sustained growth impair or aid the adoption of new techniques and does the business cycle have an important role to play in the diffusion process? In this case, of course, potential policy implications concern demand management.

Third, how does the exact nature of the innovation itself affect its diffusion? For example, are there significant differences between the diffusion of major, as opposed to minor, innovations? Similarly, can Mansfield's findings, for the U.S., that more profitable innovations tend to diffuse more quickly, be confirmed for the U.K.?

In some ways, these empirical objectives are limited, leaving a number of the questions suggested in the introduction unanswered. On the other hand, it is hoped that some of the answers generated may provide at least an aid to further research in this field concerning, for instance, explanations of international differences in the speed of diffusion.

1.3 A brief outline

Chapter 2, a discussion of past research in this field, fulfils two main functions. First, and in the absence of any comprehensive surveys in the existing literature, it provides an extended summary of what is already known about the diffusion of industrial processes. It brings together the analysis and results of a number of case studies with those of Mansfield's more general study of diffusion in the U.S. In addition, it points to those areas where there are gaps in our knowledge or where further tests are required, and thus to which the present study is directed. Second, it attempts a critical assessment of the various alternative theoretical models (fully developed or in embryonic form) which might provide a suitable framework for the present study.

Chapter 3 introduces the innovations included in the sample which is to be used throughout this study. It should be mentioned at the outset that the major criterion for the inclusion of innovations in the sample is that suitable and reliable data be available on their diffusion. Thus the sample is certainly not random, but, as will be seen, it is fairly broad based. This chapter enables the technical assumptions of previous models in this field to be evaluated and also provides a useful basis for the development of the model used in the present study.

Chapter 4 constitutes the theoretical core of this work. Using a simple model of decision making under uncertainty and incorporating the findings of the previous chapter, it develops a model of diffusion which may be seen to be an extension of previous probit models used to analyse the diffusion of new consumer durables.

The following three chapters are concerned with testing the predictions of the model against data collected on the diffusion of the sample innovations. Chapter 5 tests those predictions concerning the shape of the diffusion growth curve (which shows the growth in the proportion of firms having adopted any new innovation). Chapter 6 tests those predictions concerning firm size and inter-firm differences in the speed of adoption of innovations. Chapter 7 uses the estimates of the previous two chapters to examine the causes of inter-industry and inter-innovation differences in the speed of diffusion.

Chapter 8 examines in some detail the results obtained which are of direct relevance to the debate concerning large scale, concentration and progressiveness. Chapter 9 provides a more general discussion of the policy implications of the various empirical findings, a non mathematical summary of the study and attempts a brief overall assessment of its successes and limitations.

An appendix at the end of the monograph describes the sources and definitions used to construct the data employed.

1.4 A point of definition

So far, the term 'diffusion' has been employed fairly loosely and without precise definition. Since the term is not totally unambiguous, this introduction may be usefully concluded with a short definitional note.

Mansfield, whose contributions have dominated this area of research, conceives of a three way definition: *imitation* or *inter-firm diffusion* refers to the spread of the new process from firm to firm within any industry; *intra-firm* diffusion to the spread of the process within individual firms and *overall diffusion* to the spread throughout the industry as a whole. Thus inter-firm diffusion might be measured by the proportion of firms in an industry that have adopted, intra-firm diffusion by the proportion of any one firm's output produced using the new process and overall diffusion by the proportion of the total industry output that is produced using the new process.

Nearly always in the present study, the analysis will be directed towards inter-firm diffusion; indeed, except where otherwise stated, *the term diffusion should be interpreted henceforward as referring to inter-firm diffusion.* In other words, intra-firm diffusion is largely ignored. This can be justified on three grounds. First, in some cases intra-firm diffusion is trivial: if firms are to adopt at all, they must produce 100% of their output using the new process. This is true for many of the lumpier innovations and, in these cases, inter-firm diffusion is equivalent to overall diffusion (after allowing for differences in size between firms). Second, most of the interesting theoretical questions in this area concern the initial decision of whether or not a firm should adopt the innovation. Later decisions, where applicable, to purchase further units of the process require a quite separate analysis which can be based, perhaps, on more conventional and well-tried theories of investment. Third, comprehensive data on the increasing application of the sample processes *within* individual firms (i.e. on intra-firm diffusion) has proved almost impossible to collect. Even if willing to provide such information in principle, most firms appear not to possess it in sufficient detail.

2

A survey of past research on diffusion

2.1 Introduction

Rather surprisingly, no comprehensive survey of previous research findings exists in this area. The present chapter attempts to fill this gap and points to the main areas where more research is required and to which the present study is therefore addressed. Within the study as a whole, it serves two main purposes: first, it summarizes what we already know about the diffusion of new industrial processes and indicates those policy questions on which relevant empirical results are absent; second, it serves as a starting point in the search for a theoretical framework with which to analyse the diffusion of the innovations in the present sample.

Basically, the chapter falls into two parts. Sections 2 to 5 survey what might be termed the *mainstream literature*, the main aim of which has been to analyse various aspects of diffusion performance using cross-section data. This literature incorporates three different approaches. Most well-known is the *inter-industry/innovation approach*, pioneered by Mansfield and Griliches: this amounts to studying the diffusion of one or more innovations in a number of industries and attempting to explain, empirically, the variance of the speed of diffusion in terms of differences in the attributes of the industries and innovations concerned.

Alternatively, *the inter-firm approach*, also pioneered by Mansfield, concentrates on individual innovations diffusing in single industries and attempts to explain differences between firms in the time taken to adopt. In this case, firm-level characteristics are the explanatory variables. Third, the *international approach* attempts to explain international differences in the speed of diffusion of innovations in terms of the characteristics of the countries and industries concerned.

Section 2 acts as something of a preface to this discussion. A theoretical basis for much past research has been the assertion that the diffusion of new process innovations is analogous to the spread of infectious diseases. Therefore, as a backcloth to sections 3 to 5, section 2 provides a brief exposition of the most common mathematical model of epidemics, leading on to a discussion of the logistic curve which has been used so extensively in this area.

Whilst this mainstream literature has provided a number of significant empirical findings, the heavy reliance placed on the epidemic analogy has perhaps limited the development of economic theory in this context. Consequently, many of the more interesting theoretical questions, such as the nature of the adoption decision by the individual firm, and the influence of market structure, remain unanswered. Therefore in the second part of the chapter the search for a suitable theoretical framework is widened to include past research carried out in a number of related areas. In section 6, the modification of existing stock-adjustment models of investment is discussed. Similarly, in section 7, the possibilities of extending Salter's vintage model to this area are considered. In section 8, David's analysis of the causes of the slow adoption of mechanical reapers in the nineteenth century is introduced as a further possible basis for development. Finally the past application of probit analysis to the diffusion of *new consumer durables* is discussed in section 9.

2.2 A mathematical theory of epidemics and the logistic curve

The study of diffusion is not peculiar to economics amongst the social sciences. For instance, the spread of rumours, the use of new drugs, new teaching methods, and steel axes by aboriginal tribes have all been the subject of research by sociologists, medical sociologists, educationalists and anthropologists respectively (see Rogers, 1962). A common feature of much of this research is the analogy drawn to the spread of diseases. Consequently, a theoretical tool often used is one of the mathematical theories of epidemics. As reference to these theories is also often made by economists working in this area, an exposition of the simplest model of epidemics will provide a useful introduction to the discussion of this chapter.

The basic hypothesis of the simple epidemic model[1] is represented by the following equation:

$$m_{t+1} - m_t = \beta (n - m_t) m_t /n, \quad \beta > 0 \tag{2.1}$$

where m_t is the number of individuals, in a fixed population of n, having contracted an infectious disease at time t. Thus, the number of individuals contracting the disease between times t and $t + 1$ is proportionate to the product of the number of uninfected individuals and the proportion of the population already infected, both at time t. The magnitude of β will depend on a number of factors, such as the infectiousness of the disease and the frequency of social intercourse.

This is rationalized by assuming that each uninfected individual has a constant and equal propensity to catch the disease (as reflected by β) from contact with an infected individual, and that the number of such contacts will be determined by the proportion of the population who are already infected (assuming homogeneous mixing). If the period t to $t + 1$ is very small, (2.1) may be alternatively stated as:

$$\frac{dm_t}{dt} \frac{1}{(n - m_t)} = \beta \frac{m_t}{n} \tag{2.2}$$

This differential equation has the following solution:

$$m_t/n = \{1 + \exp(-\alpha - \beta t)\}^{-1} \tag{2.3}$$

where α is a constant of integration.

This is the equation of the well known logistic time curve. As can be seen from figure 2.1, it predicts that the proportion of the population having contracted the disease will increase at an accelerating rate until 50% infection is attained at time $t = -(\alpha/\beta)$. Thereafter infection increases at a decelerating rate and 100% infection is approached asymptotically.[2] Thus this symmetrical S shaped curve has a point of inflexion (indicating a maximum value for the rate of increase in infection) at the midpoint, 50% infection.

Of course, if m_t is alternatively defined as the number of individuals having adopted a new fashion or having heard a piece of gossip, equations (2.1) and (2.2) could be used to predict bandwagons in fashion and in gossip

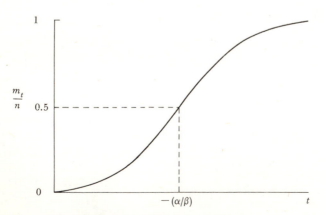

Figure 2.1   The logistic epidemic curve

dissemination. Equally, if m_t is defined as the number of firms having adopted a new technique an S shaped diffusion curve can be justified on grounds on imitative behaviour and bandwagons.

Whilst this above model is only one of an array of mathematical models of epidemics, perhaps because of its simplicity, it is by far the most commonly used in diffusion studies in the social sciences. Certainly, empirical tests are fairly straightforward using regression analysis on the linear transformation:

$$\log\{m_t/(n - m_t)\} = \alpha + \beta t \qquad (2.4)$$

The parameter β is often defined as *the speed of diffusion* and whilst this may be a little misleading,[3] it does reflect the pace of the diffusion process very neatly. For instance, suppose the speed of diffusion were measured by the time elapsing between two given levels, (m_1/n) and (m_2/n), where $1 > (m_2/n) > (m_1/n) > 0$. If (m_1/n) is attained at t_1 and (m_2/n) at time t_2, the time lapse can be derived from (2.4) as:

$$t_2 - t_1 = \left\{ \frac{\log\left[m_2/(n - m_2)\right] - \alpha}{\beta} \right\} - \left\{ \frac{\log\left[m_1/(n - m_1)\right] - \alpha}{\beta} \right\}$$

$$= \beta^{-1} \log\{m_2(n - m_1)/m_1(n - m_2)\}$$

Thus this inverse measure of diffusion speed is determined only by β and diffusion is obviously more rapid, the larger is β. As an example, suppose the two yardstick levels are taken to be 20% and 80%, the time lapse is then $\beta^{-1} \log 16$, which equals 6.9 for $\beta = 0.4$ or 13.8 for $\beta = 0.2$.

This property is very convenient for cross-section analysis of differences between the speed of diffusion of different diseases/rumours/innovations since the analysis can be directed towards a simple explanation of the determinants of β.

Unfortunately, this analytical convenience of the model has often led to its indiscriminate use, with little attention being paid to the rather stringent assumptions upon which it is based. An examination of just two of these assumptions will indicate how fragile the logistic solution is.

First, *the infectiousness of the disease must remain constant over time* for all individuals. In other words, β must be constant. Consider the consequences, however, of increasing resistance on the part of the uninfected or a reduction in the contagiousness of the disease. That is, suppose that β falls over time. To derive the point of inflexion of the growth curve, (2.2) can be differentiated and equated to zero assuming $d\beta/dt < 0$ for all t. Rearranging, it can be shown that the point of inflexion occurs when:

$$m_t/n = 0.5 + 0.5\,(d\beta/dt\,)/\beta^2 \qquad\qquad (2.5)$$

This suggests a *positively skewed* growth curve, i.e. one in which the point of inflexion occurs prior to the date at which 50% of the population is infected (as in figure 2.2).

Second, *all individuals must have an equal chance of catching the disease*. In other words, β is the same for all groups within the population. (A necessary but insufficient condition for this and the first assumption is the existence of a homogeneously mixing population.) Consider the most simple relaxation of this assumption: suppose there are two groups, 1 and 2, in the population. At time t, m_{1t} of the n_1 members of the first group and m_{2t} of the n_2 in the second group are infected. Let group 1 be less susceptible to the disease than group 2, i.e. $\beta_1 < \beta_2$. Replacing (2.2) by:

$$\frac{dm_i}{dt} = (n_1 - m_{1t})\,(m_t/n)\,\beta_1 + (n_2 - m_{2t})\,(m_t/n)\beta_2, \qquad (2.6)$$

and differentiating, setting the result equal to zero and re-arranging, this generates a point of inflexion at:

$$m_t/n = (2 + X)^{-1} \qquad\qquad (2.7)$$

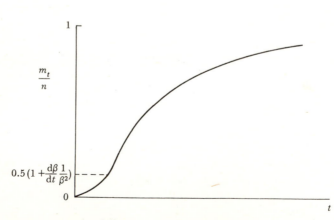

Figure 2.2   The diffusion curve for declining β

where $X = \dfrac{(n_1 - m_{1t})(n_2 - m_{2t})(\beta_1 - \beta_2)^2}{\left\{\beta_1(n_1 - m_{1t}) + \beta_2(n_2 - m_{2t})\right\}^2}$

Since $X > 0$ for all $\beta_1 \neq \beta_2$, this again implies a point of inflexion at $m_t/n < 0.5$ and thus a positively skewed S shape.

There are a number of other assumptions which may also prove to be unrealistic but which are strictly necessary for the logistic solution to obtain; for instance, a constant population is required and the possibility of cures and reinfection is ruled out. It might also be mentioned that relaxation of these assumptions does not necessarily lead to a *positively* skewed S shape: for example, if β were to increase over time, a negatively skewed curve would obtain in which 50% infection occurs prior to the point of inflexion.

2.3 The inter-industry/innovation approach

2.3.1 The theory

The above discussion relates primarily, but not exclusively, to the research considered under this heading. This approach, which has dominated the literature to date, relies on a fairly standard empirical methodology. Typically, in a first stage, the logistic curve is fitted to diffusion data on a number of different innovations in various industries and then, in a second stage, the estimated slope parameters, $\hat{\beta}$, are used as the dependent variable, in a cross-section analysis, to be explained in terms of the characteristics of the industries and innovations concerned.

By far the best known example of this approach is Mansfield's seminal paper (1961). His contribution merits a fairly lengthy discussion, partly because it constitutes the conventional wisdom in this field, but also because the use of the epidemic model is by no means obvious at first sight.

Using subscripts i and j for the ith innovation diffusing in the jth industry, the core of the model is contained in the following hypothesized relationship:

$$\lambda_{ijt} = f_i\left(\frac{m_{ijt}}{n_{ij}}, \pi_{ij}, S_{ij}\right) \tag{2.8}$$

where $\lambda_{ijt} = \dfrac{m_{ij(t+1)} - m_{ijt}}{n_{ij} - m_{ijt}}$ (2.9) and m_{ijt} is the number of firms having adopted the innovation by time t and n_{ij} is the total number of firms in the industry.

Thus equation (2.8) postulates that the proportion of 'hold-outs' (i.e. non-adopters) at time t that adopt by time $t + 1$ is some general function of: (i) the profitability of installing this innovation relative to that of alternative investments (π_{ij}), (ii) the size of the investment outlay required to install the innovation as a proportion of the average total assets of firms in the industry (S_{ij}), and (iii) the proportion of firms already having adopted by time t, m_{ijt}/n_{ij}. He argues that λ_{ijt} should be larger the higher is π_{ij} because the latter increases 'the chance that a firm's estimate of the profitability will be high enough to compensate for whatever risks are involved'. λ_{ijt} should be inversely related to S_{ij} as S_{ij} will indicate the extent of caution and financing problems associated with potential adoption. Third, and most important, the larger the proportion of firms that have already adopted, the greater are the probable competitive pressures on non-adopters and the more likely they are to accept that the innovation is highly profitable and relatively risk free. Therefore, λ_{ijt} should be higher, the larger is m_{ijt}/n_{ij}. (It should be noted, in passing, that this model, in common with most research on diffusion, attempts no explanation of the date of the initial introduction of the innovation into the industry by the first adopter. It might also be noted that 'diffusion' here is used in the sense of *inter-firm* diffusion.[4])

The model is developed by reducing the general function f to a quite specific form. This transformation is achieved, however, strictly on the basis of algebraic manipulations and assumptions: no further economic assumptions are used. More specifically, f is approximated by a Taylor's expansion which omits all third and higher order terms, the coefficient of $(m_{ijt}/n_{ij})^2$ in the expansion is set equal to zero because λ_{ijt} is not highly correlated with $(m_{ijt}/n_{ij})^2$ for the innovations in his sample, and the period t to $t + 1$ is assumed to be very short. This enables (2.8) to be written as:

$$\frac{dm_{ijt}}{dt} \frac{1}{(n_{ij} - m_{ijt})} = A_{ij} + \beta_{ij} \frac{m_{ijt}}{n_{ij}} \tag{2.10}$$

where

$$\beta_{ij} = a_{i1} + a_{i2}\,\pi_{ij} + a_{i3}\,S_{ij} \tag{2.11}$$

and A_{ij} is the sum of all remaining terms from the expansion which do not contain (m_{ijt}/n_{ij}).

Finally, by imposing the limit condition that 'as we go backward in time,

the number of firms having introduced the innovation must tend to zero',
that is:

$$\lim_{t \to -\infty} m_{ijt} = 0$$

the differential equation (2.10) has the familiar logistic solution:

$$m_{ijt}/n_j = \{1 + \exp(-\alpha_{ij} - \beta_{ij} t)\}^{-1} \qquad (2.12)$$

where α_{ij} is the constant of integration. The limit condition has, of course,
constrained A_{ij} to be equal to zero.[5]

Given the use of this limit condition, the differential equation (2.10) co-
incides exactly with that of the basic epidemic model outlined in the previous section (2.2) and the logistic solution should therefore come as no
surprise. Indeed, equation (2.8) and the ensuing mathematics seem to be
largely superfluous. One wonders why the model was not stated in the form
(2.10) immediately. Certainly none of the economic argument would be
lost by using (2.10) as a starting point and the strong assumptions involved
in suppressing all second order terms from (2.8) would be avoided.

To all intents then, this model is merely an (ingenious) application of the
simple epidemic model: 'uninfected' firms (non-adopters) are more likely
to 'catch the disease' (adopt), the more of their competitors that are already
infected (having adopted); the 'infectiousness' of the innovation is determined by its financial characteristics (profitability and cost).

Whilst this analogy is not without intuitive plausibility, it is rather limit-
ing. On the theoretical level, it is a little unsatisfactory that any model of
diffusion of new innovations should be virtually silent on one of the most
interesting aspects of the problem: decision making under uncertainty by
the individual firm. As a result the model is unable to explain one of the
important policy questions: why some firms adopt certain innovations
more quickly than other firms. This is inevitable, of course, since the model
deals only with the behaviour of firms in aggregate.

Furthermore, the implicit assumption of fixed β_{ij} limits the applicability
of the model in the real world. As argued in the previous section, the logistic
solution of (2.10) requires that β_{ij} be constant over time and that the population be homogeneous in the sense that no group(s) of firms within the
population is more or less likely to adopt the innovation at any point in
time. The consequences of either assumption being violated have already
been discussed above – basically, a symmetrical S shaped logistic diffusion
curve cannot occur in these circumstances. In the present context, it may
be noted that the implications of these assumptions are that the profitability

and cost of the innovation must remain constant over time and that they must be the same for all firms within the industry. This must follow, given the definition of β_{ij} in (2.11). Neither assumption seems to be particularly reasonable, as will be confirmed in the following chapter.

The other main proponents of this approach can be considered in less detail. Griliches (1957) also uses the logistic to describe the diffusion curve; he postulates, too, that the parameters of the curve will be determined by certain characteristics of the innovations and firms concerned. However, his choice of the logistic is not based on any underlying model or conviction: 'while there are some good reasons why an adjustment process should follow a path which is akin to a logistic, I do not want to argue the relative merits of the various S shapes'. Thus, his interest in the curve is only as a tool with which to generate parameters of diffusion which are explained in a second empirical stage.

In subsequent years a number of economists have also fitted logistic diffusion curves, justifying their choice either with direct reference to Mansfield's model or with a few passing remarks about epidemics or bandwagons (for instance, Romeo (1975), (1977), Globerman (1975), Swan (1973)). One notable exception (the only known British study) is Metcalfe (1970). Whilst he still relies on the epidemic analogy, he considers that the assumptions needed to justify the logistic are unlikely to be fulfilled in the case of the diffusion of new industrial processes. Consequently, his choice of growth curve is the logarithmic reciprocal:

$$m_{ijt}/n_{ij} = \exp(-\beta_{ij}/t) \tag{2.13}$$

This is positively skewed with a point of inflexion at $(m_{ijt}/n_{ij}) = e^{-2}$. However, this curve is rather arbitrary, being employed simply because of its skewness. Whilst good reasons have already been given for a positively skewed growth curve, there is no reason why the degree of skewness should always be the same. But the logarithmic reciprocal implies this and is just as inflexible, in its own way, as is the logistic.

2.3.2 The main empirical findings

In spite of the preceding criticisms, this approach does generate impressive results. Mansfield tests the logistic curve using weighted least squares on the transformation:

$$\log\{m_{ijt}/(n_{ij} - m_{ijt})\} = \alpha_{ij} + \beta_{ij}t \tag{2.14}$$

Using data on the diffusion of 12 innovations in the American iron and steel, coal, rail and brewing industries, he reports the coefficient of correlation between the dependent variable and time as exceeding 0.89 in all cases. At face value, then, the logistic does give an adequate description.

However, a number of qualifications might be mentioned. By its very nature, the variable $(m/n)_{ijt}$ must rise monotonically with time, therefore one would expect a high correlation between any simple transform of it and time. This is especially true given the low number of observations used: on average, only 10 per innovation and, in four cases, fewer than 6. Secondly, Mansfield reports significant auto-correlation in at least three cases; quite possibly, this is due to mis-specification of mathematical form. Perhaps a skewed curve might have been applicable in at least some cases. Thirdly, because of problems in collecting information about the dates at which smaller firms adopted the various innovations, only the largest firms in each of the industries are considered. Apart from the fact that this means that only small samples of firms are studied (on average, less than 20 per innovation), there is a chance of a significant bias in the results. If, say, large firms are liable to adopt more quickly than small firms, the heterogeneity of the populations will not be reflected by these samples. As the logistic requires homogeneity, one might expect it to provide a better fit for the samples than for the populations of firms in each industry. In the light of these qualifications, agnosticism on Mansfield's time series results is, perhaps, justified.

In a second stage, Mansfield uses the estimated slope parameters ($\hat{\beta}_{ij}$), as measures of the speed of diffusion in a cross-section analysis based on equation (2.11). π_{ij} is measured as the average pay-out period required, by firms in industry j, to justify typical investments, divided by the average pay-out period actually achieved for innovation i. S_{ij} is the average initial investment in the innovation i as a percentage of the average total assets of the firms in industry j.

The fit achieved is as follows:

$$\hat{\beta}_{ij} = \begin{bmatrix} -0.29 \\ -0.57 \\ -0.52 \\ -0.59 \end{bmatrix} + \underset{(0.015)}{0.530} \, \pi_{ij} - \underset{(0.014)}{0.027} \, S_{ij} \quad R^2 = 0.99 \qquad (2.15)$$

where figures in round brackets denote estimated standard errors.

The four alternative intercept terms correspond to the four industries. Although Mansfield is not explicit, these have been estimated, presumably, using dummy variables. (At any event, each of these intercepts has been estimated on the basis of only three observations, there being three innovations in each industry.) He draws four conclusions:

(i) '[the equation] represents the data surprisingly well'.
(ii) the coefficients of π_{ij} and S_{ij} have the expected signs.
(iii) both coefficients are significantly different from zero at the 95% level, using a 1 tailed t test. (Apparently, S_{ij}'s coefficient is significant only if an extreme observation is included.)
(iv) the differences in the size of the intercept terms are not inconsistent with more concentrated industries being slower at diffusion.[6]

These results must be judged in the light of the small sample size (12 observations) and the fact that six explanatory variables are used (including the four dummies), but, nevertheless, the overall fit is remarkable, given the nature of the dependent variable.

It would be helpful to know how much of this excellent explanation is due to the dummy intercept terms. One can conceive of β_{ij} varying due to differing characteristics of (a) the innovations and (b) the industries concerned. From this equation, we know that at least one innovation characteristic (π_{ij}) is crucial, but we are ignorant of which industry-level characteristics might be important. The differential intercept terms establish that there *are* inter-industry differences, after normalizing for innovation characteristics. Whether these differences are significant, however, is not known. Further, there is no possibility of discovering their cause, given the small industry sample size.

Unfortunately, Griliches' results can shed no light on this matter. His data refer to the diffusion of an agricultural innovation – hybrid corn – in 31 different American states between 1932 and 1956. He measures diffusion as 'the percentage of all corn acreage planted to hybrid seed', i.e. *overall*, as opposed to *inter-firm*, diffusion. The logistic is fitted to the data in much the same way, except that Griliches does not *impose* saturation levels (n_{ij}) but uses the results to decide between a number of alternatives.[7] Again, the logistic fits the data well – in none of the 25 cases does R^2 fall below 0.89, but as Durbin–Watson statistics are not reported, we cannot tell whether alternative time curves might have performed better. In his second stage, Griliches attempts to explain the inter-state variance in the three estimated parameters in a cross-section analysis, similar to equation (2.15). Whilst the fit achieved in this stage is not as high as in Mansfield's second stage (an R^2 of 0.5–0.6 is typical in explaining $\hat{\beta}_{ij}$), a number of significant determinants are detected. Almost without exception, these variables measure various aspects of the relative profitability of using hybrid seed and are usually related to inter-state geographical differences such as fertility of soil. These results have since been interpreted (Rosenberg, 1971, p. 209) as indicating 'that the behaviour of both farmers and hybrid-seed producers were firmly grounded in expectations of profit', and tend to support

Mansfield's finding of the importance of π_{ij}. On the other hand, the role of inter-industry variables, such as industrial structure and growth of market remains unexamined.

This omission is also unavoidable in Metcalfe's study of the diffusion of three innovations in the Lancashire textile industry. By studying only one industry, he effectively removes inter-industry differences and concentrates instead on innovation characteristics. Using his alternative S shaped curve (equation 2.13), he reports a satisfactory fit in each case, although once again, no Durbin–Watson statistics are quoted. Obviously, no systematic cross-section explanation of $\hat{\beta}_{ij}$ is possible given only three observations; but it is noticeable that the innovation recording the slowest speed of diffusion is also the most expensive and least profitable.

In summary then, none of these three studies establish that the chosen S shape necessarily yields the best explanation of the time series data; but, on the other hand, all three present evidence to suggest that the characteristics of the innovations do affect their speed of diffusion. The role of *industry-level* variables remains largely unexplored.[8]

A note of dissonance Even though Mansfield's and Griliches's studies were published more than a decade ago, there has been very little critical analysis of their work. One notable exception is provided by Gold, Pierce and Rosseger (1970) in their study of the diffusion of 13 major process innovations in the U.S. They claim that there is such a diversity of variables which affect the diffusion of individual innovations, that it is almost pointless to build a general model of diffusion as did Mansfield. For instance, *by-product coking* diffused only very slowly initially, as there were plentiful supplies of coking coal and organic chemicals; on the other hand, *beneficating and pelletizing* spread quickly after the first introduction, due to shortages of high grade iron ore; *machine cutting of coal*, like by-product coking, did not 'catch on' very quickly, but this was because there were a large number of variants of the technique available on the market, which led to confusion and uncertainty among potential consumers. Indeed, Gold et al. cite 'special circumstances' for all of the innovations they study.

This seems to be an unnecessarily pessimistic view. In any cross-section study, in virtually any area of economics, there are special or random influences; the point of model building is to investigate the importance of *general* factors. It may be, of course, that special factors dominate, but that, surely, is a matter of empirics. As it happens, an examination of the 'special factors' in this case suggests that many of them reduce to differences in the profitability of the innovations, or to different rates of change of profitability.

A second broad criticism made of Mansfield's approach is his use of ex-post profitability as a determinant of the speed of diffusion. They argue that many business decisions are the results of animal spirits; *expected* profitability is a more meaningful concept in this case; and that the profitability of any innovation will not be constant over the diffusion period. Mansfield's answer, one suspects, would be pragmatic – namely, that his specification was dictated by availability of data.

On a more positive note, Gold et al. note the importance of the demand facing the *adopting* industries. Of the 5 innovations introduced in slow growth periods (i.e. where demand for the industry's product over the first 15 years of the innovation's life was slow or static), none diffused rapidly. Of the 8 innovations introduced during periods of rapid growth, 3 diffused rapidly. The (rather heroic) conclusion drawn is that industry growth may be necessary, but not sufficient, for fast diffusion.

2.4 The inter-firm approach

2.4.1 The theory

The central aim of this body of research is the explanation of differences between firms in the speed with which they adopt the same innovation. Again, the innovator is Mansfield who postulates (1963a) the following relationship:

$$\log d_{ij} = \log Q_i + a_{i2} \log H_{ij} + a_{i3} \log S_{ij} + a_{i4} \log G_{ij} + a_{i5} \log A_{ij} +$$
$$+ a_{i6} \log \pi_{ij} + a_{i7} \log L_{ij} + a_{i8} \log T_{ij} + \log \epsilon_{ij} \qquad (2.16)$$

where d_{ij} is the number of years the jth firm waits before beginning to use the ith innovation, S_{ij} the firm's size, H_{ij} a measure of the profitability of its investment in the innovation, G_{ij} the firm's rate of growth, π_{ij} the firm's profitability, A_{ij} the age of its president, L_{ij} a measure of its liquidity, T_{ij} the firm's profit trend.

The two most important of these variables (both empirically and theoretically) are S_{ij} and H_{ij}. d_{ij} is likely to be inversely related to S_{ij} on three counts. First, the costs and risks of early adoption are more easily borne by large firms. Second, because of their size, there is a greater probability of large firms needing to replace old equipment at any point in time. Thus, if the innovation is embodied in new equipment, large firms have greater *opportunities* to adopt early, on average. Third, again purely because of their size, larger firms are likely to encompass a wider range of operating conditions than smaller firms. As some innovations have only limited applicability initially, there is more likelihood that large firms will have the appropriate operating conditions for adoption of the new innovation in its early years.

H_{ij}, the profitability of adoption, presents severe measurement problems as it is likely to depend on a number of the characteristics of the firm, such as its product mix, quality of inputs, etc. Statistically, there would seem to be a strong possibility of multicollinearity if H_{ij} is collinear with S_{ij} due to any returns to scale that are available in adoption of the innovation.

The other variables *hint* at a behaviouralist view of decision making: declining profits are seen as activating search and older presidents are believed to be more conservative (i.e. $\partial d / \partial T < 0$ and $\partial d / \partial A < 0$). Similarly, the role of the innovation characteristics are hinted at, but not developed. For instance, poor liquid asset ratios and low profits will hinder adoption of multi-million dollar innovations but probably not of relatively cheap innovations. It is likely, therefore, that the values of a_{i6} and a_{i7} will depend on the type of innovation, but this point is not discussed.

It should be stressed that this model is quite independent of the epidemic model discussed earlier. Nevertheless, it is surprising to note the absence of any common thread between the two models. In fact, one could argue that this model makes the epidemic model redundant since the diffusion curve may be viewed merely as an aggregation of d_{ij} over all firms in the relevant industry. In other words, once we know the distribution of d_{ij} within an industry (which requires assumptions about the distribution of S_{ij} etc.), equation (2.16) can be used to predict the shape of the aggregate industry diffusion curve.[9]

Most other research in this area follows Mansfield's ad hoc theorizing and empirical methodology quite closely. A number of authors, however, have placed more emphasis on 'attitudinal' or 'informational' variables, whilst retaining more conventional economic characteristics in their analysis. These variables will be discussed individually below. As a group, their inspiration is to be found in the sociologist Rogers' survey of diffusion studies in the other social sciences (1962). Apparently, in these other areas, the individuals who appear to be quicker to adopt new ideas, techniques etc., tend to be young, affluent, opinion-leaders, non-traditional and cosmopolite (i.e. mix with individuals outside of their own groups.)

However, these variables present many problems. Often, such characteristics are difficult to measure without resorting to the construction of arbitrary indexes (perhaps based on questionnaire answers). Sometimes circular results arise, e.g. if non-traditional, opinion leaders are found to adopt earlier, the only conclusion which can be drawn is that progressive firms adopt new innovations quickly. Further, even if firm decision making is dominated by one man, or a small group, whose personal characteristics play a significant role, such variables, given the above data problems, only merit inclusion in the analysis if their effects are independent of the economic characteristics of the firm, such as its size, growth, profits etc.

2.4.2 The main empirical findings

Mansfield has fitted equation (2.16) to data for 167 firms, adopting 14 different innovations in various American industries. Only S_{ij} and H_{ij} attain statistical significance and the latter, for only 2 of the 14 innovations. Unfortunately, H_{ij} cannot be measured directly but proxy measures have been used for 5 of the innovations. For instance, the profitability in adopting a *continuous mining machine* is heavily influenced by the proportion of the adopter's output derived from high coal seams; as data on the latter is available for most firms, Mansfield has used this to approximate H_{ij}. Needless to say, H_{ij} will be determined by many other unknown or unmeasurable factors for most innovations. This must restrict the explanatory power of this variable in practice, although it would be unfair to claim that Mansfield's approach could easily be improved in this respect.

On the other hand, S_{ij} is consistently significant, regardless of which other variables are included in the equation: depending on the exact specification of the equation, $\hat{a}_{i3}$ varies between -0.03 and -1.53, with Mansfield's preferred equation yielding an estimate of -0.4. Rather surprisingly however, whilst permitting the coefficient on H_{ij} (a_{i2}) to vary across innovations, he constrains a_{i3} to be equal for all innovations. (That is, equation (2.16) and similar equations have been fitted to the pooled data for all innovations and industries with various dummies on H_{ij} but not for S_{ij}). Statistically, this makes interpretation of this parameter particularly hazardous: one cannot be sure that it reflects inter-firm, rather than inter-industry, size effects. As an extreme example of the potential problem of interpretation, consider the hypothetical situation depicted in figure 2.3.

Industry A, comprising a few large firms, adopts its innovation quicker than industry B, which comprises many small firms. Even if there is no relationship between firm size and speed of adoption *within* each industry, a regression line fitted to the pooled data for both industries will clearly be downward sloping, apparently indicating an inverse relationship between *firm* size and d_{ij}.

Given the large number of observations at Mansfield's disposal, this ambiguity could easily have been avoided by fitting the equation separately for each of the different industries and innovations. Inter-industry size effects could then have been investigated by using t tests on the $\hat{a}_{i3}$. But as the results stand, one must remain agnostic on the role of firm size and, for that matter, industry size.[10]

The results of other empirical research are rather disappointing, being

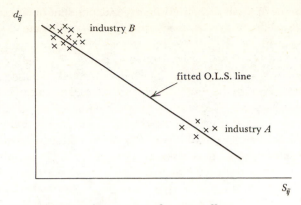

Figure 2.3   Industry versus firm size effects

characterized by low R^2, insignificant variables and rather suspect specification of the dependent variable.

Nabseth (in Williams, 1973), using data for Swedish firms adopting 6
different innovations, employs up to nine explanatory variables, of which
four approximate roughly to Mansfield's S_{ij}, H_{ij}, G_{ij} and L_{ij}, the other five
being 'attitudinal' variables. Of the first group, only S_{ij} and H_{ij} are ever significant and even then only for 2 and 1 of the 6 innovations respectively. Of
the second group, two (INF_{ij} and B_{ij}) are significant for 4 and 3 innovations.
INF_{ij} measures the date at which firm j claims to have first heard of innovation i, and B_{ij} is an arbitrary index for which firms are given ratings between
0 and 16, depending on how quickly they adopted past innovations. In other
words, there is some evidence to suggest that firms adopt more quickly, the
sooner they know of the existence of the innovation and the more progressive they have been in the past.

Hakonson (chapter 4 in Nabseth and Ray (1974)) uses the same set of
explanatory variables in his study of the diffusion of Special Presses in three
countries. He finds S_{ij} and H_{ij} to be significant with expected signs, in two
of the three countries. In common with Nabseth, he finds R^2s in the region
of 0.4 to 0.6.

Smith's results (in Nabseth and Ray (1974)) are even more disappointing.
Using much the same array of explanatory variables, R^2s of 0.1 are typical
and only an arbitrary index reflecting the extent of firms' vertical integration
ever attains significance.

Except for their patchy evidence on firm size, it is difficult to argue that
these three studies have established any strong policy conclusions and on a
more theoretical level, we still seem to be a long way from understanding the
behaviour of individual firms in this context.

Unfortunately, each of these three authors have faced a problem not encountered by Mansfield: the innovations studied had not diffused 100% at the time of investigation. Consequently observations on d_{ij} are not available for all firms in the samples considered. However, rather than discard the non-adopting firms from their samples, they have allocated to these firms an arbitrary adoption date in the future. (Nabseth and Hakonson assumed that non-adopters would all adopt in 1975, Smith assumed adoption in 1980). The likely outcome of this unfortunate assumption is biased estimates, as becomes clear from the following simple hypothetical example. Suppose that the true relationship is given by:

$$d_{ij} = \alpha_{i1} + \alpha_{i2} S_{ij} + \epsilon_{ij} \tag{2.17}$$

where ϵ_{ij} is a disturbance term satisfying all the standard criteria of the ordinary least squares model. This might generate a scatter of observations as in figure (2.4a).

However, if viewed at time d^* (i.e. the time of the research), no observations are available for non-adopters (for all j with $d_{ij} > d^*$). If, following Nabseth, Hakonson and Smith, artificial observations are constructed, such that $d_{ij} = d^{**}$ for all $d_{ij} > d^*$, a regression line fitted to the data may well diverge significantly from the 'true' line. In the hypothetical case drawn in figure (2.4b), the effect would be to bias $\hat{\alpha}_{i2}$ downwards; in general, however, the bias could work either way, depending on the size of $\text{var}(\epsilon_{ij})$, the exact choice for d^{**} and, of course, d^*.[11]

In summary, this approach has achieved only limited success in furthering our understanding of diffusion. On a theoretical level, we are nowhere

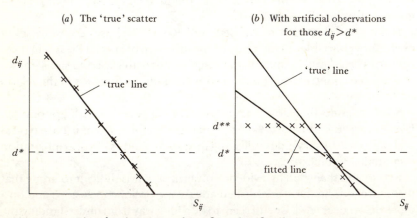

Figure 2.4   Biased estimates resulting from 'artificial' observations

nearer an economic model of the adoption decision: theory has been a little ad hoc and many of the variables suggested offer little *explanation* of individual firm's behaviour (Nabseth's *B* variable, for example.) On an empirical level, there is some evidence that the more rapid adopters will tend to be those for whom the innovation is particularly well suited, technologically. Similarly, it is probable that large firms tend to be the faster adopters, but the statistical methods employed leave a question mark surrounding this conclusion.

Having said this, the problems facing empirical research at the firm level should not be under-estimated. Clearly, there are a multitude of factors which influence the profitability of adoption for any individual firm, and, as the analysis of the following chapter indicates, many of these factors are technological. These may be very difficult to measure, even when data is freely available.

2.5 The inter-country approach

The basis of this approach has been to study the diffusion of the same innovation in a number of different countries and to explain the observed differentials in diffusion performance in terms of the characteristics of the countries and industries concerned. The empirical methodology has been somewhat less uniform than in the research discussed in the previous two sections.

Nevertheless, the Mansfield methodology is followed in a number of instances. Swan (1973), for instance, fits logistic curves to data on the diffusion of synthetic rubber in 12 countries during the post-war period. In a second stage, he 'explains' the parameters of the fitted logistics, in a cross-section analysis, using country-level explanatory variables such as the growth in output, the level of rubber imports, the level of rubber exports and the production of rubber per capita. Both his curve fitting and cross-section analysis record high R^2 and significant variables.[12] His rationalization of the logistic and explanatory variables is brief and along familiar lines; again there is no fully worked economic model.

Perhaps the most striking contribution in this area has been produced by an international consortium of economic research institutes who have studied the diffusion of ten major process innovations in six countries; Nabseth and Ray (1974) present the final report. Because each institute was responsible for studying a separate innovation, a number of quite different methodologies have been pursued and a brief summary of their conclusions cannot be comprehensive.

Having said this, a consensus view does seem to have emerged on a number of points. For instance, whilst a number of the authors concede the likelihood that the diffusion growth curve will be S shaped (usually rational-ized with reference to the epidemic model), curve fitting is not attempted in most cases. This is surely quite acceptable *if one believes that there is no economic, non-trivial, rationale for the S shape*. If the S shape results by virtue of a physi-cal, quasi-sociological law, then curve fitting reduces to a purely descrip-tive exercise designed only to generate some empirically useful measure of the speed of diffusion (in the case of the logistic, $\hat{\beta}$, the slope parameter). In the circumstances, equally acceptable indicators would be obvious and far easier to compute (for instance, the time taken for diffusion to reach some level, say 50% or 90%).

Although most of the contributors to the study do not formalize the underlying assumptions used concerning the nature of the adoption deci-sion, in nearly all cases a behavioural approach can be detected. Consi-derable emphasis is placed on the role of 'management factors' (various indices of attitudes and information receptiveness are constructed).

More generally, inter-country differences tend to be explained in terms of three groups of variables. Most popular are measurements of, or proxies for, the *profitability of the innovation* in different countries. Oppenlander attri-butes differential diffusion rates with respect to Numerically Controlled machine tools to differences in labour costs; Meyer and Herregat emphasize the role of various factor prices (e.g. scrap metal, labour, capital) in the diffusion of Basic Oxygen Steel-making; Gebhardt attributes prime impor-tance to the compatibility of the country's upstream steel-making processes to the Continuous Casting technique and so on. Second, and closely related, *technological and institutional differences* are mentioned in a number of cases. Davies, Smith and Lacci introduce the concept of a Technological Ceiling: countries are limited, to differing extents, by the nature of their clay in the extent to which Tunnel Kilns may be adopted in brickmaking; Gebhardt uses a similar concept in his analysis of Continuous Casting. Ray highlights the importance of legal restrictions to the diffusion of Gibberellic Acid in brewing, and of licensing agreements to the diffusion of the Float Glass technique in glassmaking. Third, some authors have attempted to explain diffusion differentials in terms of more conventional economic *industry characteristics*: growth and size of the market, size of firms, age of existing equipment etc. Surprisingly, however, the influence of industry structure (i.e. concentration and barriers to entry) has received little attention.

Overall, this study provides more insight into the empirical task facing future research into diffusion; the technological analysis is comprehensive and underlines the crucial role of technical factors in explaining differences in the performance of firms within the same country and between countries. On the other hand, the economic theory of diffusion has not been deve-loped beyond the epidemic model and most of the questions with which the present study is concerned (e.g. the role of industry structure, firm size, demand conditions etc.) remain unanswered.

At this stage the literature survey is now widened in order to assess whether a potentially suitable theoretical framework already exists *outside* of what was termed earlier the mainstream of diffusion research.

2.6 Stock adjustment models

The use of stock adjustment models in the analysis of investment behaviour is by now well known (see, for instance, Wynn and Holden 1975, for a summary). Two studies in particular are of potential interest in the present context, both being concerned with the analysis of investment in computers: Chow (1967) for the U.S.A. and Stoneman (1976) for the U.K.

Both authors postulate that the growth in computer usage in any time period is proportional to the extent to which the actual stock at the beginning of the period (m_t) falls short of the equilibrium stock (n_t). Both employ two alternative forms to test this hypothesis:

$$\frac{dm_t}{dt\,m_t} = \beta\,(n_t - m_t) \quad \text{or} \quad \frac{dm_t}{dt} = \beta\,(n_t - m_t)m_t \qquad (2.18)$$

and

$$\frac{dm_t}{dt\,m_t} = \beta\,(\log n_t - \log m_t) \quad \text{or} \quad \frac{dm_t}{dt} = \beta\,(\log n_t - \log m_t)m_t \qquad (2.19)$$

(where continuous time is used here to indicate the similarities with the epidemic model).

In other words, the increase in the stock of computers will be determined by the *level* of the stock (rationalized on familiar grounds of competitive pressures and as a proxy for the quality of information about computers), and the shortfall existing between actual and equilibrium stock. The only difference between (2.18) and (2.19) lies in the precise formulation of the stock adjustment mechanism. The first form is, of course, the differential equation of the standard logistic; the second is the differential equation of the Gompertz curve, which is a skewed S-shape growth curve, having a point of inflexion at $m_t/n_t = 0.37$ (as opposed to 0.5 for the logistic). Both authors prefer the Gompertz on the basis of its superior subsequent empirical performance.

On the face of it, these estimating forms appear to be very similar to the epidemic model discussed earlier. There is, however, a major difference in that n_t is itself variable. Both authors argue that the equilibrium stock will increase as G.N.P. increases because this leads to increased scope for the application of computers; similarly, the equilibrium stock of computers will be determined by the relative price of computers, since this will influence the cost savings effected by computer usage. Substituting in a specific expression for n_t, the Gompertz equation becomes:

$$\log m_t - \log m_{t-1} = \beta(b_0 + b_1 \log p_t + b_2 \log X_t) - \beta \log m_{t-1} \qquad (2.20)$$

where discrete time is used for the purpose of estimation, X_t is the level of G.N.P. and p_t is the relative price of computers (both authors go to considerable lengths to allow for quality changes in computers in measuring p_t and m_t).

This equation (and a similar one based on the logistic) is fitted to time series data on the post-war spread of computers. Chow estimates β at about 0.25 but finds only $\log m_{t-1}$ to be significant. Stoneman's results are also a little disappointing at this stage.

Consequently, and as an extra refinement, Stoneman allows β the coefficient of adjustment, to vary with certain economic variables. Briefly, he argues that the extent to which the actual stock is adjusted towards the equilibrium stock will vary between time periods, depending on (i) the extent to which firms are motivated to search for new methods of achieving their goals and (ii) the results of this search, once undertaken. This behaviouralist view of decision making suggests a number of possible determinants of β, such as the growth of profits, costs and outputs (which will influence the propensity to search) and the level of profits, the price of computers and the stock of computers (which will influence the results of and returns from the search).

Unfortunately, this refinement produces an estimating equation which is under-identified. Stoneman attempts to circumvent this problem by using ancillary information to estimate n_t. In general, however, his results are inconclusive although there is some evidence to suggest that diffusion accelerates in periods of rapid G.N.P. growth.

Abstracting from the generally unexceptional results of both Chow and Stoneman, this approach has widened the diffusion debate in a number of significant respects.

First, there has been an important switch in emphasis. The estimated diffusion growth curve is no longer merely a means of generating observations to be used in cross-industry comparisons but is, instead, an empirical *end* in itself. This results, of course, because they, particularly Stoneman, invest the diffusion curve with rather more economic meaning, based on an explicit theory of decision making. Second, both authors report a better fit for the skewed Gompertz curve than for the symmetrical logistic. Third, implicitly, they measure diffusion by the stock of computers, rather than by the number of firms having installed a computer. Consequently, their approach does not differentiate between *inter-firm* diffusion and *intra-firm* diffusion. In some ways, this is a major limitation of their approach since there is no theoretical distinction between two quite different types of decision: namely, on the one hand the decision of a non-adopter to install a computer for the first time and, on the other, the decision of an adopter to increase its stock of computers.[13] Indeed, this type of stock adjustment model is probably best suited to an analysis of intra-firm diffusion and for that reason, but also partly because of the rather arbitrary specification of the Gompertz and logistic equations, this approach will not be pursued in the present study.

2.7 The vintage approach

It is quite obvious that very little of the research surveyed so far has used conventional economic theories of decision making. The lack of interest in the standard neo-classical theories is, perhaps, understandable: concepts of perfectly malleable capital and profit maximization are somewhat hard to sustain in an area dominated by uncertainty, imperfect information and embodied technical progress. However, modifications to conventional theory do exist which might be developed to provide an economic theory of diffusion. The most obvious candidate is the vintage growth model as propounded by Salter (1960) and others.

The bare bones of the simple vintage approach may be summarized as follows. New technology is assumed to be embodied in new capital equipment and so gross investment is the vehicle of diffusion. Old equipment is only replaced or scrapped when its *operating* costs exceed the rents it earns. Similarly, new equipment is only installed if its *total* costs are covered by the revenues it earns. It is usually assumed, for analytical convenience, that plant is indivisible and that new technology cannot be introduced on old equipment. Thus, each vintage of equipment embodies the best practice technology of its date of construction, and is then committed to this technology (and a fixed labour complement) until its date of expiry.

The appearance of a cost-saving process innovation, within this framework, will have the following consequences. It will become profitable to *immediately* replace some proportion of existing equipment because the total costs of the new equipment (including a profit allowance yielding the normal rate of return) are lower than the operating costs of some old equipment. (The existing capital stock comprises a number of vintages embodying the old technology – the newer vintages being slightly more efficient than the old, due to minor improvements in specification over the years.)

At the same time, product price will fall to equality with total costs of the new innovation – having previously been equal to the (higher) total costs of the latest vintage of the old technology. This fall in price is effected by the creation of new capacity, chasing the spectre of super-normal profits to be earned from installing the new innovation.

Some of the more efficient old technology equipment will still remain: its operating costs being lower than total costs of the new innovation. This equipment will gradually be replaced over the years, given a favourable movement in factor prices and improvements in later vintages of the new innovation. The important point is that 100% diffusion will not be instantaneous, even given perfect information and cost minimizing behaviour.

The above may be formalized mathematically fairly easily, and it may be shown that the diffusion growth path will depend upon such variables as the growth in wages relative to product price, the time path of the price of the innovation and the age distribution of existing old-technology equipment. However, the simplicity of the model does depend heavily on the assumptions of cost minimization and perfect information on the one hand and indivisibility of plant and the embodiment hypothesis on the other. In principle each of these assumptions can be relaxed without destroying the essence of the model. In practice, however, it is doubtful whether the model would retain its predictive power if all four assumptions were relaxed simultaneously. For reasons to be discussed in the following two chapters, none of these assumptions seems to be particularly viable and consequently this approach has been (regrettably) discarded as a potential framework for the analysis of the diffusion of the innovations in the present study.

2.8 David's analysis of mechanical reapers

In a recent paper analysing the mechanization of reaping in the U.S. in the nineteenth century, David (1975) has produced a model which rests on a view of decision making which is not totally dissimilar to Salter's. His basic thesis is that mechanical reapers were adopted only very slowly because the majority of American farms did not own sufficient acreage for the labour savings made possible to pay for the initial outlay required to install the reapers. He argues that diffusion only proceeded as the price of reapers fell relative to wage rates and as farm sizes increased.

The model can be summarized briefly as follows. Adoption of mechanical reapers is profitable for farm i at time t if:

$$w_t(L_{iot} - L_{iNt}) \geqq p_{iNt} \tag{2.21}$$

where w_t is the wage rate, p_{iNt} the average annual cost of a mechanical reaper and L_{iot} and L_{iNt} are the annual labour requirements of the old manual method and of the new mechanical reapers respectively. (This assumes no other variable imputs.) Assuming no scale economies in either method, then

$$L_{iot} = a_1 S_{it} \tag{2.22}$$

and $L_{iNt} = a_2 S_{it}$ where $a_1 > a_2 > 0$

and S_{it} is the size of farm i at time t. $\qquad$ (2.23)

Combining these equations, the condition for profitable adoption follows easily:

$$S_{it} \geqq \frac{p_{INt}}{w_t} \frac{1}{a_1 - a_2} \tag{2.24}$$

Given that (2.24) did not hold for all i at the date when reapers were first available, diffusion would not be instantaneous but would proceed only as (a) farms increased in size. (b) the cost of reapers declined relative to wage rates and (c) reapers were improved technologically (resulting in reductions in a_2).

Whilst David does not have sufficient data to test these predictions rigorously, he does provide some evidence which indicates that (a) and (b) may have been important factors over the period considered.

As already mentioned, the vintage approach might be developed along similar lines and one would expect (b) and (c) to figure centrally in any such development. The role attributed to farm size is particularly interesting: it does *not* derive from scale economies in the usual sense, but rather, from the total lumpiness of the innovation (all farms must pay the same rental). Under these circumstances, large farms must always be at an advantage since the innovation price may be spread over a larger scale of operations. It is perhaps unlikely that this will be the case for most twentieth-century industrial innovations and, if capital costs are proportional to the scale of operations, the predictive power of the model may disappear. Nevertheless, along with the vintage model, David's approach is quite instructive in establishing the potentially important role of post-invention improvements of the technology embodied in the new innovation. It also goes some way to answering earlier criticisms of the epidemic model by establishing the individual firm's adoption decision at the centre of the analysis.

2.9 The diffusion of new consumer durables

Surprisingly, the study of the diffusion of new *products* (mainly consumer durables) has developed quite independently of the various studies on new processes already discussed. Whilst the economic agents involved are different (individual consumers, as opposed to firms), there are sufficient common factors, such as uncertainty and possibly bandwagons, to suggest that the two areas would benefit from cross-pollination.

No attempt will be made to survey this area comprehensively (see Bain, 1964, chapter 2 for such a survey), but one particular technique, which has been successfully employed on a number of occasions, does deserve some discussion. Cramer (1969), Aitchison and Brown (1957) and Bonus (1973) have each advocated the application of Probit Analysis to this field;[14] only the basic framework of their models will be outlined below and no reference will be made to their empirical findings.

The central assumption is that an individual consumer will be found to own the new product at time t if his income y_{it}, exceeds some *critical* level y_{it}^*. This critical, or tolerance, income represents the tastes of the consumer which, in turn, may be related to any number of personal or economic characteristics (generally excluding income however). At any event, y_{it}^* is usually regarded as the product of a large number of random influences. As such, the multiplicative form of the central limit theorem suggests that y_{it}^* may be lognormally distributed across consumers. Moreover, it is usually assumed that income is, itself, lognormally distributed across consumers.

These three assumptions may be written as follows:

$$P\{q_{it} = 1 \,|\, y_{it}\} = P\{y_{it}^* \leqq y_{it}\} \tag{2.25}$$

$$y_{it} \sim \Lambda\,(\mu_t, \sigma_t^2) \tag{2.26}$$

$$y_{it}^* \sim \Lambda\,(\mu_t^*, \sigma_t^{*\,2}) \tag{2.27}$$

That is, the probability that consumer i owns the new durable at time t, denoted by $q_{it} = 1$ given his income is y_{it}, is equal to the probability that his actual income is not less than his tolerance income. Log y_{it} is normally distributed with mean μ_t and variance σ_t^2, log y_{it}^* is also normally distributed with mean μ_t^* and $\sigma_t^{*\,2}$.

Substituting (2.27) into (2.25), it follows that the probability of ownership will be related to income by a 'Quasi-Engel' curve which has a positively skewed S shape, and is, in fact, a cumulative lognormal curve. Formally,

$$P\{y_{it}^* \leq y_{it}\} = \Lambda\,(y_{it}|\mu_t^*, \sigma_t^{*2}) \tag{2.28}$$

Given further assumptions about the time paths of the parameters of (2.26) and (2.27) various predictions also emerge concerning the shape of the *aggregate* diffusion curve. For instance, suppose both σ_t^{*2} and σ_t^{*2} are constant over time, and μ_t and μ_t^* can be approximated by:

$$\mu_t = \mu_0 + g_1 t \tag{2.29}$$

$$\mu_t^* = \mu_0^* - g_2 t \tag{2.30}$$

This is equivalent to assuming a constant growth rate of all incomes of g_1, with unchanged income inequalities, and a constant rate of decline in all critical incomes, with each individual's tastes remaining the same relative to his peers (implying an across-the-board change in tastes in favour of the new durable, due to bandwagon effects, greater information about the product etc.).

The aggregate diffusion curve is found by aggregating the Quasi-Engel curve over the income distribution for each point in time. Thus, at time t, the expected proportion of the population owning the durable is given by the sum of the probabilities at each income level, weighted by the probability that each income will occur. It can be shown fairly easily[15] that this leads to the following diffusion curve:

$$m_t/n = N(t|\mu_D, \sigma_D^2) \tag{2.31}$$

where $\mu_D = \dfrac{\mu_0^* - \mu_0}{g_1 + g_2}, \quad \sigma_D^2 = \dfrac{\sigma^{*2} + \sigma^2}{(g_1 + g_2)^2} \tag{2.32}$

and m_t is the number of owners out of a population of n consumers. Thus diffusion will follow a cumulative normal time curve which will be steeper (i.e. diffusion will be quicker), the smaller is σ_D^2.

A brief comparison with the epidemic model (which could easily be employed in the durable context) is quite interesting. First, this model is based on specific behavioural assumptions concerning the individual consumer. Apart from constituting an intellectually more satisfying basis, this enables the model to predict the behaviour of individual consumers (via the Quasi-Engel curve.) Second, there is a reduced need for ad hoc theorizing on the determinants of the speed of diffusion: from (2.32), we can see that diffusion will be more rapid (i.e. σ_D^2 will be smaller) the faster the growth in incomes, the faster the bandwagon effect, the more equal is the income distribution and the less variable are consumer tastes.[16] Third, the *shape* of the diffusion curve need not always be the same: given alternative assumptions to (2.29) and (2.30), which might be more appropriate for some durables and/or populations, alternatives to the cumulative normal diffusion curve are possible. Fourth, the simple model presented here does share some common features with Mansfield's epidemic model. In both cases, the diffusion curve has a symmetrical S shape – the cumulative normal is very similar in shape to the logistic. Further, just as Mansfield suggests that innovations will diffuse more quickly the higher is their profitability and the lower their cost, so too one might expect that the bandwagon effect in this case (represented by the parameter g_2) will be more pronounced, and diffusion faster, the cheaper is the durable and the greater the improvement it offers over existing products.

2.10 Conclusions

In the introduction two main aims were attributed to this survey. It is therefore convenient to summarize the main conclusions of this chapter in two parts. First, what do we know already about the diffusion of new industrial processes? The answer, suggested by sections 3 to 6, is that our knowledge is still remarkably limited and tentative. (Moreover, the case studies of N.I.E.S.R., Stoneman and Metcalfe apart, no general study of diffusion in the U.K. has yet been attempted). Probably the most common finding is that the typical diffusion growth path can be adequately described by a sigmoid curve, but whether it is symmetrical, as advocated by Mansfield and Griliches, or positively skewed, as suggested by Metcalfe, Stoneman and Chow, is less certain. In general, little attention has been directed towards the *exact* choice of S shaped diffusion curve used in these various studies. This is unfortunate since the measure of diffusion speed will clearly depend on the choice of growth curve fitted.

Mansfield, Griliches and Metcalfe all produce evidence to suggest that a major determinant of the speed of diffusion, as represented by the slope of the growth curve, is the profitability of the innovation concerned. On the other hand, there are still very few results in this literature concerning the influence on diffusion speed of the characteristics of the industry in which the innovation is diffusing.

Furthermore, little is known of the reasons why some firms adopt innovations quicker than others. The one fairly common finding identified in section 4, that large firms tend to be quicker, must be viewed with caution, owing to the strange statistical techniques used in most research in this area.

Fairly certainly, however, there are so many technological factors which will influence the behaviour of any individual firm in this context, that any empirical explanation of inter-firm differences faces an up-hill struggle without the collection of vast quantities of technical information.

Finally, it would appear from section 5 that international differences in diffusion performance can be partially ascribed to technological and institutional differences between the countries. From this finding, we must also expect that differences between industries within the same country will be sensitive to technological differences between the industries and innovations concerned.

In summary, it is clear that many of the interesting economic questions have yet to be considered in sufficient detail and it is hoped that some of the gaps identified above will be at least partially filled in the later empirical chapters of this study. Having said this it should be acknowledged that this is an area where data requirements (and often non-economic data at that) are very high. As such it would be unfair to be too critical of the early research in this field which has often been based, necessarily, on inadequate and imperfect data.

The second aim of this survey was to assess the suitability of existing theoretical models to the sorts of questions with which the present study is concerned. Unfortunately, the mainstream diffusion literature has yet to produce a totally acceptable theoretical framework. The epidemic model, used so frequently, suffers from two drawbacks. First, it depends on two technological assumptions which are unlikely to apply in this context (namely, that there are no post-invention improvements in process innovations and that all potential adopters should be equally susceptible to any new innovation). Second, by dealing only with the behaviour of firms in aggregate, it pushes aside many of the more interesting theoretical questions and substitutes a rather mechanistic hypothesis of behaviour.

Even in the literature addressed specifically to explaining inter-firm differences, no attempt is made to formulate a fully-worked theory of firm decision making. The work on international differences makes only a limited theoretical contribution; on the other hand, it does indicate the importance of incorporating technological aspects into model building, even in non-international studies. Stoneman's use of the stock adjustment model does incorporate a definite theory of decision making but the overall framework is still inflexible and somewhat ad hoc.

Perhaps the two most promising bases for theoretical development are to be found outside of the immediately relevant literature. The probit model, used in the analysis of the diffusion of consumer durables, whilst rather simplistic, does suggest a framework based on individual behaviour which is flexible enough to be used in this area. Salter's vintage model also offers an avenue which, given certain modifications, might be used.

In the light of these conclusions, two major tasks become apparent. A fairly comprehensive survey is required of the technical characteristics of the sample innovations as listed in chapter 3. Specifically, the twin technological assumptions of the simple vintage model (embodiment of new technology and indivisibility of plant) should be tested. More generally, it is essential to establish whether new innovations have certain common attributes which might influence firms' decision making. Secondly, a realistic but empirically manageable approach to the firm-level adoption decision must be provided. The following two chapters are directed to these two tasks.

3

The sample innovations

3.1 Introduction

As explained in the appendix on data sources, data on the diffusion of 22 post-war process innovations has been collected from a number of sources and, in this connection, the generous help of the National Institute of Economic and Social Research in providing so much information from their own investigations cannot be overemphasized.[1] In general, published data on the diffusion of new innovations in the U.K. is extremely scarce and, without access to the Institute's data, it is doubtful whether the empirical parts of this study would have been possible.

In addition to this data, information has also been collected on the nature of the technology embodied in these innovations from various trade and scientific journals, from the firms who manufacture the innovations and, in some cases, from the firms who have adopted them. The purpose of this chapter is to provide an analysis and summary of the common technological attributes which have emerged from this literature search. Bearing in mind the findings of the previous chapter, it is clear that the technological characteristics of new innovations must play a crucial role in model building in this area. Whilst it is suspected that most technologists, and probably most industrialists, would view much of the following analysis as obvious, it is worthy of fairly lengthy elaboration on at least three grounds. First, some of the implicit assumptions common to much theoretical work on the economics of technical progress are not substantiated for this present sample. Second, and more specifically, the epidemic model has been criticized above for its unrealistic technological assumptions; clearly these criticisms should be supported by particular examples – the present chapter provides such examples. Third, the alternative theoretical model presented in chapter 4 assumes a number of technological attributes to be common to all new process innovations – again these assumptions must be judged against the real world.

Section 2 considers how representative the present sample of innovations might be, in order that the conclusions of this chapter may be placed into some overall perspective of process innovations as a whole. Section 3 pro-

TABLE 3.1   *The sample innovations*

Innovation[†]	Industry	Average[‡] pay back	Average[‡] initial outlay	Probable[§] learning curve
(a) *Supplementary*				
1. Special Presses (SP) (first adopted in 1962)	Paper and board	1.0^a	14.7^a	A
2. Foils (1962) (F)	Paper and board	0.5^c	2.5^b	A
3. Synthetic Fabrics (1962) (SF)	Paper and board	0.25^b	0.6^b	A
4. Wet Suction Boxes (WSB) (1957)	Paper and board	4.0^b	3.0^b	A
5. Gibberellic Acid (GA) (1959)	Malting	0.5^a	0.5^a	A
6. Accelerated Drying Hoods (ADH) (1948)	Weaving	1.75^h	0.35^h	A
(b) *Involving automation*				
7. Paper Machine (PCBC) Control by Computer (1965)	Paper and board	2.0^d	100.0^d	B
8. Computer typesetting (CT) (1964)	Provincial newspapers	4.0^b	46.7^b	U
9. Electrical Hygrometer (EH) (1935)	Weaving	1.9^h	0.1^h	A
10. Automatic Size Box (ASB) (1951)	Weaving	7.0^h	2.75^h	A
11. Automatic Track Lines (ATL) (1947)	Car manufacture	3.8^a	1000.0^i	B
12. Photo-electrically controlled cutting machines (PE) (1957)	Shipbuilding	10.9^g	54.0^g	U
(c) *Replacing capital-embodied old technology*				
13. Shuttleless Looms (SL) (1958)	Weaving	4.5^e	3.5^f	U
14. Tufted Carpet Machines (TC) (1955)	Carpet manufacture	0.4^j	35.0^j	U
15. Numerically Controlled Machine Tools (NCPP) (1962)	Printing press manufacture	5.4^a	20.7^a	U
16. Numerically Controlled Machine Tools (NCTN) (1956)	Turning machine manufacture	5.4^a	20.7^a	U
17. Numerically Controlled Machine Tools (NCTB) (1957)	Turbine manufacture	5.4^a	20.7^a	U
18. Tunnel Kilns (TK) (1953)	Clay brick making	5.6^a	260.0^b	B
19. Basic Oxygen Process (BOP) (1958)	Iron and steel	6.0^a	6000.0^a	B

TABLE 3.1   *Continued*

Innovation†	Industry	Average‡ pay back	Average‡ initial outlay	Probable§ learning curve
20. Continuous Casting (CC) (1959)	Iron and steel	4.6^k	4640.0^k	B
(d) *Involving a new function*				
21. Vacuum Melting (VM) (1958)	Iron and steel	3.0^b	155.0^l	B
22. Vacuum Degassing (VD) (1955)	Iron and steel	5.0^b	164.0^m	B

Notes:

† The date of first adoption of the innovation is shown in brackets after its name.

‡ Average initial outlay is measured in thousands of pounds (in current prices). Average pay back reflects the number of years required, on average, for that outlay to be recouped from the net revenues produced by operating the process. Broadly speaking, the estimates refer to the average across firms and approximately at the mid point of the period studied. In many cases, however, scarcity of data does not permit such averages to be computed. In their place, what seems to be the most representative available estimate is reported. The sources for these estimates are as follows:

  (a) N.I.E.S.R. questionnaires to British adopters in connection with the Nabseth and Ray (1974) study.
  (b) Communication from a manufacturer of the innovation.
  (c) Barnard (1971).
  (d) Elliot Automation (1966).
  (e) Textile Council (1969).
  (f) Ormerod (1963).
  (g) Mellanby (1959).
  (h) Metcalfe (1970), but see also Davies (1976, appendix 1).
  (i) Pratten (1971).
  (j) Scott (1975).
  (k) Brisby (1964).
  (l) Barraclough (1969).
  (m) Holden (1969).

§ See section 3.3.5 for a full explanation. Briefly, A indicates innovations which are relatively cheap and technologically simple, whilst B are technologically complex and relative expensive. It is argued in the text that this distinction may have important implications for the nature of manufacturers' learning. U indicates 'unclassified', meaning that the innovation in question shares certain attributes with both group A and group B.

vides the core of the chapter and identifies six main areas in which the sample innovations appear to exhibit strong common features. In the appendix to this chapter, brief technical descriptions of the innovations are presented alongside the main technical sources used. Table 3.1 lists the sample innovations, the industries in which they have diffused, and certain key statistics such as the cost and profitability of adoption.

A more detailed discussion of these innovations, and the evidence on which the various assertions made in this chapter is based, are to be found in Davies (1976, chapter 3 and appendix 1).

3.2 Representativeness of the sample

As can be seen from table 3.1, all but one of the innovations originated in the post-war period. Whilst not random, this sample is fairly broadly based.[2] The thirteen U.K. industries in which these innovations have diffused are distributed across the industrial spectrum. Using Pratten's four way classification of industries, table 3.2 indicates that roughly 10% of all U.K. industries are covered with roughly the same proportion of all employees. At the slightly less aggregate level, the 10% figure is maintained for 'process' and 'textile' industries but exceeded slightly for 'engineering', with a compensating short fall for 'others'. Against this, however, it should be noted that *within* 'process' industries, crude steelmaking accounts for three of the sample innovations; within 'textiles', weaving for four, and within 'others', paper and board for five: these three (admittedly large) industries are, therefore, somewhat over-represented.

Turning to the innovations themselves, it is impossible to say how 'typical' they are. Nevertheless, if three basic characteristics are considered (namely function, cost and profitability), it would be fair to claim a wide variety within the sample. From the brief technical summaries provided at the end of the chapter, four main types of innovation may be identified. Six are essentially *supplementary*: their main function is to speed up existing processes; as such, they can be applied to old existing equipment as well as to new equipment. In these cases, little or no replacement of existing equipment is involved. Six other innovations *automate old manual operations* or sometimes do away with them altogether. Again, these usually imply only limited replacement of old technology equipment. Only eight of the twenty-two innovations conform to the technological assumption of the basic *vintage* model (see for instance, Salter, 1960). That is, they are embodied in

TABLE 3.2   *The coverage of the sample*

Type of industry	Total U.K. (1968)		This Sample		
	Number of census trades	Number of employees ('000)	Number of sample trades	Employees ('000)	Number of sample innovations
Process	32	1376	3	260	5
Engineering	35	2938	5	347	5
Textiles	25	1163	2	106	5
Others	49	2601	3	104	7
Total	141	8078	13	817	22

Sources: Figures for total U.K.: Pratten (1971, p. 267), and for the sample: the present enquiry.

new capital equipment and replace an old technology which is also embodied in existing equipment. It is interesting to note that even in these cases, adoption does not necessarily imply replacement of entire plants. To give one example, the Tunnel Kiln replaces the old technology Hoffman Kiln in brickmaking but the adjacent processes of clay-winning, shaping and drying do not need to be drastically altered when the Tunnel Kiln is introduced. Finally, two of the innovations *serve a different purpose* from any existing process; for example, Vacuum Degassing units are used in steelmaking to improve the quality of the product and do not necessarily involve the replacement of existing equipment.

Whilst it is dangerous to assign to any innovation a 'typical' cost or profitability (as will be argued presently, these will vary widely from firm to firm and over time), using information collected from various sources, table 3.1 shows what might be termed average (over time and across firms) estimates. As can be seen, a number of the innovations, mainly in the process industries, can cost millions of pounds to install whilst others involve an initial outlay measured only in hundreds of pounds. The potential profitability of adoption also varies substantially; in some cases the increased revenues resulting from adoption will sometimes cover the initial outlay within the first year of operation, whilst in others the pay back period may stretch over ten years.

The overall picture which emerges, then, is of a non-random sample which is nevertheless sufficiently broad based to suggest that any conclusions which can be drawn may have wider implications than merely the present sample.

3.3 Some common characteristics

3.3.1 The sources of invention and innovation

Invention and development of the processes can be attributed almost exclusively to firms or individuals outside the adopting industries. None of the processes were invented by firms in the adopting industries and in only four or five cases was any significant contribution made to development. Having said this, it is difficult in most cases to distinguish *one* crucial invention. In some instances the technology involved is by no means new, for example, Tunnel Kilns, Shuttleless Looms and Continuous Casting can all be traced back to related inventions made during the last century. Moreover, the development of most of the innovations has been international and often the result of the coming together of ideas originating from different and independent sources.

As far as one can designate a country of origin, it could be claimed that the U.K. was the originator or co-originator of six innovations as opposed to nine for the U.S., four each for Germany and Austria, and at least one each for Switzerland, Sweden and Canada. This does not tell a complete story, however, since British firms played important roles in the development of at least twelve innovations. But then this wider role also applied to the U.S. and Germany.

As suggested by Pratten (1971, p. 293), the main vehicle of new technology appears to have been the capital goods industries and, to a lesser extent, Research Associations. The Textile Research Association (better known as the Shirley Institute) was directly responsible for the three sizing innovations, and the British Iron and Steel Research Association (B.I.S.R.A.) was extremely active in the development and modifications of the steel innovations (particularly Continuous Casting and Vacuum Degassing). The role of the capital goods sector was even more substantial however. All of the sample innovations are sold and/or installed by a capital goods industry which was responsible for much of the original inventive activity and development work.

Contrary to expectation however, most of the innovations are not supplied by monopolists. Only four (all supplementary and relatively cheap) are produced by a single supplier: Giberellic Acid, Synthetic Fabrics, Electrical Hygrometers and Automatic Size Boxes. In the latter two cases, this monopoly position was allocated under licence by the Research Association. Elsewhere the norm appears to be oligopoly with between two and eight suppliers.

Two other interesting characteristics of the innovation suppliers are their close historical links with the consuming industries and their international nature. For nearly all of the innovations, producers are traditional suppliers, having supplied many previous innovations. In at least nine cases, the consuming industries constitute the main, if not the sole, market for the suppliers. For instance, the producers of Tufted Carpet machines supply a wide range of other products predominantly to the carpet industry in many different countries. For only three innovations, Gibberellic Acid, and the use of Computers in both newspaper printing and paper production, could the innovation supplier be said to be breaking into a new market. Under these circumstances, it is unlikely that many potential adopters will remain totally ignorant of the existence of a new innovation for very long. Given the international history of many of the innovations, it is not surprising to find, moreover, that the supplying industry is international in its operations. In some cases, the Paper machinery industry for example, the suppliers are foreign-owned subsidiaries; whilst in others, including those supplying the process industries, British firms compete both in the U.K. and abroad with large European firms. Consequently, it is likely that the suppliers will have ready access to improvements in the technology emanating from over-seas.

In summary, then, the conventional view of a firm inventing a new process for its own use, perhaps patenting it and then permitting its competitors to use the process under licence, is inaccurate for the sample innovations.[3]

3.3.2 *Factor savings and the coefficients of production*

Labour saving is the most obvious attribute of nearly all the innovations. This is true, almost by definition, for the automating type, and the eight vintage type innovations all have higher labour productivity than the old equipment which they replace. The main advantage of the supplementary type is in the speeding up of existing processes which, in turn, leads to more efficient use of labour (as well as other inputs). Fuel savings are less pro-nounced but still significant for Tunnel Kilns and the Steel Innovations. A straightforward assessment of capital savings is difficult, given the elusive nature of the concept in practice. Nevertheless, the supplementary innova-tions unequivocally increase the productivity of existing equipment without any increase in other inputs. On the other hand, the vintage group, with the exception of Continuous Casting, have higher investment costs per unit of capacity than do new vintages of the technology with which they compete. Where estimates of ex-ante engineering production functions are provided in the technical literature, it would appear that, for any given level of capa-city, the coefficients of production (as embodied in the labour–output ratio, for instance) are relatively fixed.[4]

3.3.3 *Variability between adopters in the profitability of adoption*

Every innovation in the sample possesses certain technical characteristics which lead to often quite large differentials in the profitability of adoption between different potential adopters. These differentials arise essentially because of heterogeneity within the adopting industries. More specifically, four main characteristics of a potential adopter may influence the returns to be gained from adoption.

(a) *The nature of the product* which is to be produced using the innovation is often a major cause of inter-firm differences. In most industries, one can usually point to a handful of main products (and sometimes, even, only one). But using a finer definition of 'product', to include real or imagined brand differences, there are often as many products as there are firms. Very often the attributes which differentiate products, in the same industry, influence the returns that can be derived from adoption of the new process.

Usually, the more differentiated and less standard is the product, the less profitable is the new process. For instance, certain quality type bricks are not easily produced under the automation of Tunnel Kilns; similarly, it is more difficult to produce carpets with a complicated design using Tufted Carpet Machines; the continuous nature of Continuous Casting makes it less beneficial for heterogeneous product mixes; Gibberellic Acid is said to impair the quality of certain beers if applied in large quantities, and so on. In fact for just over half of the sample, it is the specialist products for which potential returns from adoption are reduced (but rarely removed altogether). For certain other innovations however, the opposite is true: using Numerical Control, Vacuum Melting, Vacuum Degassing and Photo-electrically controlled cutting machines, the quality and precision of the product can be improved considerably. Although these innovations may be used for a wide variety of products, within the industry concerned, they are most beneficial for those products where quality is important.

(b) *The nature of a firm's existing processes* will also affect the returns in many cases. This is perhaps most obvious for those innovations which replace an old technology embodied in existing equipment. With the appearance of the new process, it might be expected that much existing old technology equipment will become economically obsolescent, but the extent of returns from replacement will clearly depend on the age and vintage of the equipment to be replaced.

On the other hand, the 'supplementary' innovations usually operate more efficiently on relatively new equipment. In these cases, adoption will be more profitable the younger the firm's existing equipment. As Salter notes (1960, p. 85): 'A modern machine may have higher operating costs or a greater installation cost when installed in an older plant than the same machine in a completely modern plant'. This can also be observed for a number of the more fundamental sample innovations: Shuttleless Looms are easier to accommodate in newer, better laid-out weaving sheds; Vacuum Degassing is more compatible with the Basic Oxygen Steelmaking Process than with old-fashioned Open-Hearth furnaces; Gibberellic Acid only yields large savings if the kiln, used for drying, can handle the higher output rate.

(c) *The nature of the raw materials* to be used in the new process is particularly important for at least six of the sample innovations. Both Shuttleless Looms and Tufted Carpet Machines can be run more quickly for certain types of textile; Electrical Hygrometers are less suitable for rayon and nylon; Tunnel Kilns are much easier to operate when the clay used has a low carbon content; the returns from adoption of Gibberellic Acid will depend on the type of barley used and Basic Oxygen Steelmaking can only be employed when scrap metal constitutes no more than a limited proportion of the raw material.

(d) As many of the sample innovations are technically very sophisticated, they can only be operated efficiently and balanced with existing plant if managers, staff and workers understand the technical complexities involved. Thus inter-firm variance in the *technical skills and educational attainments of managers, staff and labour force* may lead to differences in the returns to be gained from adoption. Of course, expertise may be 'bought in' at the time of adoption, but this in itself will increase the cost of the new process. Either way, firms with less skilled managers stand to gain less from adoption.

Overall then, it is clear that the potential returns to be had from adoption of probably all the sample innovations will vary between firms quite significantly. In general, exact quantifications of the extent of this variability are unavailable. However, Hakonson and Gebhardt (both in Nabseth and Ray (1974)) do provide estimates for two particular innovations: Special Presses and Numerically Controlled Machine Tools. It is clear from these estimates that the variability may, indeed, be substantial: Hakonson's estimates of hypothetical pay back periods in Sweden for Special Presses varied from as little as six months for some firms to over three years for others. Similarly, Gebhardt's data suggests that these are massive differences in the savings resulting, depending on batch sizes and the nature of the end product.

3.3.4 Economies of scale and other size-related advantages

One very striking feature which emerges from the technical literature on many of the sample innovations, and in correspondence with many of the innovation suppliers, is the possibility of scale economies for the potential adopter. Whilst the term is often used in a rather loose sense, it is clear that, for a large proportion of the sample, the savings resulting from adoption should be proportionately greater, the larger the scale of adoption. This is not surprising perhaps, although this phenomenen has received little attention in most previous research as diffusion.[5]

The most obvious examples of scale economies in the sample are to be found in the process industries. It has long been argued, of course, that certain processes and machines will exhibit scale economies in both initial outlay and operating costs per unit of output, approximating to the following mathematical form:

$$Y = aS^b \qquad (3.1)$$

where S is the capacity of the process, Y the initial outlay per unit of capacity, or operating costs per unit of capacity, and a and b are constants: $a > 0$, $b < 0$. It is conventional to argue for capital costs, that $b = -0.4$ on the basis of the well known 'six-tenths' rule of engineering.[6]

On fitting equation (3.1) to engineering data on the initial outlay required for different capacities (Davies 1976, appendix 1), b is estimated as -0.32 for Tunnel Kilns, -0.20 for Basic Oxygen and -0.45 for Automatic Track Lines. For Vacuum Degassing, there is also a close inverse relationship of the same sort between capital outlay and *ladle* capacity which, in turn, will help determine overall capacity. Moreover, Leckie and Morris (1968, pp. 442–52) have found that a form similar to (3.1), describes scale economies in the capital costs of virtually all new processes in the iron and steel industry, therefore it seems probable that similar economies are also available for Continuous Casting and Vacuum Melting, although specific data on these innovations was unavailable.

Using similar engineering data on operating costs per unit of output, b was estimated at -0.13 for Tunnel Kilns, -0.30 for Basic Oxygen, -0.21 for Automatic Track Lines and -0.52 for Vacuum Degassing. Leckie and Morris, fitting a slightly different form than (3.1), also found substantial scale economies in operating costs for many different processes in iron and steel, and so again it is not unlikely that both Continuous Casting and Vacuum Melting exhibit such economies.

Whilst it is worth recalling the limitations of ex-ante engineering data and remembering that these estimates do not apply to actual installations,[7] it does seem likely that the larger process innovations exhibit non-trivial economies to scale of adoption.

Turning to the two computer-using innovations in the present sample, it is conventional to claim (as do the manufacturers) that these, too, exhibit significant scale economies. However, this view is challenged by Stoneman (1976, pp. 60–5) who presents econometrically estimated relationships between computer price and three aspects of computer size which are not inconsistent with constant returns to scale. On the other hand, Stoneman's analysis does suggest significant economies to scale in operating costs. Furthermore, it is argued by computer manufacturers that the *quality* of service offered by computer control of Paper Machines and Computer Typesetting improves as the scale of installation increases. This is due largely to increasing scope for automation.

As far as is known, there is no engineering evidence of scale economies for the 14 other sample innovations. In most of these cases, however, the so-called *economies of large numbers* seem to be important. For example, although unit costs of Shuttleless Looms do not appear to be sensitive to the *size* of loom, they are to the *number* of looms installed (typically, looms and some of the other innovations are installed in batches). In fact similar economies are claimed for Numerically Controlled Machine Tools, Tufted Carpet Machines, Photo-electrically Controlled Cutting Machines, Computer Typesetting and Computer Control of Paper Machines. They are attributed, variously, to (a) economies in servicing and programming, (b) proportional reductions in necessary stocks of spare parts, and (c) proportional reductions in 'setting-up' time. Because labour is 'lumpy' in some processes in the textile industries (that is one operative is responsible for a number of machines), an added economy to the installation of large numbers of Shuttleless Looms and Tufted Carpet Machines derives from a better chance of optimizing the capital–labour ratio.

The extent to which these various scale economies make adoption more attractive for larger firms will depend in practice on three factors. First, how much does firm size dictate the scale of adoption? This will clearly vary across innovations and industries. For some of the more fundamental innovations, there may be little flexibility. For instance, the capacity of a Tunnel Kiln installation will be dictated by the capacity of the adjacent processes in the brickworks: clay winning, shaping and drying. In other words, the need for balance will often restrict the scale of adoption for small firms. (Local demand conditions may also restrict the small firm's ability to go in for large installations.) Having said this, in industries where plant size is typically small relative to firm size, smaller firms may be *able* to match the scale of installation of large firms (the larger firms being of greater size mainly due to their operating more, rather than larger, plants). However, even in these cases, smaller firms may be less *willing* to undertake large scale installations if this reduces the flexibility of the product mix within the plant. Given that many of the sample innovations standardize the end product, single-plant firms will be unable to install large units of the new innovations and still retain a range of products. Again, the Tunnel Kiln is a good example. Whilst large multi-plant firms may be willing to turn over one entire plant to the production of standard common bricks, leaving other plants to produce quality facing bricks, the one-plant firm must produce both types of brick in the same plant and may therefore be forced to employ two smaller kilns, one for each brick type.

A second possibility which might reduce the advantages to large firms would be the existence of scale economies in the old technology being replaced. This can be discounted immediately, however, for the six innovations replacing manual operations and the six supplementary innovations. Of the other ten innovations, there is concrete evidence in only one case: Continuous Casting. Pratten (1971, p. 303) provides some detail on this example in his comprehensive survey of scale economies in production processes. However, he does conclude that 'many new processes are increasing the economies of scale and increasing their range, and though some new techniques ... reduce the economies of scale, the impression gained from the industry studies was that these are exceptional cases'.

Thirdly, if there are upper limits to the range of capacities for which scale economies apply, this may reduce the advantage to very large firms. For example, Bruni (1964) suggests that at certain very high capacities, stresses appear in the raw materials used to construct some large processes. The data which is available for the sample innovations does suggest upper limits for Basic Oxygen, Automatic Track Lines and Tunnel Kilns, but in each case, these limits appear to be at capacities in excess of anything ever installed in the U.K.

Overall then, it does seem probable that for many of the sample innovations, there are strong technological reasons why larger firms should find adoption more attractive. Moreover, there are a number of other factors which should re-inforce this tendency:

(a) Large firms may be able to use the new innovation more intensively. The importance of avoiding 'down-time' for Computer Typesetting and Computer Control of Paper Machines was stressed by computer manufacturers. Similarly, large firms may be able to operate Shuttleless Looms for longer runs, not least because they are often able, by virtue of localized monopsonist power over labour, to demand shift working.

(b) Large firms are perhaps more likely to employ the skilled management and staff needed to understand the technical intricacies of most new innovations.

(c) Most of the large innovations often require more than a year for proper installation. This can lead to loss of output (where building on an old site) and problems of liquidity in the change-over period. Similarly, periods of retraining (and thus further loss of production) may be needed for managers, staff and workers. Because of their greater resources, larger firms may be better able to absorb these disruptive effects.

(d) There is, perhaps, a higher probability that large firms will have the ideal conditions for adoption. As explained above, although all of the sample innovations are suitable for most firms in the appropriate industries, they are more suitable for some than others, (in that they possess the most appropriate produce, inputs etc.). As Mansfield notes (1968, p. 156), 'large firms, because they encompass a wider range of operating conditions, have a better chance of containing these conditions'. A second possibility, also noted by Mansfield, is that larger firms, just because of their size, are more likely to have a unit of the old technology needing replacement (perhaps failing to earn rent or nearing the end of its physical life). At least this is true so long as there is no pronounced tendency for large firms to have newer capital equipment than small firms.

(e) As noted below, many of the sample innovations require high capacity usage if substantial savings are to be effected. Larger firms may be better able to optimize their technology mix so as to operate the new innovation at full capacity permanently, whilst satisfying the fluctuating residual by retaining some units of the old technologies. Indivisibilities may prevent many small firms from following this option.

3.3.5 Post-invention improvements: the group A/group B distinction

Rarely, if ever, does the technological development of a new process cease once it has been adopted for the first time. Typically, the manufacturers of new processes continue to devote resources to effect post-invention improvements for some time after the date of introduction. More generally, both the manufacturers and consumers of new processes will benefit from 'learning by doing'. The case for learning by doing is, by now, well known:[8] as manufacturers have more and more experience at producing new equipment (and consuming firms have acquired experience of using the equipment) they attain a better understanding of the technical relationships involved and their workers acquire on-the-job skills. In consequence, it is to be expected that the cost of producing the new process and the operating costs involved in using the process will fall in real terms for a number of years following the initial introduction. Moreover, these learning effects are often quite substantial: 'At one firm it was suggested that the costs for the initial batch produced may be as much as three times the average costs of a machine tool after it had been in production for eighteen months or so. Another 'rule of thumb' suggested was that the average cost for the first production batch could be reduced by more than one third' (Pratten 1971, p. 167). Turning specifically to the innovations in the present sample, there is considerable, if piecemeal, evidence of learning by doing. For instance, the price of an average Computer Typesetting installation in 1973 was claimed to have been only 25% of the 1964 price. Similarly, the price of Gibberellic Acid fell from £8.75 per gram in 1962 to £0.58 in 1974.[9] In such cases the costs of producing the innovation have presumably declined substantially. Examples may also be found of later vintages of the same innovation proving to be substantially more productive than earlier vintages. For instance, Lacci, Davies and Smith (in Nabseth and Ray (1974)), show that labour productivity of Tunnel Kilns installed between 1964 and 1968 was significantly higher than of those installed between 1960 and 1964 which, in turn, was higher than that of Tunnel Kilns installed before 1960. Similarly, Reynolds (1968) presents some data on the output per man-hour of Tufted Carpet Machines which implies an increase of at least 25% between 1958 and 1963 machines.[10]

Interestingly a number of conclusions drawn in previous work on learning by doing can be confirmed for the present sample. Not surprisingly, the *scope* for learning appears to be greater the more technically sophisticated the process innovation, and the more discontinuities or breaks in production there are for the innovation manufacturer. Likewise, both factors tend to produce significant learning effects for a *longer* period. On the other hand, discontinuities in production tend to produce more 'forgetting' and duplication of mistakes, especially in the early years. Another tendency which is quite pronounced, especially for the more sophisticated innovations including Continuous Casting, Vacuum Degassing and the other innovations in the process industries), is that of 'teething troubles'. As Rosenborg (1976, p. 526), claims, 'Innumerable "bugs" may need to be worked out.' In other words significant technological stumbling blocks appear both in the production and the use of the innovations in the early years. Moreover, some of the innovations are so lumpy that each potential adopter will only ever need to purchase one or two units of them. From the manufacturers' point of view, this means greater heterogeneity in their installations; this is emphasized by the complexity of most of the lumpy innovations, which tends to produce significant inter-site differences because of different operating conditions.

For these reasons, it is necessary to identify two basic types of innovation. *Group A* can be defined as technologically simple, probably relatively cheap and produced off-site. *Group B* are more sophisticated, expensive innovations which are produced on a one-off basis, often requiring lengthy periods of installation on the adopter's site.[11] Learning effects (as reflected by declining labour inputs, both in the *production* of the innovation and *when using* it) for group A might be initially quite large, but soon falling away drastically. For group B, they are likely to be much longer lived and, in the long run, more substantial. Nevertheless, over the early years, whilst the manufacturer is overcoming teething troubles and building up a portfolio of knowledge about his customers' different operating conditions, learning may be quite limited for group B.

This distinction may be stylized graphically as in figure 3.1. In the long run, the learning curves of both Groups will settle down to the familiar form hypothesized in most of the existing literature on learning by doing:

$$L_t = \alpha t^{\beta}, \alpha > 0, \quad -1 < \beta < 0 \tag{3.2}$$

where L_t is, say, the labour input per unit of output in the production of vintage t of the new process or, equally plausibly, the labour input per unit of output when using vintage t of the new process.

In the short run, however, an 'initial period' is hypothesized for group B innovations. During this period, teething troubles are encountered and 'forgetting' takes place and gradually innovation makers build up a portfolio of knowledge about their various potential customers' characteristics and technical idiosyncracies. For the duration of this period learning is limited and only accelerates appreciably after a number of years. Thus, in the short term, and perhaps even in the medium term, the learning curve might exhibit more of a rough exponential shape.

This distinction, if valid, is important for the study of inter-firm diffusion. When considering inter-firm diffusion, it is only the first installation of the innovation for each firm which matters. As such, the period concerned may constitute only a small part of the life of the innovation. In the steel industry, for example (but also many others), a technology may reign supreme for as long as a century, yet it may be only two decades or less before all firms have made their *first* purchase of the technology. Consequently, whilst the long run learning curve for these innovations may be approximated by equation (3.2), for the relatively short periods considered here, an exponential curve may be more appropriate.

Finally, three other lesser aspects of technological learning might be mentioned. In some cases the range of operating conditions for which the innovation is suitable is extended widely in the very early years.[12] For instance, initially, the main advantage of Vacuum Degassing lay in its ability to remove hydrogen in the production of steel and, because this advantage is only crucial for certain types of steel, the process was much more desirable for some firms than for others. As the technology developed, however, another major technical advantage emerged: more efficient de-oxidisation of steel. This property is of much more general appeal to steelmakers and so the process took an added significance for a much wider range of steel-

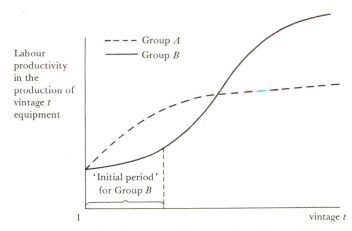

Figure 3.1   The learning curves for group A and group B innovations

makers (see Flux, 1965, and Holden, 1969.) Similar, if less pronounced, widening of the technology occurred for three or four other sample innovations but in each case before the innovation in question had been introduced in the U.K.[13] Second, in a few cases, the economies of scale exhibited by the process appear to have increased in the early years (Vacuum Degassing, Basic Oxygen Steelmaking and Continuous Casting most noticeably), but again these changes were achieved long before the innovations had 'taken-off' in the U.K. Third, the so-called 'Sailing Ship Effect' could be observed in two cases (Tunnel Kilns and Basic Oxygen Steelmaking). This is said to occur when the introduction of a new innovation leads to a sudden spurt of improvements in the old technology.[14] In both instances, however, this effect could only be identified in countries other than the U.K.

3.3.6 The short-run cost curve and other cyclical considerations

For a number of fairly obvious reasons, the attractiveness of adoption of a new innovation is likely to vary across the trade cycle. Over half of the sample innovations are typified by high fixed costs relative to the old technology. These are due, variously, to the need to employ highly paid and highly skilled staff and workers, high capital charges and high start-up costs. Although variable costs are lower, reasonably high output rates are still required for these to outweigh the fixed cost differential.

This applies to the six continuous processes (usually replacing old batch-type processes) and the six innovations automating old manual operations.

There is a further set of eight innovations which produce unit cost savings mainly by speeding up existing processes (without an increase in most inputs), or by removing bottlenecks. For these too, therefore, adoption is only worth while given sufficient demand. Similarly for Shuttleless Looms, most of the cost savings only result from long production runs which also depend on reasonably healthy demand conditions.

Clearly, then, the returns to be gained from adoption will vary according to demand conditions and expected capacity usage. This may be particularly important if firms' investment decisions are based on simple rules of thumb, such as the pay-back method, which weight immediate returns as over-whelmingly important.

On the other hand, as has been already mentioned, many of the innovations require lengthy building programmes which lead to short-run disruption and output losses – these may *encourage* adoption in periods of low demand when disruption and output losses may be less real.

3.4 Implications

As the present chapter has included a certain amount of technological discussion, it is perhaps useful to summarize the main implications which may be drawn. First, and rather negatively, neither the Mansfield epidemic model nor a Salteresque vintage approach seem to be applicable to a majority of the sample innovations. It was argued in the previous chapter that the epidemic model assumes (1) that all potential adopters of any process innovation must be equally 'susceptible' and (2) that the profitability and cost of innovations must remain constant over the diffusion period. From the findings of section 3, these assumptions may be rejected: the profitability of adoption will clearly vary from firm to firm within the same industry and, given the probable importance of firm size, it is unlikely that this variation will be in any sense random. Similarly, if learning by doing is as significant as claimed, it is unlikely that the profitability and cost of many innovations will remain constant over time. Whilst the vintage approach cannot be totally ruled out as a possibility, the fact that so few of the sample innovations replace an old technology embodied in existing equipment would imply that significant modifications to the basic vintage model would be necessary if it was to attain any explanatory success in this context.

Second, a multitude of technical factors have been identified as important in determining the profitability of adoption of any process by any firm. This goes a long way to explaining the poor explanatory power of the previous research attempting to explain the speed of adoption of individual firms as noted in the previous chapter.

More positively, a number of pointers have emerged which help the model building of the next chapter. The adoption decision at the individual firm level is likely to be determined by a large number of characteristics of the firm including, perhaps crucially, its size. Learning by doing will clearly be of some importance in the diffusion process and the distinction drawn in the chapter between group A and group B innovations should be acknowledged in any theoretical model of diffusion.

Finally, a number of findings of more general interest have emerged. Perhaps most significant is the generally rather passive role played by most consuming industries in the invention and development of the new processes which they are to adopt. In contrast, the various capital goods industries are very much the vehicle of technical progress.

These conclusions must be modified, of course, by the proviso that, strictly, they apply only to the innovations in the present sample. Having said this, it has been established in section 2 of this chapter that the sample, whilst not random, is fairly broadly based.

Appendix A.3   Brief descriptions of the sample innovations[15]

1—4 Special Presses, Foils, Synthetic Forming Fabrics and Wet Suction Boxes   The paper machine represents the major technical stage in the process of making paper and board from the raw material of woodpulp or waste paper; it transforms the web (a dispertion of fibres in water) into paper sheet. The paper machine itself consists of three sections (the wire section, the press section and the dryer), one role of each being to reduce the water content of the web. Each of these innovations is applied to the press section. In each case the speed of the paper machine is increased and the quality of the end product is improved. It should be stressed that these innovations are not substitutes for each other. Moreover they may be adopted without replacement of the paper machine involved.

Major sources of technical information. Nabseth and Ray (1974, chapter 4), Ray (1969) and Nissan (1969) for Special Presses. Barnard (1971), Hart, Utton and Walshe (1973, pp. 151–3) for Foils. Cruden and Wild (1971) and Hampson (1971) for Synthetic Forming Fabrics and *The Paper Maker* (1962) for Wet Suction Boxes. In each case, communications with various manufacturers and their advertising literature provided useful ancillary information.

5 Gibberellic Acid   The malting industry transforms grain (usually barley) into malt, most of which is used by the brewing industry. It has three main processes: steeping (soaking the grain in water for two to three days); germination (in which the drained barley loses weight and is transformed from a hard mass into soft malt; this may take from seven to ten days) and drying and curing (in which excess moisture is removed from the malt in a kiln, lasting up to twenty-four hours). Gibberellic Acid is an additive which is used to reduce germination time to as little as five to six days. Other side advantages include reduction of malting loss, and increases in the yield and quality of the extract. The adoption of Gibberellic Acid requires the purchase of specialized machinery such as moving spray booms, reservoirs and pipelines.

Major Sources. Nabseth and Ray (1974, pp. 215–16), Northam (1962), Ray (1969) and I.C.I.

6, 9, 10 Accelerated Drying Hoods, Electrical Hygrometer and Automatic Size Box   The sizing process is a preparatory stage prior to weaving in the textile industry, in which the warp threads are impregnated with size in order to prevent the threads from disintegrating in weaving. The Electrical Hygrometer is a simple instrument which helps the operative measure the dryness of the warp; as such it increases the speed of the process and thus reduces the labour input per unit of output. The Accelerated Drying Hood

comprises a fan and motor covered by metal covers and its purpose is to increase drying capacity. The Automatic Size Box automatically controls the proportions of size paste and water applied to the warp; this leads to important savings in the amount of size needed, increases in the weavability of the warps and does away with the minor sub-process of pre-boiling the size.
Major Sources. Metcalfe (1968 and 1970).

7 Paper Machine Control by Computer   Process control by computer is, of course, a classic example of automation. In this case, the computer has control over a number of variables in the paper making process – machine speed, thick stock flow, clay flow, flowbox pressure and slice gap etc. In layman's English, it controls the speed of the whole process, the rate at which various materials are added to the basic wood pulp and the speed of various sub-sections of the process. Consequently, the operators acquire greater and more immediate control over the paper machine, leading to increased machine speeds without any loss in quality. Down-time is also reduced for a number of reasons, for example, switching from producing one grade of paper to another can be effected very quickly. It is also claimed that because paper quality is more consistent, waste due to 'off-specification paper' is substantially reduced.
Major Sources. Elliott Automation (1966), various editions of *Paper Technology* and, on computers in general, Stoneman (1976).

8 Computer Typesetting   This innovation is applicable to the 'composing room' in a printing works; it is, perhaps, self-explanatory – a computer is responsible for 'setting-up' the page in terms of number of words per line, spaces between words and between lines, and in the case of newspapers, classified ads and display ads are stored, sorted and up-dated. These functions provide savings in composing room labour, e.g. reducing paste-up time and improving the appearance of the newspapers. As composing staff comprised nearly 22% of the printing work force in 1967, this can be seen to be a relatively major innovation.
Major Sources. Manpower Research Unit (1970), Data Systems (1973), communications with, and advertising literature of, the three major producers.

11 Automatic Track Lines   The Automatic Track Line, as used in car manufacture, 'replaces some, or many, individual machines, makes it possible for several metal-working processes on one piece of equipment to be amalgamated and caters for the internal transport, from one process to the next, of the work in progress' (Ray, 1969, p. 76).
   It is, then, basically a series of machines operating on a continuous supply

of engine parts, e.g. blocks. The main economic advantages are savings in labour and the removal of potential bottle-necks.

Major Sources. Ray (1969), *British Industry Week* (2 February 1968), Pratten (1971).

12 Photo-electrically Controlled Cutting Machines   Steel plates are used extensively in the construction of all new ships above a certain size. Traditionally, plate was bought from the steel industry and cut by hand by relatively skilled workers, after having previously marked the appropriate shapes in the plate, also by hand. This innovation in the shipbuilding industry eliminates the marking process and automates the cutting process. Basically, a drawing of the shape required is placed in the control side of an automatic burning machine which then cuts the plate to the appropriate shape with the help of a photo-electric device. Savings are therefore possible in direct labour costs and from more economical use of steel plate, and increased precision.

Main Sources. Ray (1969), Mellanby (1959), the Research Association.

13 Shuttleless Looms   The Shuttleless Loom is certainly one of the most revolutionary recent innovations in the weaving stage of textile production. In the traditional process, the cotton threads are woven by a thread-carrying shuttle moving to and fro across a series of threads arranged lengthwise. Shuttleless looms use other methods of transmitting the single thread across the lengthwise threads (weft insertion). The Sulzer loom, for example, draws the weft from a stationary supply package mounted on the side of the loom, as opposed to the traditional method of carrying the supply with it. The major advantages derive from higher possible speed and the reduced labour time in replacing weft supplies. In addition to the higher production from a given floor space and increased labour productivity, the quality of the end product is often improved because of fewer weft breakages and less strain on the lengthwise threads.

Main Sources. Smith's chapter in Nabseth and Ray (1974), Ray (1969), Ormerod (1963).

14 Tufted Carpet Machines   The Tufted Carpet Machine is probably the most fundamental innovation in the modern carpet industry. Basically, it has transformed carpetmaking by replacing a weaving process with what amounts to a giant sewing machine: pile yarn is inserted into a woven backing by a row of needles, the inverted tufts being held in place by the 'untwisting' effect of the yarn and by the addition of latex to the back of the carpet.

This constitutes the largest and most important part of the carpet making process and major savings are usual, particularly in operatives.

Main Sources. Reynolds (1968), Scott (1975) and correspondence with the machine suppliers.

15, 16, 17 Numerically Controlled Machine Tools   Numerically Controlled Machine Tools are simply machine tools which are controlled and monitored in their operation by a computer of some sort. Because continually changing processes can be handled on the same machine, this allows flexible automation of the old technology. The major economic advantages are: (1) labour savings, as one numerically controlled machine tool can often do the job of two or three conventional machines, (2) savings on other tools, such as templates, jigs and fixtures, (3) quality improvement arising from the greater accuracy and uniformity of the end-product, (4) reduced levels of stocks of finished products (arising from the greater flexibility of production mentioned above) and (5) it is often possible to use the innovation to produce part designs that are impracticable using conventional machine tools.
Main Sources. Ray (1969) Crookall (1968) and Gebhardt's chapter in Nabseth and Ray (1974).

18 Tunnel Kilns   There are three main stages in brickmaking: quarrying of clay, forming the clay into brick shapes and burning or baking the clay into the finished product in a kiln. The kiln represents the most expensive piece of equipment in most brickworks. The old traditional kilns usually consist of a circular series of chambers and the fire moves continuously round the kiln through the chambers in which the bricks are placed. The Tunnel Kiln, on the other hand, involves a stationary firing zone and the bricks move on a wagon at a very slow speed through a long tunnel. The main advantages of this innovation are: (1) labour savings (primarily due to less physical handling of the bricks), (2) fuel savings (fuel is wasted by the old technology as the heat must be built up in each of the chambers separately), (3) easier working conditions (as operatives do not need to enter the kiln to extract the baked bricks) and (4) reduced chances of the kiln walls cracking.
Main Sources. Davies (1971), Davies and Smith's chapter in Nabseth and Ray (1974), Pratten (1971).

19 Basic Oxygen Process   To obtain steel from 'pig iron' the latter must be refined, namely unwanted chemical elements (carbon, sulphur, silicon, manganese and phosphorous) must be removed by oxidization. Traditionally, steel was refined using the Acid and Basic Bessemer process, in which air is blown from underneath into the hot metal bath in a convertor; or in Open Hearth furnaces in which burning fuel gas is passed over the top of the pig iron.

The Basic Oxygen Steelmaking process uses pure oxygen (rather than air) which is blown from above on to the surface of the hot metal bath. The main advantages are shorter 'tap-to-tap time' (that is quicker output from the same amount of metal input), improved quality of steel and lower fuel and capital costs.

Main Sources. Ray (1969), Nabseth and Ray (1974), Leckie and Morris (1968).

20 Continuous Casting   The process which typically follows refining in the steel industry is the casting of the molten steel traditionally into ingots, which are then rolled into semi-finished products such as billets, blooms or slabs.

Traditionally, casting has been an intermittent process: after each ingot is cast, casting is stopped in order to 'trim off' large quantities at the top and bottom of each ingot. After the metal is cooled sufficiently, the ingots are removed from the moulds, reheated and transferred to blooming mills where they are rolled into the semi-finished product.

Continuous casting turns this process into a continuous one: the liquid metal is poured into the mould at the same rate as the solid metal emerges at the other end, to be passed through straightening rollers and cut into pieces of the required length.

Major advantages arise from the displacement of the 'soaking pit' and blooming mill and from the improved yield (because of the displacement of 'trimming-off').

Main Sources. Ray (1969), Nabseth and Ray (1974), Iron and Steel Board (1963) and U.N.E.C.E. (1968).

21 Vacuum Melting   Vacuum Melting is a process used for refining those very high grade steels which must be able to cope with extreme temperatures and high stress. Traditionally, the main source of high quality alloy engineering steels has been the electric arc furnace. However, as the consumers of high quality steel have required an increasingly pure product, the electric arc has become inadequate in removing sufficient oxygen, hydrogen, sulphur, etc. The basis of vacuum melting is the removal of unwanted gases by melting the steel in an air-free chamber. There are three variations on this theme: vacuum induction melting, the consumable electrode vacuum remelting process and electro-slag remelting; in each case the main advantage is a better quality product, reduced costs in selecting raw materials and reduced rejection rates of the end product.

Main Sources. Barraclough (1969).

22 Vacuum Degassing   To simplify crudely, vacuum degassing provides the same functions for bulk steelmaking that vacuum melting does for certain special steels, namely the liberation or removal of unwanted elements (usually gases) from the finished ingots. One important difference is, however, that vacuum degassing units are often used in conjunction with the conventional methods of melting and refining. The advantages are mainly concerned with the quality of the end product: better hydrogen removal avoids lengthy and costly heat treatment, reduces the tendency of the steel to hair line cracking and improves its hardenability, weldability etc. Productivity is improved due to the reduction in subsequent processing and because cheaper bulk low carbon steels may be used to make sophisticated end products.

Main Sources. Flux (1965), Holden (1969) and correspondence with B.S.C.

4

A new model of diffusion and the diffusion growth curve

4.1 Introduction

In this chapter, the above discussion of the technological characteristics of new processes is incorporated into a simple model of decision making at the firm level. Initially, the main objective is to examine the implications for the aggregate industry diffusion curve. This shows the growth over time in the proportion of firms having adopted a given innovation. In later chapters the implications for inter-firm and inter-industry differences will also be outlined and tested.

As a preliminary to a mathematical formalization of the model, section 2 provides a discussion of the role of information flows and search behaviour in the individual firm's decision of whether or not to adopt the new process innovation. Section 3 sets out the adoption decision within a probabilistic framework which has much in common with the probit models of consumer durables described in chapter 2. Section 4 touches briefly on the predictions of this model concerning inter-firm differences in the speed of adoption. Section 5 introduces the assumption of the lognormal firm size distribution as a convenient means of aggregating the behaviour of individual firms and generates the basic predictions of the model concerning the behaviour of the industry as a whole. Sections 6 to 8 consider some alternative predictions which emerge, concerning the shape of the diffusion growth curve, when various assumptions are relaxed or modified. Section 9 provides a non-mathematical summary of the chapter.

4.2 Imperfect information, search behaviour and the adoption decision

This section suggests eight propositions, concerning the diffusion of information about new innovations, the behaviour of individual firms in seeking out information and the methods used to appraise the viability of adoption. Coupled with the findings of the previous chapter, these propositions form the basis of the model which is used throughout the rest of this study.

Proposition 1: All potential adopters[1] of any innovation are aware of its existence almost immediately it first becomes available commercially. This seems probable for two reasons. First, given the typically small number of potential adopters of most innovations,[2] it is relatively easy for the innovation supplier to inform all potential customers of his new product (either through salesmen or advertising literature). This probability is reinforced by the traditional supplier–consumer link which is common in most of the industries studied here and which has been mentioned already in section 3.3. To give an example from the present sample, it is known that I.C.I., the sole producer of Gibberellic Acid, informed all malt-making firms of the existence of its innovation once it was commercially available. Second, in most consuming industries, inter-firm communications are probably sufficiently regular and frequent to ensure that a 'word of mouth' effect reinforces any advertising campaign by the suppliers. Czepiel's findings (1974) in connection with inter-firm contacts in the U.S. steel industry are particularly relevant in this context. Firms were asked whether they had regular opinion/advice relationships with other firms in the industry. Apparently, all but one of the thirty-two firms questioned had such contacts – on average, with two or three other firms in the industry. Rather surprisingly, direct informal inter-personal contacts among decision makers in different firms occurred about once a week. Under the circumstances then, it is unlikely that any firm will remain ignorant of the existence of any major innovation for very long. Having said this, the *depth* of this initial information concerning the new process will surely be rather limited for many potential adopters. After all, it was suggested earlier (section 3.3.3) that the profitability of adoption for many new processes will vary widely depending on the operating conditions, such as the nature of existing processes, inputs and products, of the potential adopter. In which case, it is unlikely that the innovation supplier will possess sufficient knowledge and/or experience to provide each individual customer with immediate detailed information as to how the process will perform given his own peculiar requirements.

Proposition 2: The quality of information available to the non-adopter should improve with the passage of time. One of the implications of the epidemic model, as employed by Mansfield, is that as more of their competitors adopt (and presumably make their experiences available to other firms), non-adopters are able to piece together a more informed view of the new innovation. Of course, this need not necessarily involve any conscious exchange of information: non-adopters should be able to glean some information about the capabilities of the innovation simply by observing changes in price or quality of the product of the firms which have already adopted. On the other hand, some managers might derive 'kudos' from informing their peers of their experiences with a new, technically advanced, innovation.

Although the discussion of the present chapter will intentionally avoid much mention of inter-industry differences (these will be discussed at length in chapter 7), it might be noted, in passing, that the extent of such inter-firm exchange of information may depend on the competitive structure of the industry concerned. For instance, Martilla (1971) reports that in the competitive U.S. greeting card industry very little technical information was exchanged. But in the more localized, and thus less competitive, envelope industry, information was frequently shared among friendly firms.

The other major source of improvements in information seems to be the innovation suppliers. Ozanne and Churchill (1968), in their study of the adoption of an automatic machine tool in the U.S., report that visits from salesmen often instigated potential adopters' first *serious* interest in the innovation. This was usually followed by an increased interest on receipt of a formal 'pricing and tooling proposal'. Hakonson's data[3] confirms that suppliers (and trade journals) are often an important source of further information. Similarly Rogers (1962) claims that many (mainly sociological) studies support the hypothesis that impersonal information sources, such as advertising literature, are important to the potential adopters at what he calles the 'awareness stage'.

Proposition 3 : Information may also be improved by 'active search' on the part of non-adopters. In addition to the above reasons for improved information, which will fall like 'manna from heaven', i.e. with little effort by the information-recipient, it seems probable that more *active* search will often further improve the quality of information. For instance, Czepiel (1974) found that, on average, firms approached 5.5 of their competitors asking for information about Continuous Casting, before they finally decided to adopt the innovation. Moreover, many of these firms were contacted on numerous occasions. Similarly, both Martilla (1971) and Webster (1970) report that potential adopters often undertook lengthy search activity before adopting new techniques and that, as search proceeded, an increasing number of opinions were sought (often from engineers outside of the firms involved).

An important distinction should be drawn at this point between this so-called active search and the virtually costless information which might accumulate according to Proposition 2. Clearly, active search is by no means automatic but, rather, requires some stimulus. As such, the Behavioural Theory of the Firm (Cyert and March, 1963) offers an interesting rationale: search is only undertaken when the firm's goals are threatened or unfulfilled. Thus, it is problem-oriented and probably initially simple-minded and localized: managers may only look outside their own firms if initial search is unproductive. Of course, Cyert and March offer a quite general explanation of the motives for information search; in the present context of a new process innovation a number of special features might operate. Consider the position of the non-adopter: given mounting pressures arising from increasing numbers of its competitors having adopted the new cost-saving innovation, it is probable that a number of its goals may be increasingly jeopardized. for instance, market share, sales growth and profit goals will all be harder to attain, and increasingly so, the more of the non-adopter's competitors that have adopted.

In addition, there may be more *general* changes in the economic environment across the business cycle (e.g. labour shortages and other capacity constraints, static or falling demand, import competition etc.) which might also be expected to activate search as goals become more difficult to attain. Whilst there is no certainty that this search will always be directed specifically towards gathering information concerning the new innovation, this is more likely the more significant and conspicuous the new innovation is. This, in turn, may be determined by the extent of the supplier's initial advertising campaign and of inter-firm information exchanges. One interesting implication of this theory of search behaviour is the possibility that the quality of information acquired by the non-adopter may improve at a non-uniform rate across the trade cycle. For instance, if most goals are threatened at times of falling demand, most efforts to improve information concerning the new innovation may occur at the trough of the trade cycle.

Proposition 4: Information search will be both more necessary and more sustained for group B innovations. It was argued earlier (section 3.3.5) that the relatively cheap and technically simple group A innovations are subject to major improvements in specification in the early years but thereafter, as learning by doing by manufacturers slows down, there will be fewer improvements in later vintages. Correspondingly, much of the effective information search by potential adopters may well be concentrated in the early years of life of these innovations: on the one hand, localized search may be sufficient to gather an accurate picture of the capabilities of these simple innovations, on the other hand, protracted search in later years is unlikely to unearth any significant new findings, since most of the major post-invention improvements in the technology will have been effected already. For group A innovations then, the information available may be quite accurate for most potential adopters at a relatively early stage.

This may not be true, however, for the group B innovations which have been defined above as relatively expensive, technically complex and subject to substantial post-invention improvements for many years after their first commercial introduction. For these innovations, not only will more substantial and lengthy information search be required, but also such search may continue to yield new information for many years as later vintages of the process embody significant improvements in specification.

Proposition 5: At any point in time there may be significant differences between potential adopters in their understanding of any new process innovation. It is fairly obvious that firms will differ in their ability to gain and process technical information, and one might hypothesize that differences between managers in their technical education, propensity to attend industrial conferences and to read technical journals may be important in this respect. Håkanson (in Nabseth and Ray (1974)), following Carter and Williams (1957, chapter 16), has suggested that these differences may be reflected in the size of R and D departments, the extent of overseas interests and whether or not firms belong to a trade or research association.

Rather more interesting is the possibility that firm size may be a useful indicator of information receptiveness. Mansfield (1968, p. 156) has argued, for instance, that large firms may be better able to absorb and process information because they have larger engineering departments. It is also possible that large firms may *receive* more frequent information from the innovation suppliers (because they present larger potential markets for the innovation) and from other firms in their own industry (if, because of their size, they have regular contact with more firms). On the other hand, information may be less efficiently diffused within large firms because of bureaucratic control loss.

Proposition 6: Typically, firms will assess the viability of adoption of the new process innovation using 'target' rates. Given the uncertainty and imperfect information which must surround most firms' evaluation of whether or not to adopt a new process innovation, it should come as no surprise to find that previous research in this area has found little evidence of optimizing behaviour in this context. For instance, Stoneman (1976, p. 109), after summarizing a number of sample surveys on the evaluation methods used by firms when deciding whether or not to adopt computers, concludes that 'the majority of computerization projects that are evaluated use satisficing rather than optimizing techniques'. He goes on to add that these surveys suggest 'that simple standard operating rules are used for evaluation, e.g. mainly payback rates and discounted cash flow. The importance of the use of payback rates is that it is a procedure that implies dependence on current prices and thus avoids prediction of the future as the [behavioural] theory would suggest.' This conclusion is supported by an earlier study concerning the financial methods used by 116 British firms in the 1950s in deciding whether or not to invest in new innovations (Carter and Williams, 1958, chapter 5). Apparently, 18 of these firms used a standard yardstick or target by which to judge whether adoption was worth while; for most of these the standard was a payback period ranging from one to ten years. Another 34 claimed to make estimates of the likely costs and revenues, but said that no single payback period was always used, or that they could not necessarily rely on these arithmetic calculations; 'commercial acumen' was also used. The remaining

64 firms reported that they made no explicit calculations, but that they acted rather on the basis of hunches or crude rules of thumb.

Moreover, past work on the evaluation methods used by British industry for more general investments suggests that these findings, particularly the frequency of use of payback methods, are quite typical (see, for instance, Lund and Miner, 1972).

Thus it seems reasonable to assume that, typically, potential adopters will use yardstick or target payback/rates of return when deciding whether or not to adopt the new innovation. That is, adoption will only be sanctioned if and when the estimate of the profitability of adopting (often based on imperfect knowledge) is sufficiently favourable to satisfy the target rate. One might also add that in some circumstances, the yardstick will be little more than an implicit notion of what is required.

Proposition 7: For most potential adopters targets will be relaxed as diffusion proceeds. Again, the behavioural theory of decision making offers some support for this proposition. First, as search improves the quality of information available, potential adopters may require less of a risk premium from adoption and similarly, as more of their competitors adopt, they may conclude that the innovation is not a particularly risky investment. Second, to the extent that goals become increasingly difficult to fulfil as diffusion proceeds, these goals and, perhaps, the yardsticks or targets may be revised downwards (see Cyert and March, 1963, p. 121). For both reasons, widespread adoption by competitors may lead to more favourable attitudes to the innovation by non-adopters. Furthermore, the more general factors leading to non-fulfilment of goals, as noted above, may have a similar influence. For instance, if goals become more difficult to attain in the trough of the business cycle, one might expect to observe a softening of attitudes towards the new innovation. Once more, the group A/group B distinction may be important here. Because of the slowing down in post-invention improvements in group A innovations, the rate of increase in competitive pressures and reductions in the potential adopter's assessment of risk may both begin to level off, once the initial substantial improvements have been effected. For group B innovations, however, there may initially be considerable resistance to relaxing targets. This will be due not only to the fact that these innovations often experience teething troubles, but also because potential adopters anticipate further substantial improvements in the technology.[4] Having said this, the competitive pressures on non-adopters are likely to be more substantial than for group A innovations and, in the long-run, there may be an overwhelming pressure on non-adopters to relax their yardsticks. Similarly, just because these innovations are surrounded initially by considerable risk, the scope for relaxation of risk premiums as information improves is much more substantial.

Proposition 8: Targets for the innovation may vary considerably between firms in the same industry. There are good reasons to suppose that, at the same point in time, potential adopters may differ quite considerably in the targets which they require the process to achieve. Under most industry structures (excepting perfect competition), firms may be permitted a wide variety of goals and differences in attitudes to risk might be expected. As Rosenborg puts it (1976, p. 523): 'Since the technological future is, inevitably, shrouded in uncertainty, it is not surprising both that different entrepreneurs will hold different expectations, and also that entrepreneurial behaviour will further differ due to varying degrees of risk aversion on the part of decision makers.' Moreover, the target rate may well reflect the relative bargaining strengths of various members in the management coalition within the individual firm. For example, a research intensive firm with scientists or engineers on the board of directors may be more favourably disposed to new innovations than might a craft-based family business.[5]

Firm size may be an important indicator of attitudes, and thus targets.[6] On the one hand, large firms may employ relatively low yardsticks in this context, (1) because the consequences of failure may not be proportionately so disastrous, (2) because the cost of the finance necessary may be lower and (3) to the extent that they employ more scientifically trained managers who might be expected to argue for early adoption. On the other hand, because management is not usually the function of the owners of large corporations, even low risk and obviously profitable innovations may be required to achieve very high targets by the managers. After all, new innovations usually involve extra management problems such as the reorganization of shifts, factory lay-out, the *rate* of production and, perhaps, the employment of new technical staff.

Needless to say, many other hypotheses have been suggested concerning the determinants or indicators of attitudes for different firms although often they have proved difficult to test: for instance, the education and age of management, the degree of internal financing, profit trends, growth performance etc. Undoubtedly one could argue at length on these and other possibilities. For present purposes, however, it is sufficient to note that differences in attitudes will exist and will, presumably, be reflected in an equivalent variability between firms in the yardstick or targets used in evaluating the advisability of adoption.

The present section may now be concluded with a few final observations. Various evidence from past empirical studies of decision making under uncertainty has been used to formulate eight hypotheses, or propositions, concerning the behaviour of individual firms when facing a new process innovation. Whilst a number of these propositions are seemingly trivial, they are all required in the model developed below. To the extent that they derive from any specific theory of the firm, that theory may be identified as behavioural. Nevertheless, it is not unlikely that similar propositions could be derived from an alternative profit maximizing model which acknowledges the constraint placed on maximizing by imperfect information and the fact that search involves non-trivial costs.

Using these propositions alongside the more technological findings of the previous chapter, the basic theoretical model can now be presented relatively briefly.

4.3 A probabilistic statement of the adoption decision for the individual firm

A few preliminary comments are necessary at the outset. First, for the sake of brevity, the analysis applies to 'any' new process innovation diffusing within a single industry. No attempt will be made, at this stage, to identify how certain parameters of the model will vary between different industries and innovations. Having said this, the distinction drawn earlier between the two broad types of innovation (group A and group B) plays an important role in the analysis and, consequently, the different implications for these broad types will be examined simultaneously throughout.

Second, since the model is concerned with *inter-firm* diffusion only the first adoption by each firm is considered. Thus the term 'adoption' implies only that the firm begins to produce some of its output using the new process innovation. (Of course, in many cases, especially group B innovations, the innovations are so lumpy that if a firm is to adopt at all, it must change over 100% of output to the new process, but this is not always the case).

Third, in common with virtually all other studies of diffusion, the initial introduction of the new innovation into the industry is taken as given. That is, diffusion commences once the first potential adopter (sometimes known as the innovator) has already adopted. No attempt is made to identify or explain the behaviour of the innovator.

It is assumed that the new process innovation is embodied in capital equipment supplied by a capital goods industry which has no vested interest in any firm in the consuming industry. All n potential adopters in the latter industry know of the existence of the innovation once it is first commercially available. Thus no potential adopter is prevented from adopting by total ignorance or patent restrictions. (Although it is quite possible that patents will restrict the number of suppliers.)

It is to be assumed that all firms use simple satisficing methods in deciding whether or not to adopt the innovation. In which case the adoption decision may be formulated simply using the following two definitions.

Let ER_{it} be firm i's expectation of the pay-off period associated with adoption *at time t* (that is, its expectation of the period elapsing before the initial outlay will be recouped from increased net earnings), and

Let R_{it}^* be a yardstick or target which i views as the maximum pay-off period acceptable.

Then denoting the state of firm i having adopted the innovation by time t as $q_{it} = 1$ and the state of not having adopted as $q_{it} = 0$, it is assumed that:

$$q_{it} = 1 \quad \text{if } ER_{i\tau} \leq R_{i\tau}^* \quad \text{for some } \tau \leq t$$
$$q_{it} = 0 \quad \text{if } ER_{i\tau} > R_{i\tau}^* \quad \text{for all } \tau \leq t \qquad (4.1)$$

Thus it is assumed that for i to be using the innovation by t, then at some earlier date, or at t, the firm's expectation of the profitability of adoption was (is) sufficiently favourable (i.e. ER sufficiently low) to satisfy its required target.[7]

For convenience, this expression will be referred to, henceforward, as the *ownership condition*. Shortly, an alternative somewhat looser, but analytically simpler, formulation will be introduced, but for the moment, the analysis is most easily conducted by turning immediately to the proposed specifications for ER and R^*.

Consider first, therefore, the expected pay-off (ER) which, to repeat, is an inverse measure of the expected profitability of adoption. Clearly, ER will reflect not only the *actual* profitability of adoption, but also the extent and quality of information about the innovation which firm i has at time t. On the basis of the findings in section (3.3), on the determinants of profitability, and the above assumptions concerning information (Propositions 2, 3 and 5), suppose that ER varies between firms and over time as follows:

$$ER_{it} = \theta_1(t)\, S_{it}^{\beta(1)} \epsilon_{1it} \qquad \text{where } \beta(1) \gtrless 0 \qquad (4.2)$$

$$\epsilon_{lit} = \prod_{j=1}^{r} X_{ijt}^{\nu(j)} > 0 \qquad (4.2.1)$$

and

$$\theta_1(t) > 0; \quad (d\theta_1/dt)/\theta_1 < 0 \text{ for all } t \qquad (4.2.2)$$

Thus the expectation of the pay-off period resulting from adoption at time t is a multiplicative function of *firm size*, S_{it}, and r other characteristics of the firm (the X_{ijt}).[8] The r other characteristics are left unspecified but it is suggested that they will include, say, g technical attributes of the firm, such as the nature of its product(s), existing processes and inputs (which were identified in 3.3.3 as potential determinants of the actual profitability of adoption) and, say, $r - g$ other attributes (such as the educational attainment of managers, research intensity) which might reflect the firm's ability to collect and process information concerning the innovation (see Proposition 5 above). Firm size is considered to be a particularly important determinant, partly because of the hypotheses discussed above concerning the information receptiveness of large firms, but mainly because of the advantages to large scale adoption mentioned in 3.3.4. For these reasons, it seems probable that $\beta(1)$ will normally assume negative values (remembering that ER is an inverse measure of expected profitability) but this assumption is unnecessary.

(4.2.2) assumes that ER will decline monotonically with time for all i. This may be explained in terms of successively improved later vintages of the process resulting from learning by doing by the innovation supplier(s) (see 3.3.5) and the strong likelihood that incoming information resulting from search will tend to improve most firms' views of the profitability of adoption.[9]

However, because of the suggested differences between group A and group B innovations in the nature of the learning curve, and in the returns from information search (see section 3.3.5 and Proposition 3), it will be assumed that the rate of decline in ER will differ between the two groups as follows:

$$\mathrm{d}[\,(\mathrm{d}\theta_1/\mathrm{d}t)/\theta_1\,]/\mathrm{d}t > 0 \text{ for group A innovations} \qquad (4.3\mathrm{a})$$
$$= 0 \text{ for group B innovations} \qquad (4.3\mathrm{b})$$

In words, for group A innovations, this reflects a slowing down over time in learning by manufacturers and in the returns from information search (and thus a slowing down in the rate at which potential adopters' expectations improve), but no such slowing down for the more expensive and complex group B innovations, at least over the diffusion period.

Turning to inter-firm and inter-temporal variations in R_{it}^{*}, the target or critical pay-off period against which adoption is assessed, a similar mathematical formulation is suggested (on the basis of Propositions 7 and 8):

$$R_{it}^{*} = \theta_2(t)\, S_{it}^{\beta(2)}\, \epsilon_{2it} \quad \text{where } \beta_2 \lessgtr 0 \qquad (4.4)$$

and

$$\epsilon_{2it} = \prod_{j=1}^{u} Y_{ijt}^{\phi(j)} > 0 \qquad (4.4.1)$$

and

$$\theta_2(t) > 0, (d\theta_2/dt)/\theta_2 > 0 \quad \text{for all } t \qquad (4.4.2)$$

Thus R_{it}^* is a multiplicative function of the firm's size and u other characteristics of the firm (the Y_{ijt}). Again, the u other characteristics are left unspecified, but it is suggested that they will include, perhaps, the age of management, the degree of internal financing, profit trends, growth performance and other variables influencing attitudes to risk. The sign of $\beta(2)$ is uncertain: it was argued earlier that there are arguments both ways as to whether larger firms will use lower target rates in assessing adoption. (4.4.2) implies that R^* should increase monotonically with time for all i (reflecting relaxations in the risk premium and the effect of competitive pressures). However, it seems reasonable to suppose that the general shape of the time path for θ_2 will vary between group A and group B innovations. More specifically, let:

$$d[(d\theta_2/dt)/\theta_2]/dt < 0 \text{ for group A innovations} \qquad (4.5a)$$
$$= 0 \text{ for group B innovations} \qquad (4.5b)$$

Thus it is assumed that the relaxation in R^* will level off over time for group A innovations but will be more sustained for group B innovations (see Proposition 7).

This completes the basic specification of the model, but in order to ease the ensuing algebra considerably a modification to the initial formulation of the adoption decision is now required. Because some of the questions raised by this modification have implications beyond merely the present context a short digression is perhaps called for.

A simplifying assumption   As it stands, the initial formulation of the ownership condition, equation (4.1), rules out the possibility that an adopter at time $\tau < t$ subsequently 'disadopts' and no longer uses the innovation at t. In general, this should be considered a suspect assumption: one can easily conceive of circumstances under which an adopter may later regret adoption and cease to use the innovation. For instance, the innovation in question may be superseded, prior to 100% diffusion, by a further, technologically superior, innovation or, more generally, there must always be a possibility that a given innovation does not match up to expectations and is scrapped some time after adoption.

As it happens, in the context of the present sample of innovations, this does not appear to be an objectionable assumption. All of the sample innovations are 'successful' and none has been superseded by a further new innovation during the periods considered here. No case could be found of any firm 'disadopting' any of these innovations.

Having said this, (4.1) does not lend itself very easily to the manipulations required below by the present model (in particular, the aggregation procedure). For this reason, rather than due to any dissatisfaction with the realism of this formulation, it is now replaced by a somewhat looser, but analytically more convenient, formulation.

Assume now that i will have adopted by t,

$$q_{it} = 1 \text{ if } ER_{it} \leqq R_{it}^* \tag{4.6}$$

This revised form of the ownership condition states that firm i will be using the innovation at t only if its expectation at t is sufficiently favourable to satisfy its target rate at t. Quite clearly this formulation does not preclude the possibility of disadoption. An adopter at some $\tau < t$ will only continue to use the innovation at t so long as $ER_{it} \leqq R_{it}^*$ (that is, only so long as it *would* readopt if given the choice over again at t). More precisely *the state of disadoption* by t is defined by:

$$\begin{aligned} & ER_{i\tau} \leqq R_{i\tau}^* \text{ for some } \tau < t \\ \text{but} \quad & ER_{it} > R_{it}^* \end{aligned} \tag{4.7}$$

Unfortunately, this may overstate the likelihood of disadoption (and thus (4.6) may understate the likelihood of ownership) at t. To see why this is so, consider the three conditions which must obtain in practice for a firm to have disadopted by t. First, it must have adopted at τ, second, the original installation at τ (and any subsequent installations prior to t) must no longer be in use at t, and, third, readoption at t must be considered insufficiently profitable. But (4.7) captures only the first and third of these conditions and whilst $ER_{it} > R_{it}^*$ is necessary for i to be in the state of disadoption, it is not sufficient. After all, there may be sound financial reasons for continuing to operate a process, once installed, even where subsequent developments are such as to render readoption insufficiently profitable, given the choice over again.[10]

Now if the model is to be based on this formulation (as indeed it is), credibility can only be retained if there are reasons for supposing that any overstatement of the likelihood of disadoption is insignificant. It is believed that this is the case in the present context, just because of the undoubted success of all the innovations in the present sample. As already mentioned, no instances have been found of actual disadoption but, more important for (4.6), neither is there any evidence of firms continuing to use an innovation whilst expressing regret at having adopted in the first place.[11] In other words, there is no evidence that the two conditions in (4.7) have ever been satisfied for any firms considered in the present sample. If this is true then (4.6) can be justified as an acceptable statement of the condition of owner-ship for i at t. Indeed, if the possibility of (4.7) is ruled out, this revised formulation is identical to the original formulation, (4.1).

In the appendix to this chapter, this discussion is reopened in the light of subsequent estimates of the parameters of (4.2) and (4.4) and it is sug-gested that, unless these estimates are wildly inaccurate, there are strong grounds for supposing that ER/R^* declines monotonically with time for all i. Quite obviously this is a sufficient condition for attaching zero probability to (4.7). In these circumstances it is believed that the ana-lytical simplicity afforded by equation (4.6) is at the cost of little loss of realism.[12]

Using this simplified version then, the ownership condition can be re-written:

$$q_{it} = 1 \text{ if } (ER_{it}/R^*_{it}) \leq 1 \tag{4.8}$$

At this point some simplifying definitions ease the exposition:

let $\beta = \beta(2) - \beta(1) \gtreqless 0$

$\epsilon_{ut} = \epsilon_{2it}/\epsilon_{1it} > 0$

and $\theta_t = \theta_2(t)/\theta_1(t) > 0$

where $(d\theta/dt)/\theta > 0$ for all t (4.9)

and from (4.3) and (4.5)

$d[(d\theta/dt)/\theta]/dt < 0$ for group A innovations
$\qquad\qquad\qquad = 0$ for group B innovations

In which case,

$$ER_{it}/R^*_{it} = \left[\theta(t)S^\beta_{it}\epsilon_{it}\right]^{-1} \tag{4.10}$$

and the ownership condition may be again re-expressed as:

$$q_{it} = 1 \quad \text{if } S_{ait} \leq S_{it} \text{ for } \beta > 0$$
$$\text{or if } S_{ait} \geq S_{it} \text{ for } \beta < 0 \tag{4.11}$$

where S_{cit} is henceforward referred to as *critical firm size* and

$$S_{cit} = (\theta_t \epsilon_{it})^{-1/\beta} \tag{4.12}$$

Finally, it is at this point that it is convenient to formally interpret the ownership condition in a probabilistic framework. *Let P_{it} be the conditional probability of ownership (having adopted) given that the firms is of size S_t.* Then

$$
\begin{aligned}
P_{it} = P(q_{it} = 1 \mid S_{it} = S_t) &= P(S_{cit} \leq S_t) \text{ for } \beta < 0 \\
&= P(S_{cit} \geq S_t) \text{ for } \beta > 0
\end{aligned} \tag{4.13}
$$

In other words, given that its size is S_t, the probability that firm i will have adopted by t is equal to the probability that its size is not less than its critical size, S_{cit} (or for $\beta < 0$, equal to the probability that its size is not more than S_{cit}).

This bout of algebra has thus permitted a simple re-expression of the ownership condition which will prove particularly convenient for the development of the model in the following sections. But because equations (4.9)–(4.13) are central to all that follows, a few words of interpretation may be helpful at this stage.

First, the sign of β indicates whether or not the probability of ownership is positively related to firm size: thus if $\beta > 0$, larger firms will have a greater probability of ownership at any point in time. (Given the strong technological advantages of scale noted in the previous chapter, this is, perhaps, the more likely outcome.) Second, critical size, as defined in (4.12), will tend to decrease over time for $\beta > 0$, or increase for $\beta < 0$; either way, this increases the probability of ownership at any given firm size. However, (4.9) implies that the time path for critical size will differ between group A and group B innovations. Third, critical size will vary between firms, depending on the host of factors (other than size) which influence each firm's adoption decision; these are reflected by ϵ_{it}.

4.4 The distribution of critical size: inter-firm differences in behaviour

The exact implications of (4.13) for inter-firm differences in the speed of adoption will depend quite crucially on the specification of ϵ_{it} and, although these implications are not considered in depth until chapter 6, an assumption about the distribution of ϵ_{it} is essential at this point.

From (4.9), ϵ_{it} is the ratio of two separate error terms, each of which is the product of a large number of characteristics of firm i ($X_{ij}, j = 1, \ldots, r$ and $Y_{ij}, j = 1, \ldots, u$ in equations (4.2.1) and (4.4.1)). Now, so long as the

X variables (reflecting largely technical characteristics) and the Y variables (reflecting largely economic or financial variables) are broadly independent, then the multiplicative form of the central limit theorem suggests that ϵ_{it} *will be lognormally distributed across firms for all t.*[13]

It will be assumed, in addition, that the geometric mean value of ϵ_{it} is unity, for all t. This is quite unexceptional since $\theta(t)$ can be left to reflect any changes over time in ER and R^* which are common to all firms. If the variance of $\log \epsilon_{it}$ is denoted by σ_t^2, these assumptions may be written, using Aitchison and Brown's notation (1957, p. 7) as:

$$\epsilon_{it} \sim \Lambda\,(0, \sigma_t^2) \tag{4.14}$$

or what comes to the same thing, as:

$$\log \epsilon_{it} \sim N(0, \sigma_t^2)$$

Thus (4.14) means that the logarithm of ϵ_{it} is normally distributed across firms at time t with mean zero and variance σ_t^2.

As the lognormal distribution features extensively throughout the remainder of this study, this is probably an appropriate point at which to describe the remaining notation to be employed in this context. Figure 4.1 portrays the lognormal density function (this is equivalent, of course, to the familiar bell-shaped normal function when measuring $\log \epsilon_{it}$ on the horizontal axis). Figure 4.2 portrays the cumulative counterpart of this curve: the lognormal distribution function. This shows the probability that a firm chosen at random will record a value for ϵ_t not more than some number, say E. As can be seen, this probability increases with E according to a positively skewed S shaped curve (with a point of inflection occurring prior to 50% probability). Hereafter, this will be written:

$$
\begin{aligned}
&P\{\epsilon_{it} \leq E\} = \Lambda\,(E \,|\, 0, \sigma_t^2) \\
\text{or} \quad &P\{\log \epsilon_{it} \leq \log E\} = N(\log E \,|\, 0, \sigma_t^2)
\end{aligned}
\tag{4.15}
$$

Now given the assumption of lognormal ϵ_{it} and since β and θ_t are assumed constant across firms at t, it follows immediately that critical size will also have a lognormal distribution, the mean and variance of its logarithm being $-(\log \theta_t)/\beta$ and $(\sigma_t/\beta)^2$ respectively (see Aitchison and Brown, 1957, theorem 2.1, p. 11). In turn this means that the ownership probability, (4.13), may be rewritten:

$$
\left.
\begin{aligned}
&P_{it} = \Lambda\,\{S_t \,|\, (-\log \theta_t)/\beta,\, (\sigma_t/\beta)^2\} \text{ for } \beta > 0 \\
\text{or} \quad &P_{it} = 1 - \Lambda\,\{S_t \,|\, (-\log \theta_t)/\beta,\, (\sigma_t/\beta)^2\} = \\
&\quad\quad = \Lambda\,\{1/S_t \,|\, (\log \theta_t)/\beta,\, (\sigma_t/\beta)^2\} \text{ for } \beta < 0
\end{aligned}
\right\}
\tag{4.16}
$$

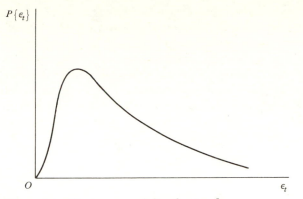

Figure 4.1   The lognormal distribution for ϵ_t

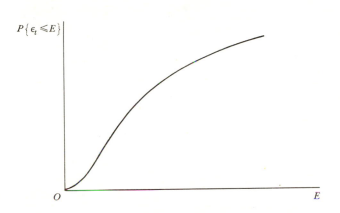

Figure 4.2   The lognormal distribution function

The implications of (4.16) will be developed and discussed fully in chapter 6. Very briefly, it suggests that, for $\beta > 0$, the probability of having adopted increases monotonically with firm size (or decreases monotonically for $\beta < 0$). Moreover, the relationship between the probability and firm size will describe a skewed, cumulative lognormal S shape, as in figure 4.2 (or its complement for $\beta < 0$).

4.5 The industry diffusion curve: the basic predictions

The probabilistic counterpart of the level of diffusion is the probability that a firm chosen at random will have adopted by time t. If this is denoted by

Q_t, then, for $\beta > 0$, it can be restated as the probability that a firm chosen at random will have actual size not less than critical size:

$$\left.\begin{aligned} Q_t &= P(S_{ct} \leqq S_t) \text{ for } \beta > 0 \\[6pt] &= P(S_{ct} \geqq S_t) \text{ for } \beta < 0 \end{aligned}\right\} \tag{4.17}$$

The purpose of this section is to build on the above predictions concerning conditional probabilities to examine the time path for Q_t, and thus diffusion.

Conceptually, the link between the P_{it} and Q_t is straightforward: Q_t is simply the weighted sum of all possible values of P_{it}, where the weights are the probabilities that each firm size will actually occur. In other words, to derive Q_t, the P_{it} must be aggregated over the firm size distribution. Thus if $dF_t(S)$ is the probability at t that a firm chosen at random will be of size S_t, it follows (Cramer, 1969, p. 37) that:

$$Q_t = \int_0^\infty \Lambda \{S_t | (-\log \theta_t)/\beta, (\sigma_t/\beta)^2\} dF_t(S) \quad \text{for } \beta > 0 \tag{4.18}$$

(For the moment, the analysis will proceed on the assumption of $\beta > 0$, the implications of negative β will be discussed presently.) Now if this aggregation is to be at all manageable, a fairly simple assumption is required concerning the form of the firm size distribution. Since there is considerable evidence that nearly all real world firm size distributions are positively skewed, the most convenient and realistic answer is probably to assume a lognormal distribution of firm size.[14] Indeed, past research on empirical firm size distributions indicates that for many industries, the lognormal does provide a fairly close approximation. Moreover, the assumption of lognormality has been tested for the industries in the present sample and the results, using the χ^2 and the more powerful Kolmogoroff–Smirnov tests of normality are very encouraging. The hypothesis that the observed firm size distribution was lognormal could be rejected for only one of thirteen industries, and even in this case, it is suspected that this result derives from a failure to compile a complete list of small firms operating in the industry concerned: the brick industry.[15]

Therefore, it is with reasonable confidence that the present aggregation problem proceeds with the assumption that the *logarithm of firm size is normally distributed with mean μ_{st} and variance σ_{st}^2*. In which case, the frequency distribution is:

$$dF_t(S) = d\Lambda (S_t | \mu_{st}, \sigma_{st}^2). \tag{4.19}$$

Substituting (4.19) into (4.18), then by the convolution property of normal distributions (Aitchison and Brown, 1957, p. 11 and p. 139):

$$Q_t = \Lambda \{1 \mid -(1/\beta)(\log \theta_t + \beta\mu_{st}), (\sigma_t/\beta)^2 + \sigma_{st}^2\} \quad \text{for } \beta > 0 \tag{4.20}$$

or, what comes to the same thing using the standard normal distribution function:

$$Q_t = N \left\{ \frac{\log 1 + (1/\beta)(\log \theta_t + \beta\mu_{st})}{(\sigma_{st}^2 + \sigma_t^2/\beta^2)^{1/2}} \mid 0, 1 \right\}$$

This, then, is an expression for the probabilistic counterpart of the *level* of diffusion at t. The next task is to investigate the time path of this expression.

Consider first the outcome when the parameters of the firm size distribution remain fixed over the diffusion period and when, likewise, the variance of the error term (and thus critical size) remains constant. Thus, assume:

$$\mu_{st} = \mu_s; \sigma_{st}^2 = \sigma_s^2; \sigma_t^2 = \sigma^2 \quad \text{for all } t \tag{4.21}$$

In these special circumstances, the only variable over time in (4.20) is θ_t and from earlier restrictions on its derivatives (see equation 4.9), the following alternative time paths seem reasonable:

$$\theta_t = \alpha t^\psi \text{ for group A innovations}$$

and

$$\theta_t = \alpha e^{\psi t} \text{ for group B innovations}$$

$$\tag{4.22}$$

where $\alpha < 0; 0 < \psi < 1$ and $t = 0$ denotes the date at which the first manufacturer decided to begin commercial production of the innovation. In words, this implies that θ_t increases monotically with time for all innovations, but that the rate of increase tends to tail off for the group A type. (The implications for mean critical size are obvious from 4.12.) Substituting these two alternatives into (4.20) and rearranging slightly:

$$Q_t = N \left\{ \frac{\psi \log t + \log \alpha + \beta\mu_s}{(\beta^2 \sigma_s^2 + \sigma^2)^{1/2}} \mid 0, 1 \right\} \quad \text{for group A} \tag{4.23a}$$

or

$$= N \left\{ \frac{\psi t + \log \alpha + \beta\mu_s}{(\beta^2 \sigma_s^2 + \sigma^2)^{1/2}} \mid 0, 1 \right\} \text{ for group B} \tag{4.23b}$$

These rather clumsy expressions may be simplified by introducing the following definitions of convenience:

$$\mu_D = -(\log \alpha + \beta \mu_s)/\phi \, ; \, \sigma_D^2 = (\sigma^2 + \beta^2 \sigma_s^2)/\phi^2 \tag{4.24}$$

In which case,

$$Q_t = N \left\{ \frac{\log t - \mu_D}{\sigma_D} \,\middle|\, 0, \, 1 \right\} \quad \text{for group A} \tag{4.25a}$$

or

$$= N \left\{ \frac{t - \mu_D}{\sigma_D} \,\middle|\, 0, \, 1 \right\} \quad \text{for group B} \tag{4.25b}$$

That is,

$$Q_t = N(\log t \,|\, \mu_D, \, \sigma_D^2) = \Lambda \, (t \,|\, \mu_D, \, \sigma_D^2) \quad \text{for group A} \tag{4.26a}$$

or

$$Q_t = N(t \,|\, \mu_D, \, \sigma_D^2) \quad \text{for group B} \tag{4.26b}$$

These two alternative forms of (4.26) imply that Q_t increases with $\log t$ according to a cumulative normal curve for group A and that Q_t increases with t according to a cumulative normal curve for group B innovations. Equating Q_t to diffusion, this means diffusion will follow a *cumulative lognormal time path for group A innovations but a cumulative normal time path for group B innovations.*

As can be seen from figure 4.3, this implies that the technically complex and expensive group B innovations should follow a symmetrical S shaped diffusion curve not dissimilar to the logistic curve.[16] For the less costly and relatively simple group A innovations, however, the diffusion curve should take on a positively skewed shape which predicts that the increase in adopters will peak at an early stage, but will slow down quite noticeably thereafter. Interestingly, these predictions hold for negative, as well as positive, β. Returning to equation (4.16) and this time combining P_{it} for $\beta < 0$ with the lognormal firm size distribution, it can easily be shown that the expression which emerges for Q_t is simply the complement of that for $\beta > 0$ shown in equation (4.20). Substituting in the specific forms for θ_t and re-expressing using the standard normal distribution function, it follows

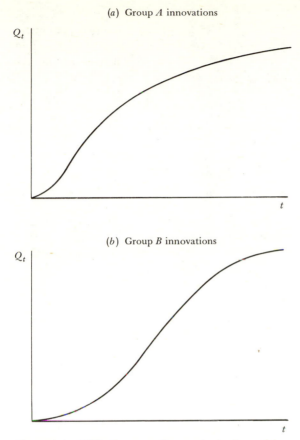

(*a*) Group *A* innovations

(*b*) Group *B* innovations

Figure 4.3   Diffusion according to the basic model

that for group A innovations, for instance:

$$Q_t = 1 - N \left\{ \frac{\log 1 + (1/\beta)(\log \alpha + \psi \log t + \beta \mu_s)}{(\sigma_s^2 + \sigma^2/\beta^2)^{1/2}} \middle| 0, 1 \right\} \quad \text{for } \beta < 0.$$

Now because of the symmetry of the standard normal, this may be re-written:

$$Q_t = N \left\{ \frac{-(\psi \log t + \log \alpha + \beta \mu_s)}{\beta(\sigma_s^2 + \sigma^2/\beta^2)^{1/2}} \middle| 0, 1 \right\} \quad \text{for } \beta < 0 \qquad (4.27)$$

from which (4.25a) follows exactly as for $\beta > 0$. Q_t still increases monotonically with $\log t$ as for $\beta > 0$, since, although the coefficient on $\log t$ now has the opposite sign compared to that in (4.23a), β is of course negative. In exactly the same way, the cumulative normal prediction obtains, as before, for negative β. In fact it will be seen in chapter 6 that, without exception, β appears to be positive for the innovations in the present sample and from now on β will always be assumed positive unless otherwise stated. Nevertheless, the fact that the basic predictions of the model are insensitive to the sign of β is comforting.

It will be argued in later chapters that this distinction between the two types of growth curve, shown in figure 4.3, has potentially important implications, especially for the later stages of the diffusion period. It will also be argued that the parameter, σ_D, may usefully be interpreted as a measure of the speed of diffusion in either case. In the remainder of this chapter, however, the analysis concerns various modifications which may arise when one or more of the assumptions in (4.21) is violated or when θ_t contains a cyclical component.

4.6 The diffusion curve, allowing for industry growth

The above predictions have been derived on the assumption that the parameters of the firm size distribution remain constant over time: this effectively abstracts from the possibility that the adopting industry may be growing over time. In this section, this assumption, as embodied in equation (4.21), is relaxed in three ways.

Suppose *first* that the adopting industry grows (or contracts) at a steady rate over time and that all firms within the industry grow (contract) at the same proportionate rate. Abstracting from exit or entry, this means that the variance of log size, σ_{st}^2, remains constant, but that median firm size, $\exp(\mu_{st})$ in the lognormal, will grow at exactly the same rate as the industry as a whole. In this case, if the aggregate industry size is denoted by S_{It} at time t and by S_{Io} at the start of the period then:

$$\log(S_{It}/S_{Io}) = \mu_{st} - \mu_{so} \qquad (4.28)[17]$$

Now *suppose that the industry grows at the exponential rate δ*, it follows that:

$$\mu_{st} = \mu_{so} + \delta t \quad \text{where } \delta \lessgtr 0 \qquad (4.29)$$

Consider the implications for a group B innovation: substituting (4.29) into (4.23b), algebraically the only change is that the coefficient on t is now $\psi + \beta\delta$. This means that the cumulative normal prediction still holds, with the parameters of the diffusion curve now redefined as:

$$\mu_{D1} = -(\log \alpha + \beta\mu_{so})/(\psi + \beta\delta); \; \sigma_{D1}^2 = (\sigma^2 + \beta^2\sigma_s^2)/(\beta\delta + \psi)^2$$

$$(4.30)$$

Alternatively, if industry size grows according to a linear-in-logs function of time at rate δ, it follows that:

$$\mu_{st} = \mu_{so} + \delta \log t \quad \delta \gtreqless 0 \tag{4.31}$$

If this is substituted into (4.23a), the cumulative lognormal prediction for group A innovations still obtains, with the parameters of the growth curve redefined as in (4.30).

It should be noted in passing that σ_{D1}^2 is thus inversely related to the rate of growth of industry size (for $\beta > 0$). As already mentioned, it will be argued later that σ_{D1} is an excellent measure of diffusion speed. As such, this simple modification to the basic model suggests faster diffusion in high growth industries, ceteris paribus. In chapter 7 this prediction is investigated further.

Needless to say, however, (4.29) and (4.31) describe a very simple (and for present purposes very convenient) picture of industry growth. Strictly speaking, the basic predictions only remain unaltered given the happy coincidence that all industries in which group B innovations are diffusing exhibit exponential growth (4.29), whilst those in which group A innovations are diffusing exhibit linear-in-logs growth (4.31). There is, of course, no reason why this coincidence should occur. On the other hand, the time periods considered here are relatively short and, unless any of the industries have grown particularly quickly, it is not unlikely that *both* (4.29) and (4.31) will offer reasonable *approximations* to the trend growth in μ_{st} and thus, in turn, in the logarithm of industry size. (Indeed, this assertion is largely confirmed in curve fitting exercises in chapter 5.) Even abstracting from this problem, however, there is no doubt that industry size will fluctuate over the trade cycle and thus around its underlying trend. In order to investigate the consequences of both these problems, consider now a *second* modification in which μ_{st} is variable and its time path cannot be described perfectly by either of the two simple forms, (4.29) or (4.31). For instance, suppose that industry growth in a group B innovation industry is approximated as above by an exponential curve, but that at each t a residual is observed:

$$C_t = \log S_{It} - \log \hat{S}_{It} = \log (S_{It}/\hat{S}_{It}) \tag{4.32}$$

where

$$\log \hat{S}_{It} = \log \hat{S}_{Io} + \delta t \quad \text{for group B} \tag{4.33}$$

In which case, from (4.28),

$$\mu_{st} = \mu_{so} + \delta t + C_t \quad \text{for group B} \tag{4.34}$$

If this expression is now substituted into (4.23b), the cumulative normal prediction still holds, albeit with an interesting modification. After simple manipulation,

$$Q_t = N\{t + (\delta + \phi/\beta)^{-1} C_t | \mu_{D1}, \sigma^2_{D1}\} \quad \text{for group B,} \tag{4.35b}$$

Thus the group B diffusion curve is cumulative normal if plotted against $t + (\delta + \phi/\beta)^{-1} C_t$. What this means for the *time* path of diffusion depends, quite obviously, on how C_t changes over time and on the values of δ, β and ϕ. First and most simply, if the exponential curve does provide a good approximation to the *underlying trend* in μ_{st}, then C_t is a variable with no trend and which merely fluctuates over the trade cycle. This will have the effect of speeding diffusion up in times of rapid growth and slowing it down in times of slow growth. Figure 4.4b shows how this might work out in practice. Second, if there is one or more breaks in the trend growth path for S_{It} (namely, changes in the value of δ) then corresponding changes occur in μ_{D1} and σ^2_{D1}. The implications of this are similar to the case, discussed presently, of variable σ^2_{st} over time (see figure 4.5). Third, if the exponential does not provide a good approximation to the underlying trend in μ_{st}, then, not only will C_t fluctuate, but it will also itself trend over time. This could lead to the diffusion curve deviating systematically from the cumulative normal predicted in the basic model. Each of these possibilities assumes greater importance, of course, the smaller is ϕ, i.e. the slower is the growth rate of θ_t, that is, the weaker are the trend dynamic influences on the adoption decision.

Turning briefly to group A innovations and defining now

$$\log \hat{S}_{It} = \log \hat{S}_{Io} + \delta \log t \quad \text{for group A} \tag{4.36}$$

and thus

$$\mu_{st} = \mu_{so} + \delta \log t + C_t \quad \text{for group A} \tag{4.37}$$

a similar picture emerges. Figure 4.4a shows the implications of purely cyclical fluctuations in C_t: the underlying lognormal diffusion curve remains, but with cycles superimposed upon it. Formally, the diffusion curve is:

$$Q_t = N\{\log t + (\delta + \psi/\beta)^{-1} C_t \mid \mu_{D1}, \sigma_{D1}^2\} \quad \text{for group A} \tag{4.35a}$$

Third, and finally, consider now the possibility that the variance of log size, σ_{st}^2, changes as the adopting industry grows or contracts. From (4.24) or (4.30), this implies variable σ_D^2 or σ_{D1}^2. Now if σ_D^2 varies over time, then the diffusion curve will comprise of a number of segments, taken from different cumulative lognormal (or normal) curves, each with different variances. (Interpretation is clarified at this point if it is remembered that the larger is σ_D^2, the 'more spread out' is the distribution and, thus, the flatter are the cumulative curves shown in figure 4.3). Now suppose that size inequalities, and thus σ_D^2, increase gradually over time. The group B diffusion curve, for instance, will then become an amalgam of small segments from many (and successively flatter) cumulative normal curves (figure 4.5c). Alternatively, for a gradual decrease in the value of σ_{st}^2 over time, the sectors come from successively steeper cumulative normal curves (figure 4.5d). The upshot is that, for increasing σ_{st}^2 the upper tail of the diffusion curve is elongated, i.e. a positive skew emerges (which might make the diffusion curve indistinguishable from the basic group A diffusion curve). But for decreasing σ_D^2, the upper tail of the curve is compressed (i.e. a negative skew emerges). The analysis is similar for the group A diffusion curve except that here, increasing σ_{st}^2 tends to accentuate the positive skew of the basic curve, whilst decreasing σ_t^2 will tend to reduce, or even reverse, the skew (this might make the diffusion curve

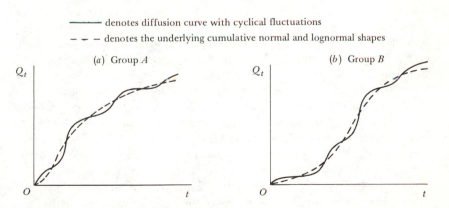

——— denotes diffusion curve with cyclical fluctuations

– – – denotes the underlying cumulative normal and lognormal shapes

Figure 4.4 Diffusion with cyclical fluctuations

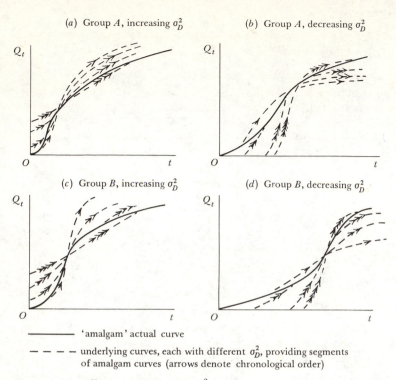

(a) Group A, increasing σ_D^2 (b) Group A, decreasing σ_D^2

(c) Group B, increasing σ_D^2 (d) Group B, decreasing σ_D^2

——————— 'amalgam' actual curve

– – – – underlying curves, each with different σ_D^2, providing segments of amalgam curves (arrows denote chronological order)

Figure 4.5   Diffusion with variable σ_D^2

indistinguishable from the basic Group B diffusion curve, especially if the tendency for σ_D^2 to decline exactly offsets the inherent skewness of the basic curve).

Now just how far these possibilities will jeopardize the explanatory power of the basic model is perhaps an empirical matter. It must again be noted that the time periods studied here are of relatively short duration and, except in industries undergoing fairly rapid structural change, it would be surprising to find drastic systematic changes in the variance of log size. Unfortunately, lack of data precludes any tests of this for the present sample of industries. Indeed, more generally, there is surprisingly little evidence on the stability or otherwise of σ_{st}^2 in industries at the level of disaggregation considered here (but see Engwall, 1974, p. 75, for examples of relative stability). All that can be said with confidence is that fluctuations or trends in σ_{st}^2 will have less proportionate influence on σ_D, the smaller is β and/or the larger is σ_t^2 (the variance of all other influences on the adoption decision). Beyond this, the curve fitting exercises of the next chapter provide the best (although indirect) test of the practical importance of these modifications.

4.7 The diffusion curve, allowing for changing inter-firm differences

For completeness, one other possible modification to the basic predictions should be mentioned. So far σ^2 has been assumed constant over time. This implies that inter-firm variance in R and ER, after allowing for the effects of firm size, remains constant over time. Whilst this does not seem an unreasonable approximation, one can conceive of certain circumstances when it may be suspect. Perhaps the most likely cause of changes in σ^2 would be changes in the nature of the technology involved. As will be described in the next chapter, there are at least two sample innovations in which such modifications during the diffusion period appeared to alter inter-firm differentials in the profitability of adoption.

Analytically, the effects of variable σ^2 are as variable σ_{st}^2 (discussed in the previous section) and no additional comment is necessary.

4.8 The diffusion curve, allowing for a cyclical component in θ_t

It has been assumed so far that the changes over time in ER and R which are common to all firms can be approximated by simple functions of time alone: equation (4.22) specifies these functions, which differ between the two broad types of innovation. However, there are grounds for supposing that the profitability of adoption, search activity and investment yardsticks might all vary across the business cycle: section 3.3.6 and Propositions 3 and 7 provide some discussion on this matter.

If these cyclical fluctuations are at all significant, this suggests that θ_t, which represents all dynamic influences on ER and R, should include a cyclical component as well as the trends already specified. A simple respecification of equation (4.22) which acknowledges this possibility, without unnecessarily complicating subsequent empirical tests, is as follows:

let $\theta_t = \alpha t^{\phi} e^{\Omega C(t)}$ for group A innovations   (4.38a)

and $\theta_t = \alpha e^{\phi t} e^{\Omega C(t)}$ for group B innovations   (4.38b)

where $\Omega \gtrless 0$ and C_t is defined in (4.32)

In some respects this specification is somewhat arbitrary, especially in the choice of functional form and the measure chosen to reflect cyclical variations in θ_t. On the other hand, C_t should suffice as a useful empirical cyclical indicator: in general, it should display positive values in times of boom but will fall below zero when the industry is growing at

slower than the trend rate. (There are, of course, many other candi-
dates as measures of cyclical variations but relevant data may not always
be available at the level of disaggregation required here.) Because it is
not certain how, if at all, *ER* and *R* will vary over the business cycle
(there are arguments both ways) the sign of Ω is left unspecified. It
should be clear that were Ω positive this would imply that the probability of adoption increases more rapidly in times of boom, whilst the
reverse is implied by negative Ω. If this respecification of θ_t is included
in (4.23) alongside the modifications concerning μ_{st}, it follows that the
time series predictions must be restated as:

$$Q_t = N\{\log t + (\beta + \Omega)(\beta\delta + \phi)^{-1}C_t \,|\, \mu_{D1}, \sigma_{D1}^2\} \quad \text{for group A} \quad (4.39a)$$

and

$$Q_t = N\{t + (\beta + \Omega)(\beta\delta + \phi)^{-1}C_t \,|\, \mu_{D1}, \sigma_{D1}^2\} \quad \text{for group B} \quad (4.39b)$$

These predictions differ from those earlier derived from variable
μ_{st} (equations 4.35), only in the coefficient attached to C_t and, unless
$\Omega = -\beta$, this again implies fluctuations around the underlying diffusion
curves predicted by the basic model (as in figure 4.4).

The findings of sections 5 to 8 can now be summarized briefly as follows.
The basic predictions of the model are that the time path of diffusion will
be cumulative lognormal for group A innovations and cumulative normal
for group B innovations. These predictions are stated in equations
(4.26) and shown graphically in figure 4.3. They are based on the assumption
of constant σ_{st}^2, σ_t^2 and μ_{st}. Allowing for the possibility of steady growth
or contraction over time in μ_{st}, because of growth or contraction in industry size, the basic predictions remain unchanged (given certain assumptions about the form of this growth) although the parameters of the
diffusion curve must be redefined as in equation (4.30). This has implications for inter-industry differences in the speed of diffusion but leaves
the time series implications unchanged. Extending the analysis to allow for
cyclical fluctuations in μ_{st} and/or cyclical influences on the adoption
decision (equations 4.35 and 4.39 respectively), diffusion is still inherently cumulative lognormal or normal, but cyclical fluctuations around
the trend should be observed. Only if there are breaks in the growth path
of μ_{st} or significant fluctuations in σ_{st}^2 or σ_t^2 over time are the basic predictions jeopardized. It is suspected that major changes in these parameters
would be required to invalidate these predictions but this is probably
best resolved by the empirics.

4.9 Summary and interpretation

Bearing in mind the high algebraic content of this chapter, a non-mathematical review of the main assumptions and predictions of the model is called for.

The model is based on the simple premise that potential adopters of a new innovation will adopt when their assessment of the profitability of adoption is sufficiently favourable to suggest that the initial outlay required can be recouped within an acceptable time period. Firms will differ, however, in three respects: (a) their ability to acquire and understand the technical information on which this assessment is to be based, (b) their attitudes to risk, and (iii) the broad goals to which they aspire. Therefore, even if the profitability of adoption is identical for all firms, one would not expect to observe identical behaviour by those firms. In fact, the findings of the previous chapter suggest that the profitability of adoption will *not* be the same for all firms and this constitutes another reason for expecting quite different behaviour between firms in this context. It is suggested that a significant proportion of these differences may be accounted for by differences in the size of firms. A second major assumption concerns the phenomenon of learning by doing by the manufacturers of the innovation. It is argued that this generates a stream of post-invention improvements to the typical innovation which increase the profitability of adoption over time. This, coupled with competitive pressures on non-adopters and improved information resulting from search, will increase the chances of adoption with the passage of time. An important distinction is made between simple (group A) innovations, for which most of the post-invention improvements will be effected relatively quickly, and the more complex and expensive (group B) innovations, for which learning by doing may be more sustained and, eventually, more substantial.

From this simple framework, an expression is derived in section 4 which suggests that the probability of adoption will vary across firms according to their size. (This prediction is investigated further in chapter 6.) Then, assuming a lognormal firm size distribution, the analysis moves on from this prediction, concerning individual firms, to predictions concerning the behaviour of the industry in aggregate: namely, the industry diffusion curve, which describes the growth in the proportion of firms having adopted the innovation. In sections 5–8 a number of interesting predictions have emerged concerning the diffusion curve.

(1) The curve will be S shaped for all innovations. This is hardly surprising and is in broad agreement with past models of diffusion.

(2) The exact form of the S shape will differ between broad types of innovation. Relatively cheap and technologically simple (group A)

innovations will diffuse according to a positively skewed cumulative log-normal time path, whilst more complex and expensive (group B) innovations will exhibit symmetrical cumulative normal diffusion curves (see figure 4.3). The reason for this difference is, essentially, the difference which might be expected between the learning curves of these two types of innovation noted above. The significance of this distinction will be examined in more detail in later chapters. At this point, it is merely noted that the cumulative lognormal curve implies that the increase in adopters will peak at a relatively early stage but slow down quite noticeably thereafter. This might imply that group A innovations will never be adopted by an entire industry, even although some firms may be particularly quick to adopt.

(3) Under certain circumstances, the demand conditions facing the adopting industry may have an important influence on diffusion. First, the speed of diffusion (as reflected in the parameters of the diffusion curve) may be sensitive to the growth rate of industry output (and thus demand). Second, diffusion may speed up and slow down over the trade cycle. However, these cyclical fluctuations should not affect the long term growth path of diffusion – it will retain its underlying S shape (see figure 4.4).

Finally, it should be noted that this model provides a framework for the explanation of *inter-industry* differences in diffusion speed (in terms of the differences between the parameters of the diffusion curve: μ_D and σ_D^2). These will be discussed in chapter 7.

Appendix A.4 The likelihood of 'disadoption'

In section 3 of this chapter, equation (4.6) has been adopted as the revised form of the ownership condition which forms the basis for the theoretical model employed in this study. This formulation can, in principle, overstate the likelihood of disadoption (and thus understate the likelihood of ownership); however, it was argued in the main text that this should not be the case for any of the present sample innovations, all of which are highly successful. This appendix examines this argument in more detail.

So long as ER/R^* declines monotonically with time for all i, this is a sufficient condition for there to be no firms actually ceasing to use the innovation concerned (having earlier adopted). More important for the present argument, however, it is also a sufficient condition for the state of adoption as defined by (4.6), and shown in (4.7), not to occur. Therefore, if it can be shown that ER/R^* does decline monotonically with time for all i, (4.6) is identical to (4.1) and either formulation is an acceptable description of a world in which disadoption does not occur in practice.

In terms of equation (4.10), using discrete time and assuming β positive (which is reasonable given the findings of the following chapter) this requires that, for all i and t:

$$(1/\beta)(\log \theta_t - \log \theta_{t-1}) > -(1/\beta)(\log \epsilon_{it} - \log \epsilon_{i(t-1)})$$
$$- (\log S_{it} - \log S_{i(t-1)}) \qquad \text{(A.4.1)}$$

This condition is more likely to be fulfilled, (a) the more rapid is growth in θ_t (which reflects the factors tending to cause upward revisions in expectations concerning the profitability of adoption and downward revisions in the target rates required from adoption), (b) the more stable over time are the non-size influences on ER_{it} and R^*_{it}, and (c) the faster is the growth in size of adopting industries.

In arguing that this condition is likely to be fulfilled for the present sample of *successful* innovations, the assumption is, of course, that $\log \theta_t - \log \theta_{t-1}$, will typically attain sufficiently large positive values as to outweigh any 'freak' negative changes which may occur in ϵ_{it} or firm size.

As it happens, the results of the following chapters do provide sufficient information for *estimates* of $(1/\beta)(\log \theta_t - \log \theta_{t-1})$ to be derived for all innovations at all t. Whilst these estimates are, themselves, based on a model which assumes the potentially erroneous (4.6), they do at least provide some feel for the magnitude of values which must occur for (A.4.1) to be violated.[18]

The table shows the mean and minimum observed values of $1/\beta(\log \theta_t - \log \theta_{t-1})$ over the diffusion periods of the sample innovations.[19]

TABLE A.4.1   *Mean and minimum observed values for $1/\beta$ ($\log \theta_t - \log \theta_{t-1}$)*

Range of values	No. of innovations for which minimum value lies in range	No. of innovations for which mean value lies in range
0–0.029	0	0
0.03	3	0
0.06	2	0
0.09	1	0
0.12	3	2
0.20	5	5
0.3 and above	8	15

Note: These estimates have been derived by using the specific forms for θ_t of equations (4.22) and (4.38) and the estimates of ϕ/β and Ω/β provided in table 7.1 and, indirectly, in table 5.3.

Perhaps the most striking feature of these results is that θ_t/β appears to increase strictly monotically with time for all innovations: in no case does $1/\beta(\log \theta_t - \log \theta_{t-1})$ ever fall below 0.03. This, in itself, must greatly reduce the chances of the violation of (A.4.1). Assuming, for the moment, ϵ_{it} constant over time for all i in all industries, (ER/R^*) will indeed decline monotonically for all firms whose annual growth rate ($\log S_t/S_{t-1}$) never falls below a *critical* rate of -3%. In fact for 16 of the 22 innovations, this critical rate is as low as -12% and even for the remaining 6, a 12% decline is not incompatible with (A.4.1) so long as it occurs at a time in the diffusion period when θ_t proceeds at an average or faster pace (see column 3 of the table). Bearing in mind that the feasible sets of adopters for each innovation have been defined so as to include only those firms surviving the diffusion period (see the appendix on data sources), the chances of such relatively large contractions in individual firm sizes must be small.

Of course the picture becomes more confused if ϵ_{it} does not remain constant over time: large negative annual changes would clearly increase the chances of short-run reversals in the general downward trend in (ER/R^*). But a fairly good case can be made for rough constancy of the ϵ_{it}. It is perhaps unlikely that the random variables represented (the X_{ij} and Y_{ij} in (4.2.1) and (4.4.1)) will change by much in any firm from year to year; for example, the technical characteristics of the firm and the educational attainment of its managers should both remain virtually unchanged over short periods. It should also be recalled that any systematic changes, common to all firms, over time are already reflected in this model by θ_t.

In summary then, assuming rough stability in the random influences on the adoption decision (after allowing for all systematic across-firms trend changes), this 'evidence' does point to a general applicability of condition (A.4.1).[20] In view of the highly successful nature of the sample innovations this is probably to be expected of course.

5

The empirical diffusion growth curves

5.1 *Introduction*

As reported in chapter 3, data has been collected on the diffusion of twenty-two process innovations in U.K. manufacturing industries since the war. This and the following two chapters describe the results of testing various predictions of the above model against this data. The present chapter is concerned solely with the time series predictions, that is the diffusion curve.

It is perhaps worthwhile emphasizing, at the outset, the significance of the diffusion curve to the present study. First, it has been argued in chapter 4 that the *shape* of the diffusion curve will be determined by the nature of the innovation concerned (and, under certain circumstances, it is possible that cyclical fluctuations in the growth of the adopting industry will also affect the shape of the diffusion curve). Both of these predictions are unique to the present model and, as such, they permit a useful test of the model. Second, once diffusion curves have been fitted to the data, estimates will be available for various parameters of the model. In chapter 7, these estimates for each of the innovations will be used in a cross-section analysis, aimed at discovering the determinants of the speed of diffusion. In other words, the present chapter also serves as an intermediate empirical step towards answering the most important question with which this study is concerned, namely, why some innovations diffuse faster than others.

Section 2 restates the basic time series predictions of the model in a form which is amenable to simple curve fitting and then considers which statistical technique might be most appropriate to the task in hand. Section 3 explains how the variables have been measured and discusses one or two measurement problems which have occurred. In section 4, the basic predictions of the model are tested against the data. Section 5 extends the analysis by testing the more complicated predictions of the model concerning the influences of cyclical factors on diffusion. Section 6 attempts to explain why a small number of innovations do not, at first sight, follow the predictions of the model. Finally, section 7 examines the significance of the group A/group B distinction in the light of the estimates of this chapter.

5.2 The estimating equations and the estimation technique

The time series predictions of the model are contained in the later sections of the previous chapter. Here, they will be summarized in three parts and estimating equations will be derived.

First, section 4.5 provided the *basic predictions*: the (simple and relatively cheap) group A innovation will follow a cumulative lognormal diffusion curve, whilst the (more complex and expensive) group B innovation will follow a cumulative normal diffusion curve:

$$Q_t = N(\log t \,|\, \mu_D, \sigma_D^2) \quad \text{for group A} \tag{5.1a}$$
$$\text{(4.26a repeated)}$$

$$Q_t = N(t \,|\, \mu_D, \sigma_D^2) \qquad \text{for group B} \tag{5.1b}$$
$$\text{(4.26b repeated)}$$

Initially, these predictions were derived using the assumptions of rough constancy over time in (i) median firm size, (ii) the variance of log firm size, and (iii) the variance of log critical firm size. (One implication of these assumptions is that the aggregate size, say output, of the adopting industry should remain constant over time.) However, it was shown in section 4.6 that, given certain types of steady growth in the adopting industry, these basic predictions still hold, with the parameters of the curves redefined as μ_{D1} and ω_{D1}^2 (see equation 4.30).

For estimation purposes, both forms of (5.1) can be linearized by the following transformation:

$$Q_t = N(z_t \,|\, 0, 1) \tag{5.2}$$

Following Gaddum (1945) and Aitchison and Brown (1957, p. 68), z_t may be defined as the *normal equivalent deviate* of Q_t (although it is sometimes referred to as the *normit*.) Given values for Q_t, z_t can be read off from standard normal tables (for instance, at $Q_t = 0.95$, $z_t = 1.645$). Rearranging equations (5.1) in terms of the standard normal function, it follows that:

$$z_t = (\log t - \mu_D)/\sigma_D \quad \text{for group A} \tag{5.3a}$$

$$z_t = (t - \mu_D)/\sigma_D \qquad \text{for group B} \tag{5.3b}$$

At first sight, there seems no reason why these equations should not be estimated using ordinary least squares; however, it must be remembered that Q_t refers to the probability that a randomly selected firm has adopted at time t. For empirical purposes this can only be measured by the proportion of firms having adopted, m_t/n. This is a perfectly reasonable assumption, of course (see for instance, Bonus, 1973, pp. 659–60), and it may be rationalized by postulating m_t/n to be a random variable, binomially distributed around a mean Q_t, with variance of $Q_t(1 - Q_t)/n_t$, where n_t is the sample size at time t. It should be clear, however, that to employ z_t as a dependent variable in a regression equation would violate one of the assumptions of the standard linear regression model: the dependent variable, and thus the disturbance term, is not homoscedastic.

In fact this problem is always encountered when using probit analysis; in the past, two alternative estimators have been advocated as appropriate under the circumstances: maximum likelihood and the so-called minimum normit χ^2 method. As there are no conclusive grounds for preferring one to the other, the minimum normit χ^2 method has been used here as it is computationally simpler.[1] The minimum normit χ^2 method amounts, in the present context, to the following weighted regressions:

$$z_t = a_1 + b_1 \log t \quad \text{for group A (cumulative lognormal)} \tag{5.4a}$$

$$z_t = a_2 + b_2 t \qquad \text{for group B (cumulative normal)} \tag{5.4b}$$

where z_t refers hereafter to the normal equivalent deviate of the level of diffusion (m_t/n) in year t. The regression estimates of a and b may therefore be interpreted from (5.3) as:

$$a = -\mu_D/\sigma_D, b = 1/\sigma_D$$

or $\tag{5.5}$

$$a = -\mu_{D1}/\sigma_{D1}, b = 1/\sigma_{D1}$$

where steady growth in the adopting industry is assumed.

Second, and as a modification to these basic predictions, it was shown, in sections 4.6 and 4.8 that, under certain circumstances, the diffusion growth curves will exhibit cyclical fluctuations around their underlying trend shapes (see, for instance, figure 4.4). This modified prediction results if cyclical components are introduced into μ_{st} and θ_t. These, in turn, reflect cyclical fluctuations in the growth of aggregate industry size and the possibility that the profitability of adoption, search activity and information flows may all vary across the business cycle. Formally, this led to the following revised predictions:

$$Q_t = N\{\log t + (\beta + \Omega)(\delta\beta + \phi)^{-1} C_t | \mu_{D1}, \sigma_{D1}^2\} \quad \text{for group A} \qquad (5.6a)$$
$$\text{(4.39a repeated)}$$

and

$$Q_t = N\{t + (\beta + \Omega)(\delta\beta + \phi)^{-1} C_t | \mu_{D1}, \sigma_{D1}^2\} \quad \text{for group B} \qquad (5.6b)$$
$$\text{(4.39b repeated)}$$

where C_t may be thought of as the deviation from trend output in the adopting industry. It is defined by equations (4.32), (4.33) and (4.36).

As for the basic predictions, the estimating forms of these equations are derived by measuring Q_t by the level of diffusion at t and transforming into normal equivalent deviates of diffusion by equation (5.2). Thus,

$$z_t = a_1 + b_1 \log t + c_1 C_t \quad \text{for group A} \qquad (5.7a)$$

$$z_t = a_2 + b_2 \log t + c_2 C_t \quad \text{for group B} \qquad (5.7b)$$

where a and b are defined as in (5.5) and

$$c = (\beta + \Omega)/(\beta\delta + \phi)\sigma_{D1} \qquad (5.8)$$

Third, it was also shown in sections 4.6 to 4.8 that the parameters of the diffusion curves will not be stable over time under three circumstances: (1) variable σ_s^2, the variance of log firm size, (2) variable σ^2, reflecting the variance across firms in expected profitability and target rates, (3) breaks in the trend growth path of industry size and thus μ_{st}. In any of these circumstances, it makes more sense to think of the diffusion curve comprising a number of different segments, each with different parameters. In consequence, observed diffusion curves may diverge from the predicted curves as shown, for example, in figures (4.5). It must be said that there is no formal method of testing for the occurrence of any of these three possibilities. Broadly speaking, however, in terms of the above estimating equations, they imply non-constancy over time in the regression coefficients a, b and c. As such, in the following curve fitting exercises which, of course, assume constant coefficients, any evidence of mis-specification of functional form may be taken as indicative that one or more of these three forces is at work. Section 6 of the present chapter re-examines this matter.

5.3 Data and measurement of variables

The appendix at the end of the book details the sources and definitions of the data on aggregate industry size and diffusion employed to construct the C_t and z_t variables. This section merely discusses certain problems of measurement.

5.3.1 The dependent variable, z_{jt}

As explained already, z_{jt} is the normal equivalent deviate of the level of diffusion of *innovation j* in year *t*, where diffusion is defined by the proportion of firms in the relevant industry who have adopted, m_{jt}/n_j. Given information on diffusion, z_{jt} may be read off from standard normal tables. To repeat, this transformation is required in order to linearize the estimating equations.

　　Data on this variable is on an annual basis and has been collected from a number of different sources. In some industries, n_j does not correspond with the total number of firms, since some firms are unable to adopt for technical reasons. Strictly speaking, then, n_j is the number of potential adopters at time *t*. As explained in the appendix on data sources, n_j is assumed constant over the diffusion period for all *j*.

5.3.2 Time

The apparently trivial question of how to 'measure' time also merits some brief discussion. The specification of θ_t in equations (4.22) suggests that *t* should measure the number of years elapsing since the date when the innovation supplier first decided to market the innovation. In general this date is not known exactly and the convention used here is to designate the year in which the innovation was first *adopted* as $t = 1$ (and then with each succeeding year, *t* increases by 1 unit of course.) In the case of the cumulative normal curve (equations 5.4b and 5.7b) the exact choice of time origin does not affect the overall fit of the equation or the values of $\hat{b}$ and $\hat{c}$. On the other hand, the intercept term, *a*, *is* sensitive to the choice of year in which $t = 1$ and thus, because this choice is rather arbitrary, the estimate $\hat{a}$ is, itself, a little arbitrary.[2] As will be seen in later chapters, this matters very little since *a* has no particular economic significance. A more serious problem is encountered, however, when estimating the cumulative log-normal curve. In this case, as the variance of log *t* will depend on the choice of origin, then so too will $\hat{b}$ (and the overall goodness of fit). Consequently, equations (5.4a) and (5.7a) have been fitted using a variety of different time origins, subject to the constraint that the year of first adoption should not be designated as some $t > 5$.[3] In every case in the following tabulations, the equation based on the origin which gives the best overall fit is reported.

5.3.3 The cyclical variable, C_{jt}

It should be recalled that the variable C_t fulfills two functions in the present model. It reflects variations around the trend growth path in aggregate industry size, S_{It} which gives rise to its use as a measure of cyclical fluctuations in activity (as such, one might expect a high correlation with industry unemployment, capacity age etc.) and, given certain assumptions, it will reflect cyclical fluctuations in the logarithm of median firm size. It is defined by:

$$C_t = \log S_{It} - \log \hat{S}_{It} \qquad\qquad \text{(4.32 repeated)}$$

where trend size is to be estimated as follows:

$$\log \hat{S}_{It} = \hat{A} + \hat{B} \log t \quad \text{for industries in which group A innovations} $$
$$\text{are diffusing (5.9a)}$$

and

$$\log \hat{S}_{It} = \hat{A} + \hat{B}t \quad \text{for industries in which group B innovations}$$
$$\text{are diffusing. (5.9b)}$$

Note then that different functional forms are assumed for trend growth, depending on the nature of the innovation concerned. It was argued earlier that this arbitrary distinction has no theoretical justification but that for practical purposes, either form may yield acceptable approximations for most industries. In terms of equations (4.34) and 4.37), the $\hat{B}$ are estimates of the growth parameter δ and will be used as such in chapter 7. For present purposes, however, it is the residuals generated when fitting (5.9) which are of interest. From (4.32) these provide estimates of C_t. Thus as a preliminary stage, (5.9) have been fitted by least squares regression for each adopting industry to time series data on S_{It}: the output of the industry at time t. The data employed is discussed in the appendix on data sources.

It should be stressed that the data available for S_{It} is rather deficient in a number of respects. First, it has proved impossible to obtain *any* reliable time series data for the output of the Lancashire weaving industry since 1935. Unfortunately therefore, three of the innovations (ASB, ADH and EH) have had to be excluded from all the experiments involving this cyclical variable. For a second group of industries, data is available, but at a rather aggregate level: this problem derives from the very fine industry definitions used in the present study. For example, no data is available on the output of the printing press industry, therefore the more aggregate series of output produced by 'other mechanical engineering' has been used in its stead. Whilst this is admittedly an extreme example, similar if lesser problems apply to a number of the other sample industries. Third, in some cases, time series data on 'deliveries' rather than output has had to be used: of course, this should reflect general trends in output, but, needless to say, stock fluctuations could jeopardize the applicability of this proxy (for more details, see the appendix on data sources.)

Subject to these qualifications, the results of fitting (5.9) to the data which is available are quite interesting. From the residuals observed from these equations, remarkably symmetrical cyclical patterns emerge, with no obvious evidence of an underlying trend in any case. This latter finding is significant in that it indicates that (5.9) adequately reflect the trend growth paths of industry output for all of the sample industries. Whilst this is not particularly surprising for the group B cases, after all (5.9b) implies exponential growth, it is less expected for the log-linear form (5.9a) fitted for the group A cases. This particularly convenient result arises partly because the periods studied are relatively short and partly because most of the industries grew only relatively slowly over these periods. Under these circumstances, (5.9a) is obviously just as capable of a reasonable description of the underlying trend as is the intuitively more likely (5.9b)

5.4 Results: the basic model

In this section, the results of fitting equations (5.4) to the data are described. It should be recalled that these test the simple prediction of the model that group A innovations diffuse according to a cumulative lognormal diffusion curve, whilst group B innovations diffuse according to a cumulative normal curve.

As shown earlier in table 3.1, of the sample of 22 innovations, eight have been identified as falling quite clearly into the group A type, seven are of the group B type and the remaining seven share some characteristics with both groups, these are referred to below as 'Unclassified'.[4]

Columns 2–4 of table 5.1 show the results of fitting the cumulative lognormal (equation 5.4a) to the data for the eight group A innovations and the cumulative normal (equation 5.4b) for the seven group B innovations.

At face value, the results are fairly encouraging: in all cases the $\hat{b}_j$ are significantly different from zero at the 99% level[5] and for 11 of the 15 innovations, $\overline{R}^2$ are 'high' (exceeding 0.815) and the Durbin–Watson (D–W) value leads to an acceptance of the hypothesis of no positive autocorrelation at the 5% level.

On the other hand, one might expect most S shaped curves to offer a reasonable description of this sort of data; after all, m_{jt}/n_j will typically increase with time whilst lying, by definition, between 0 and 1. Therefore to

TABLE 5.1 *Estimated diffusion curves for group A and group B innovations*

Innovation j	'Appropriate curve'[†]			'Inappropriate curve'[‡]		The logistic[§]	
	$\hat{b}_{ij}$	$\overline{R}^2$	D–W	$\overline{R}^2$	D–W	$\overline{R}^2$	D–W
Group A	(a) *Cumulative lognormal*			(a) *Cumulative normal*			
SP (1962–70)	1.49(9)	0.93	1.66	0.85	0.55*	0.78	0.33*
F(62–70)	2.11(11)	0.93	1.51	0.91	1.12(*)	0.87	0.79*
SF(62–70)	1.23(15)	0.96	1.74	0.90	1.02(*)	0.87	0.89*
WSB(57–70)	0.44(7)	0.79	0.95*	0.90	1.30(*)	0.90	1.28(*)
ASB(51–65)	0.34(29)	0.98	2.09	0.80	0.38*	0.78	0.35*
ADH(48–63)	0.31(9)	0.82	2.15	0.43	0.27*	0.40	0.27*
EH(35–55)	0.55(26)	0.97	0.88*	0.76	0.21*	0.71	0.23*
GA(59–67)	0.77(15)	0.96	2.16	0.86	1.15(*)	0.85	1.01(*)
Group B	(b) *Cumulative normal*			(b) *Cumulative lognormal*			
BOP(58–68)	0.15(7)	0.84	1.40	0.81	1.36	0.78	1.22(*)
VD(55–68)	0.15(15)	0.94	0.95*	0.77	0.37*	0.94	1.24(*)
VM(58–68)	0.19(10)	0.91	1.41	0.75	0.99*	0.90	1.43
CC(59–69)	0.11(9)	0.63	0.58*	0.79	1.07(*)	0.54	0.47*
ATL(47–60)	0.18(13)	0.924	1.79	0.84	1.25(*)	0.916	1.78
TK(53–71)	0.09(29)	0.98	1.65	0.90	0.60*	0.96	1.19(*)
PCBC(65–70)	0.14(5)	0.82	1.85	0.78	1.83	0.76	1.47

Notes: For innovation abbreviations, see table 3.1. The diffusion time periods are shown in brackets. t values for $\hat{b}_{ij}$ are shown in brackets. * denotes a D–W value indicating evidence of positive autocorrelation at the 5% level; (*) denotes an inconclusive D–W value.

† 'Appropriate' denotes the curve predicted by the model, given the innovation's classification, i.e. equation (5.4a) for group A and (5.4b) for group B. The regressions reported for the cumulative lognormal use the time origin for t which appears to yield the best fit.
‡ 'Inappropriate' denotes the opposite of the model's predictions, i.e. (5.4a) for group B and (5.4b) for group A.
§ The $\overline{R}^2$ for the logistic have been computed after transforming estimated residuals into the same units as for the two other curves.

add some sort of perspective to these results, two further sets of regressions have been computed. First, the two curves are fitted for the 'wrong' innovations, i.e. the cumulative normal (5.4b) to the data for the group A innovations and the cumulative lognormal (5.4a) to the group B innovations. This provides a crude test of the hypothesis that the nature of the data is such that the curves will provide a good fit, even when used for innovations for which the model suggests they are 'inappropriate'. As can be seen from columns 5 and 6 of the table, there is only limited support for this hypothesis however. When used in this inappropriate way, the two curves record suspect D–W values in all but 2 cases and the average $\overline{R}^2$ is only 0.8, as opposed to 0.89 when using the curves for the 'appropriate' innovations. It is also apparent that the cumulative normal performs 'better' for group B than for group A innovations and the cumulative lognormal better for group A than for group B innovations.

Second, to provide an alternative yardstick, Mansfield's form of the logistic curve has also been fitted for all 15 innovations (see equation 2.14). Again, the results are fairly encouraging for the present model: autocorrelation can only be ruled out for 3 innovations (column 8 of the table) and the average $\overline{R}^2$ is only 0.80.

However, at this stage one must query the strength of the $\overline{R}^2$ and the Durbin–Watson statistics as criteria for choosing between alternative functional forms. It is not clear, for instance, how good a test for autocorrelation the D–W statistic is in this context, given the unusual transformation of the dependent variable in the estimating equations, and the uncertain nature of the disturbance terms. Similarly, $\overline{R}^2$ is clearly a very crude criterion in this, and indeed any, context.

Having said this, there is probably little to be gained from searching for more sophisticated test statistics with which to compare the 3 alternative curves. Pesaren's Monte Carlo studies (1974, p. 164) illustrate quite clearly the near impossibility of establishing conclusively that one particular specification is 'better' than another closely related specification when, as here, the number of observations is relatively low. Instead, this part of the discussion is concluded by noting that the curve predicted by the model records a higher $\overline{R}^2$ than the logistic for 13 of the 15 innovations (see columns 3 and 7.) It would be rather difficult to argue that such a 'success rate' is due to chance.

A crude test of this is possible by calculating the probability that the model could record a higher $\overline{R}^2$ in 13 of the 15 tests *if in fact it was not 'superior' to the logistic*. Formally, suppose that the outcome of a comparison of $\overline{R}^2$ is random, and that the probability that the model will record a higher $\overline{R}^2$ in any one test is 0.5. If this is so, the probability of its recording a higher $\overline{R}^2$ in 13 of the 15 tests (using the binominal distribution) is only 0.0049.

Quite obviously this test procedure requires some faith in the ability of $\overline{R}^2$ to detect the correct specification[6] (and had more observations been available, some tests of predictive success might have been more appropriate). Nevertheless, 0.0049 is sufficiently low to support a guarded claim for the superiority of the model in the present context.

Turning now the the seven sample innovations *not* considered in table

5.1, namely the unclassified innovations, the model offers no clear prediction as to the shape of the growth curve. Because they share certain characteristics with both group A and group B, perhaps some sort of hybrid learning, and thus diffusion, curve is most likely for these innovations. As a first step, both equations (5.4a) and (5.4b) have been fitted to the data. As shown in table 5.2, for four of this group (1–4 in the table) both curves seem to offer a reasonable fit, although the D–W values cast some doubt on the cumulative normal (being in the inconclusive range in each case). Very tentatively, the apparent marginal superiority of the lognormal might suggest some slowing down in the learning effect (as for group A innovations) *but* the rather better performance of the normal here, as compared to the fits it achieves for group A innovations in table 5.1, suggests that the deceleration in learning may be less pronounced than for the typical group A innovation.

For the other three innovations in this group (5–7 in the table) the learning curve appears to have exhibited an alternative form. In fact, these three are basically the same innovation (Numerically Controlled Machine Tools, NC) diffusing in different industries: the manufacture of printing presses (PP), turning machines (TN) and turbines (TB).

For the first few years after innovation, Numerical Control exhibited most of the characteristics of a group B innovation: the complexity of the technology and the large diversity in the operating conditions of potential customers led ᴜ teething troubles and probably limited the scope for learning.[7] Yet the innovation does differ from group B innovations in that machine tools can be produced 'off the peg' and in relatively large numbers.

TABLE 5.2   *Estimated diffusion curves for 'unclassified' innovations*

Innovation j	Cumulative lognormal			Cumulative normal			Logistic	
	$\hat{b}_{1j}$	$\overline{R}^2$	D–W	$\hat{b}_{2j}$	$\overline{R}^2$	D–W	$\overline{R}^2$	D–W
1. TC (1955–68)	0.24(8)	0.82	1.47	0.05(6)	0.71	1.26(*)	0.71	1.18(*)
2. CT (64–72)	1.33(9)	0.89	1.69	0.19(6)	0.82	1.13(*)	0.74	0.78*
3. PE (57–65)	0.56(8)	0.94	1.75	0.14(7)	0.78	1.06(*)	0.75	1.09(*)
4. SL (58–70)	0.72(6)	0.98	1.89	0.12(17)	0.97	1.13(*)	0.95	0.88*
5. NCPP (62–70)	0.51(20)	0.98	3.36	0.13(7)	0.85	0.91*	0.82	0.80*
6. NCTN (56–70)	0.87(6)	0.69	0.36*	0.15(10)	0.86	0.47*	0.84	0.44*
7. NCTB (57–70)	0.89(7)	0.74	0.63*	0.16(12)	0.91	1.15(*)	0.90	1.22(*)
Shortened time periods								
6a. NCTN (62–70)	0.79(9)	0.95	1.66	0.19(8)	0.78	0.66*	0.75	0.65*
7a. NCTB (62–70)	1.06(9)	0.92	2.23	0.20(8)	0.86	1.12(*)	0.86	1.13(*)

See notes to table 5.1

Thus once the initial phase was completed (probably by the early 1960s), one might expect that the technology entered into a group A phase of rapid, if relatively short-lived, learning. This hypothesis is certainly consistent with the rather poor fit offered by both curves (and the logistic) for TN and TB (6 and 7) in the table, since the time periods considered include *both* learning phases. However, because numerical control was only introduced in the printing press (PP) industry after the group B phase had ended, one might expect the lognormal to perform rather better, as it appears to have done. As a further test of this hypothesis, for the turning (TN) and turbine (TB) industries, both curves have been re-estimated for the shortened time period *excluding* the years prior to 1962 (namely, excluding the group B phase). As shown in the table (6a and 7a), in both cases, the cumulative lognormal now produces a more convincing fit, as hoped for, whilst the cumulative normal (and the logistic) still offer unsatisfactory explanations.

Overall then, the results so far are encouraging. It seems fair to claim that the basic predictions of the model are not inconsistent with the observed diffusion paths for all but four of the twenty-two sample innovations. In section 6, possible explanations for these four failures are explored but first, in the next section, the more general form of the model, allowing for cyclical variations, is tested.

5.5 Results: the cyclical diffusion curve

In this section the results of fitting equations (5.7) to the data are described. With the inclusion of the extra variable C_t, constructed as described above, there exists the additional problem of specifying an appropriate lag. The model, and thus (5.7), is based, of course, on the *decision to adopt* whilst the data on diffusion levels reflects the dates at which firms first *started to use* the innovations. The extent of the time lag between the decision and first use will obviously vary between innovations, depending on how long they take to install, and whether any experimentation period is necessary. Consequently, equations (5.7) have been fitted with a number of alternative lags on C_t (no such lags are required on the time trend, of course). In general, there is insufficient information to permit a definite view on the most appropriate lag for each innovation, therefore experiments have been conducted assuming: no lag or a one year lag for the simple group A innovations; a one, two or three year lag for group B innovations and no lag, a one year or two year lag for the unclassified group. (Bearing in mind the results of the previous section for the unclassified group, an underlying lognormal diffusion curve, i.e. (5.7a) has been assumed.) Very crudely then, the various lags employed correspond to intuitive notions of the length of installation and delivery periods which one might expect for each of these broad types of innovation.

In table 5.3, the results reported refer to the equation (i.e. the lag on C_t) which produces the highest $\overline{R}^2$ for each innovation. Only those results are reported for which the estimated coefficient, $\hat{c}_j$, exceeds its estimated standard error. This immediately rules seven of the innovations out of the reckoning and, remembering that no data was available on C_t for the three Lancashire weaving innovations, this leaves only twelve innovations for which there is the slightest suggestion of a significant cyclical influence.

Taken at face value, the results are unimpressive. At the 95% level, the estimated t values on the $\hat{c}_j$ indicate that for only five of the innovations is there a significant influence which can be attributed to the cyclical variable. Whilst a 'success' rate of 5 from 19 is sufficiently high to suggest that there may be something in this hypothesis in some cases, there is obviously little to commend more than a brief analysis of these results. Nevertheless, a few passing comments are perhaps in order. First, the five innovations for which C_t is significant come from each of the three groups. Second, for four of the five, the variable appears to have a negative influence. This might suggest that plans to adopt have been made more often in terms of low economic activity – perhaps because the disruption costs are lowest in such periods and perhaps due to non-fulfilment of firms' goals activating information search more frequently when demand is low. On the other hand, for four of the seven innovations for which $\hat{c}_j$ records a value greater than 1, but is not significant at the 95% level, $\hat{c}_j$ is positive. Third, this cyclical variable appears

TABLE 5.3   *Estimated diffusion curves allowing for cyclical factors*

Innovation j	$\hat{b}_{ij}$	$\hat{c}_{ij}$	$\overline{R}^2$	D–W	Lag on C_{jt}
(a) *underlying cumulative lognormal (5.7a)*					
SP	1.68(8)	− 7.41(1.2)	0.93	1.90	0
F	2.18(9)	− 10.57(1.5)	0.94	2.06	0
SF	1.25(15)	− 6.29(3.5)[†]	0.98	1.77	1
GA	0.78(20)	− 22.00(2.5)[†]	0.97	1.73	0
TC	0.26(17)	2.69(4.9)[†]	0.90	1.76	2
PE	0.57(12)	2.78(1.3)	0.95	2.17	0
NCTN	0.80(17)	− 3.81(2.7)[†]	0.97	1.78	1
NCTB	1.07(10)	2.65(1.1)	0.92	2.66	1
(b) *underlying cumulative normal (5.7b)*					
BOP	0.15(7)	− 3.53(2.2)[†]	0.88	1.87	3
ATL	0.18(15)	1.73(1.6)	0.94	1.52	3
TK	0.09(30)	0.99(1.5)	0.98	2.02	3
PCBC	0.14(5)	−4.16(1.0)	0.82	2.04	3

See notes to table 5.1. All $\hat{b}_{ij}$ are significantly different from zero at the 95% level; † denotes a $\hat{c}_{ij}$ value significant at the 95% level.

to be most prominent for the innovations in the paper industry: four of the five paper innovations appear in the table. Interestingly, for each of these innovations, $\hat{c}_j$ is negative, indicating perhaps that the potential adopters in this industry are consistent in their reaction to the business cycle, regardless of the nature of the innovation. Fourth, the values of $\hat{b}_j$ (the coefficient on time or log time) have changed little, if at all, from the values reported in tables 5.1 and 5.2. This indicates no significant collinearity between t and C_t which, in turn, implies that the *trend* growth is S_{It} has been satisfactorily removed by the two alternatives described in section 5.3.3 above.

There are at least two alternative explanations of these generally disappointing results. The easy rationalization is to blame the poor quality of data used.[8] More positively, the definition of c in equation (5.8a) suggests an explanation within the terms of the model. Assuming β to be typically positive (and the results of the following chapter offer support for such an assumption), then, if Ω is typically negative, it is possible that the net effect of cyclical variations will be zero or only marginal in some cases. This might imply that search behaviour is typically less intense in times of rapidly growing demand and that this cancels out any tendency for the profitability of adoption to be higher when greater scales of output are possible. (It should be recalled that large positive values of C_t indicate expansion of output (demand) at faster than the trend rate.) But, intriguing though this possibility may be, there is really insufficient evidence to permit any strong conclusions in this respect.

Whilst further tests of the cyclical hypothesis, using better quality data, are perhaps called for, the most reasonable conclusion at this stage is that in most cases the trend growth in diffusion is sufficiently powerful to 'swamp' any minor fluctuations across the trade cycle.

5.6 Results: the 'unexplained' innovations in detail

Returning now to the conclusions of section 5.4, it was noted that the basic model was incapable of satisfactorily explaining the observed diffusion paths for four of the sample innovations (VD, CC, WSB, and EH). Clearly, the results of the previous section indicate that this position remains unchanged even when cyclical factors are allowed for. If the model is to be reconciled with the data for these innovations, the explanation must run along the lines that either μ_D or σ_D^2 did not remain constant over the diffusion period (see the last paragraph of section 2).

As it happens, there is suggestive evidence that, for three of these four innovations, this may have been the case. For instance, the technical literature suggests that post-invention improvements in Vacuum Degassing (VD) reduced the inter-firm differences in the potential profitability of adoption, whilst for Continuous Casting (CC) these inter-firm differences were gradually acknowledged to be much larger than was first supposed.[9]

In terms of the model then, σ^2 (and thus σ_D^2) probably declined over the diffusion period for VD, whilst increasing over the period for CC. As both innovations are clearly group B, the analysis of section 4.7 predicts a negatively skewed diffusion curve for VD, but a positively skewed curve for CC (see figures 4.5c and d) An inspection of the residuals generated when fitting (5.4b) tends to confirm these hypothesis: for VD, a U shaped series of residuals emerges and for CC, an inverted U shaped series is observed.[10]

For Electrical Hygrometers (EH), on the other hand, it is possible that the rapid post-war decline in the adopting industry (Lancashire weaving) may have been reflected in a structural break, just after the war, in the time path for μ_{st}[11]. Unlike the other two sample innovations in this industry (ADH and ASB), EH originated in the inter-war period.

As explained in section 4.6, this may have resulted in a diffusion curve composed of two segments, each cumulative lognormal (EH is a group A innovation) but with different parameters. This hypothesis is certainly consistent with the results obtained when fitting the cumulative lognormal separately to each sub-period (table 5.4). As can be seen, in contrast to the results observed for the cumulative normal and logistic curves, the cumulative lognormal generates D–W values which do not indicate auto-correlation in either period, although the test is just inconclusive for the second period.

In other words, it can be argued that the model is at least consistent with the observed diffusion curves for VD, CC and EH. Not only are there special features in these cases which suggest that μ_D and σ_D^2 will not have remained constant but, also, the consequences of these special features are as predicted by the model. Having said this, it should be acknowledged that the reconciliation of theory and data is, in each case, necessarily imprecise.

Finally, for the other innovation for which the model's prediction was off-target (Wet Suction Boxes in paper-making) no special features were apparent and this must remain unexplained.

TABLE 5.4 *Electrical Hygrometers: diffusion before and after 1948*

Time Period	Cumulative lognormal			Cumulative normal		Logistic	
	$\hat{b}_1$	$\overline{R}^2$	D–W	$\overline{R}^2$	D–W	$\overline{R}^2$	D–W
1935–47	0.667	0.998	2.302	0.863	0.556*	0.793	0.810*
1948–55	0.206	0.824	1.209[(*)]	0.772	0.936*	0.763	0.929*

See notes to table 5.1.

5.7 Implications of the cumulative lognormal/normal distinction

Now that the curve fitting exercises of this chapter are complete, it is well worth asking whether the distinction between the cumulative lognormal and normal diffusion curves has any substantive implications.

With this question in mind, figure 5.1 shows a pair of 'typical' cumulative lognormal and normal diffusion curves. In order to simplify the comparison, it is assumed that in year 1, diffusion is 1% in both cases. Given this restriction, and abstracting from cyclical variations, the remainder of the two curves can be derived once the values of σ_D (or b in terms of the estimating equations, 5.4) are specified. In the lognormal case, b_1 is set equal to the mean $\hat{b}_{1j}$ for the sample group A and unclassified innovations, that is, $b_1 = 0.824$. In the normal case, b_2 is set equal to the mean $\hat{b}_{2j}$ for the sample group B innovations, that is, $b_2 = 0.144$. (See tables 5.1 and 5.2).

Formally, the two 'typical' curves are derived as follows. Let $(m/n)_A$ be the level of diffusion of the 'typical' group A innovation at t and z_{At} be its normal equivalent deviate. From the initial condition that $(m_t/n)_A = 0.01$ at $t = 1$, it follows that $z_{A1} = -2.326$ (from standard normal tables). Thus, from (5.4a),

$$-2.326 = a_1 + b_1 \times 0 \quad \text{at } t = 1$$

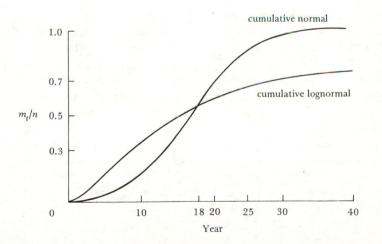

Figure 5.1 A comparison of 'typical' cumulative lognormal and normal diffusion curves

and, in general,

$$z_{At} = -2.326 + 0.824 \log t \quad \text{where } 0.824 = b_1 \tag{5.10a}$$

In exactly the same way, an expression for the normal deviate of diffusion along the 'typical' cumulative normal curve can be derived as:

$$-2.326 = a_2 + b_2 \times 1 \quad \text{at } t = 1$$

and, in general,

$$z_{Rt} = -2.470 + 0.144t \text{ where } 0.144 = b_2 \tag{5.10b}$$

Using these two forms of (5.10), it is a simple matter to read off values for the z_t, and then translate into corresponding figures for the level of diffusion at different values for t.

As can be seen from the figure, quite significant differences do emerge between the two alternative time paths of diffusion. The cumulative lognormal curve, starting from the same point as the cumulative normal, shows substantially more rapid growth in the early years: it attains 20% diffusion 5 years earlier than the cumulative normal. Thereafter, however, as the cumulative normal continues to accelerate, but cumulative lognormal diffusion to decelerate, the gap closes gradually until year 18, when diffusion is 50% in both cases. Then, as diffusion increases from 50%, both curves begin to flatten off, but the cumulative lognormal much more noticeably. Indeed, by year 26, cumulative normal diffusion is near completion, whilst the cumulative lognormal has still a long way to go, at something less than 70%. In fact, even 40 years after the first appearance of the innovation, it will still only have diffused less than 80% along the lognormal curve.

Of course, if different values are assumed for the b parameters, quite different conclusions are possible. For instance, figure 5.2 compares three alternative cumulative lognormal diffusion curves. Again, for comparability, each is assumed to attain 1% diffusion in year 1, but the 'fast' and 'slow' curves are based on the maximum and minimum observed values, b_{1j}, in the sample; the 'average' curve is merely the 'typical' curve of figure 5.1 repeated. As can be seen, in the 'fast' case, diffusion is virtually complete by year 9, whilst, in the slow case, diffusion has hardly attained 10% even by year 30. Similar, if less pronounced, differences emerge if the maximum and minimum sample observed values, $\hat{b}_{2j}$, are inserted into the cumulative normal curve (figure 5.3).

These three figures provide a number of simple and fairly obvious conclusions. First, on the average, whilst group A innovations will tend to

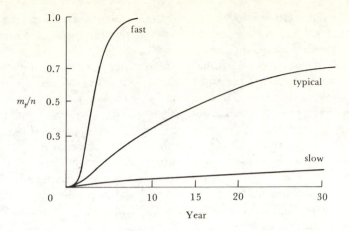

Figure 5.2   Alternative cumulative lognormal diffusion curves

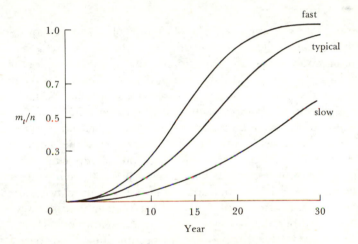

Figure 5.3   Alternative cumulative normal diffusion curves

diffuse more rapidly in the early years, in the medium and long run they will diffuse more slowly than group B innovations. Second, it seems likely that many group A innovations (including, perhaps, the above 'typical' case) will never be adopted by a significant minority of the population, especially if, as is likely, new alternative technologies appear to supersede them before, say, year 40. Third, since even in the 'slow' cumulative normal curve, shown in figure 5.3, 90% diffusion is attained by around year 40, there is probably a higher chance that most group B innovations *will* diffuse completely. On the other hand, where cumulative lognormal diffusion is rapid, 100% appears to be attainable within a decade – there is no evidence of such rapid diffusion in the observed range of sample cumulative normal diffusion curves.

In general then it seems reasonable to conclude that in most industries most firms will eventually adopt and use all major processes (albeit different vintages of those processes). But there may be large numbers of firms not using relatively minor (perhaps supplementary) processes, even many years after those processes first become available. A prime reason for this difference, as argued in terms of the present model at least, is that competitive pressures and post-invention improvements in the major processes make their widespread adoption almost unavoidable. The competitive disadvantage from failing to adopt the more minor innovations is perhaps less significant and may be obscured by other inter-firm productivity differences.

5.8 Conclusions

In general, the results reported in this chapter offer support for the time series predictions of the model introduced in the previous chapter. With only four exceptions, the diffusion curves of the sample innovations may be satisfactorily explained by the theoretical curves predicted by the model. Moreover, of the four exceptions, in three cases there are special features which can explain the failures of the basic predictions *within the framework of the model*. It is also interesting to note that when fitting alternative curves, which the model deems to be inappropriate (i.e. the logistic and for group A, the cumulative normal and for group B, the cumulative log-normal), apparently less satisfactory results are achieved. This may be interpreted, tentatively, as indicating that a good fit is not automatic whatever the exact form of the S shaped curve being used. However this conclusion must be qualified by pointing to the real difficulties of estab-lishing, statistically, the superiority of one functional form over others where, as here, the number of observations is relatively limited.

Turning to another prediction of the model, there is only limited evidence that cyclical factors have much influence on the shape of the typical diffusion curve. However the results on this score are not com-pletely insignificant and further research (and data collection) may be called for.

Finally, it has been shown that there are very real differences between the typical group A and group B diffusion curves. If the figures dis-cussed in the previous section are at all representative, this does have implications for the wider study of technical progress in general. Some of these implications will be discussed in the final chapter.

6

Firm size, the speed of adoption and the 'Industrial Engel Curve'

As was explained in section 2.4, much of previous empirical analysis in the diffusion field has been directed to explaining differences in the speed at which firms in a given industry adopt the same innovation. It is probably fair to claim that the only robust finding to emerge to date is that larger firms tend to adopt more quickly on average than do smaller firms.[1]

The purpose of this brief chapter is to develop and test the predictions of the present model in this respect. It should be acknowledged at the outset, however, that the model can have only a limited predictive power in this particular area since the only firm level variable to have been explicitly identified in the core equations of the model is firm size.[2] As such, the two most interesting questions which can be answered are whether speed of adoption is positively or negatively related to firm size and whether firm size *on its own* can account for a substantial proportion of inter-firm differences in behaviour. As an interesting by-product however, the empirical tests of this chapter also shed some light on the validity of certain assumptions concerning critical size which were made in the basic time series model of chapter 4. In section 1, the concept of the 'Industrial Engel Curve' is introduced and a prediction concerning its shape is generated. Section 2 explains how this prediction can be tested against data collected for the present sample of innovations. In section 3, the results of fitting the curve to the sample data are described. Section 4 explains how the estimated parameters can be used to assess the explanatory power of firm size as a determinant of inter-firm differences in behaviour. Section 5 considers the implications concerning speed of diffusion and firm size and contrasts present findings with those of previous research.

6.1 The 'Industrial Engel Curve'

At at intermediate stage in the development of the model in Chapter 4, the following relationship was derived:

$$P_{it} = P\{q_{it} = 1 \mid S_{it} = S_t\} =$$

$$= \Lambda \{S_t | (-\log \theta_t)/\beta, (\sigma_t/\beta)^2) \text{ for } \beta > 0$$

$$\text{or} = \Lambda \{1/S_t | (\log \theta_t)/\beta, (\sigma_t/\beta)^2\} \text{ for } \beta < 0 \qquad (4.16) \text{ (repeated)}$$

Thus, for a given innovation at time t, the probability of adoption is related to firm size according to a cumulative lognormal function for $\beta > 0$.

Now this prediction is analogous to the Quasi-Engel curve of previous probit models concerning the diffusion of new consumer durables (see section 2.9). There, the Quasi-Engel curve relates the probability of ownership of the consumer durable to the consumer's income. Since firm size fulfils much the same role in the present model as does income in these previous models, it is perhaps permissable to designate (4.16) the 'Industrial Engel Curve'.

It should be clear that this curve is merely the cumulative form of the critical size distribution (S_d) discussed in section 4.4. Figure 6.1 illustrates the general shape of the curve for $\beta > 0$, which is a positively skewed rising S shape, implying that the probability of adoption increases monotonically with firm size at t. Alternatively, for $\beta < 0$, the general shape is the complement of that in (6.1). That is, the probability of having adopted declines monotonically with firm size at time t. (It may be noted that this applies to both group A and group B innovations and is quite independent of the assumption, made in chapter 4, that the firm size distribution is also lognormal.) Although the general S shape of the curve will hold at all points in time, the parameters of the curve may change. Indeed for $\beta > 0$, the mean will decrease over time (given the positive relationship between θ_t and t earlier assumed). This results in upward shifts in the curve (i.e. to

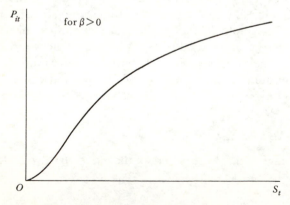

Figure 6.1   The Industrial Engel Curve

the left), indicating that the probability of adoption is increasing for all firm sizes. For $\beta < 0$, as θ_t increases, the curve shifts upwards to the right as diffusion proceeds.

On the other hand, if, as seems likely, β and σ^2 are fairly constant over time (and the results of the previous chapter indicate that this was probably true for all the sample innovations except Vacuum Degassing and Continuous Casting), then the variance, $(\sigma/\beta)^2$, will likewise remain constant. This will mean a fixed degree of skewness for the curve.

6.2 The empirical Industrial Engel Curve

An estimating equation with which these predictions may be tested can be derived as follows. First, rewrite (4.16) in terms of the standard normal distribution function:

$$P_{it} = N \left\{ \frac{\log S_t + (\log \theta_t)/\beta}{(\sigma_t/\beta)} \,\middle|\, 0, 1 \right\} \quad \text{for } \beta > 0 \tag{6.1}$$

$$\text{or } P_{it} = N \left\{ \frac{-\log S_t - (\log \theta_t)/\beta}{(\sigma_t/\beta)} \,\middle|\, 0, 1 \right\} \quad \text{for } \beta < 0 \tag{6.2}$$

Then, defining the normal equivalent deviate of P_{it} by z_{it}^1,

$$P_{it} = N(z_{it}^1 | 0, 1) \tag{6.3}$$

where $z_{it}^1 = a^1 + b^1 \log S_{it}$ \hfill (6.4)

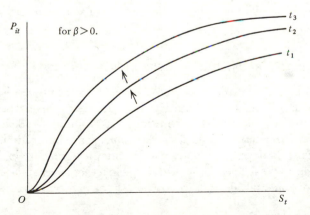

Figure 6.2   The shift over time in the Industrial Engel Curve

and $a^1 = (\log \theta_t)/\sigma_t \, ; \, b^1 = \beta/\sigma_t$　for $\beta > 0$ 　　　　　　　(6.5)

or $a^1 = -(\log \theta_t)/\sigma_t \, ; \, b^1 = -|\beta/\sigma_1|$ for $\beta < 0$ 　　　　　(6.6)

(Note that b^1 in (6.6) is negative since β/σ_t is the, necessarily positive, standard deviation of critical size.)

Whilst the probabilities P_{it} (and thus the z_{it}^1) are obviously not directly observable, equation (6.4) may be estimated as follows. For each innovation, all potential adopters are grouped into r size classes at time t. The proportion of firms having adopted in class k ($k = 1, \dots , r$) is designated $\overline{P}_{kt}$ and $\overline{z}_{kt}^1$ is its normal equivalent deviate (read off from normal tables); the mean size of firm in class k is designated S_{kt}. Equation (6.4) may then be estimated for each innovation at any point in time, as:

$$\overline{z}_{kt}^1 = a^1 + b^1 \log S_{kt} \quad k = 1, \dots , r \tag{6.7}$$

In other words, as for the diffusion curve in the previous chapter, probabilities are replaced by observed frequencies.

Consider now the potential value of this equation to the entire model. First, from equations (6.5) and (6.6), the sign on the estimate $\hat{b}$ provides information on the sign of β. If indeed $\beta > 0$, then $\hat{b}^1$ should be positive, indicating an upward sloping Industrial Engel Curve (which means the probability of ownership increases with firm size.) Second, if the relationship between the $\overline{z}_{kt}^1$ and $\log \overline{S}_{kt}$ is found to be linear, then this confirms the cumulative lognormal shape of the Industrial Engel Curve. In turn, this means that critical size and ϵ_t are also both lognormally distributed. Third, if when equation (6.7) is estimated for the same innovation at different points in time, the $\hat{b}^1$ are found to be fairly similar, this would suggest that (σ/β) is stable over time. It will be recalled that constant σ was one of the assumptions on which the basic time series predictions of the model were based.

6.3　*The data and estimates of the Industrial Engel Curve*

The data which has been used to test these predictions is outlined in the appendix on data sources. Unfortunately the empirics in this particular area have been rather limited by data constraints. To achieve the ideal and estimate (6.7) for each year throughout the diffusion of each innovation, not only must the date of adoption be known for all adopters, but so too must the size of each firm in each year. It would also help if there were sufficiently large numbers of potential adopters to provide, say, at least eight size classes in each case.

In the event, there are so few firms in most of the adopting industries that, typically, only three to five meaningful size classes can be constructed (in two cases, only two separate classes are possible). In addition, for four innovations, the only cross-section data available refers to just one year, the firms having already been classified into classes at source. Further, for most of the industries concerned, time series data on individual firms' sizes is just not available.

This all places two important constraints on the scope for estimation. First, although it has proved possible to estimate equation (6.7) for all but one of the innovations for at least one year in the diffusion period, for only a few could the equation be re-estimated at different points in time.[3] Second, in nearly all cases, the equation has been fitted to only three, four or five observations.

Because of this second problem it would be pointless to use the more sophisticated estimators that are technically called for. Instead, straight lines have been fitted by eye to the observations on the $\bar{z}_{kt}^{1}$ and $\log S_{kt}$. Whilst this is clearly not ideal, under the circumstances, it is probably the best that can be done.[4] To quote Aitchison and Brown (1957, p. 33): 'Although [this graphical method] can hardly be regarded as a rigorous statistical test of lognormality it provides a quick method of judging whether the population may feasibly be lognormal. Moreover, the parameters [of the distribution] may be estimated.'

It should be stressed, therefore, that this data and estimator do not, in general, permit strong conclusions to be drawn, although they do provide a set of results which are very consistent with expectations. The results can be summarized briefly as in table 6.1.

The estimates, $\hat{b}_{j}^{1}$ for the 21 innovations are reported (in reciprocal form) in table 6.1. In all cases, $\hat{b}^{1} > 0$ which indicates upward sloping observed Industrial Engel Curves. This result is remarkably pervasive and taking all 21 innovations together, there are but two pairs of adjacent observations (out of a total of 50) for which an increase in log size accompanies a decline in $\bar{z}^{1}$. This suggests that 96% of all observations are consistent with the probability, P_{it}, increasing monotonically with firm size. Thus whilst standard errors cannot be attached to the $\hat{b}_{j}^{1}$ it does seem reasonable in this case to conclude that the evidence points strongly to $\beta > 0$ as the typical case. Of course β positive is not required by the model of chapter 4 but this finding is not unexpected, given the strong technical reasons why larger firms should find new processes more profitable.

Second, for none of the innovations could the hypothesis of linearity be rejected at the 95% level. In every case, a χ^{2} shows no significant divergence from linearity and thus the null hypothesis of lognormality may be accepted. To repeat the above caution, this result must be seen in the perspective of the low number of observations and the weakness of the χ^{2} test. Neverthe-

TABLE 6.1   *Estimated Industrial Engel Curves*

Innovation j†	$(\widehat{\sigma/\beta})_j = 1/\hat{b}_j^1$	$\{1 + (\widehat{\sigma/\beta})^2/\sigma_s^2\}_j^{-1}$	$-(\widehat{\beta/\psi})_j^{\ddagger}$
SP (9)	1.825	0.469	−0.276
F (5)	1.800	0.476	−0.195
SF (5)	1.425	0.591	−0.381
WSB (14)	2.900	0.259	−0.787
GA (9)	3.350	0.120	−0.389
ASB (6)§	2.450	0.213	−1.070
ADH (9)§	1.150	0.552	−1.880
EH (22)§	0.860	0.687	−1.189
BOP (11)	0.960	0.554	−4.808
VD (14)	3.125	0.133	−2.024
VM (11)	1.650	0.390	−2.591
CC (11)	3.750	0.090	−2.427
ATL (−)¶	2.810	0.112	−2.155
TK (19)	1.212	0.652	−5.208
PCBC (6)	2.625	0.299	−2.336
TC (12)	2.375	0.405	−2.208
CT (9)	1.340	0.253	−0.473
PE (11)	0.645	0.628	−0.968
SL (16)	1.687	0.504	−0.311
NCPP (9)	2.250	0.354	−0.854
NCTN (15)	1.200	0.488	−0.744
NCTB (14)	2.234	0.282	−0.432

† For the key to the innovation abbreviations, see table 3.1. The figure in brackets after each abbreviation denotes the number of years after the first introduction of the innovation to which the data employed relates.

‡ Note that $(\widehat{\beta/\psi})$ for group B innovations are not directly comparable with those for group A or unclassified innovations.

§ For EH, ADH and ASB, $(\widehat{\beta/\psi})$ have been estimated assuming $\delta = 0$. For these innovations, data for estimating δ_j is unavailable.

¶ For ATL, there are insufficient firms to compute an Engel curve, but because this innovation had diffused 100% at the time of writing, (β/ψ) could be estimated directly from (6.13b), (σ/β) has then been estimated from $\hat{\sigma} \, DI_j$ (from chapter 5) σ_{sj}^2 and $(\widehat{\beta/\psi})_j$ according to (6.14).

less, it would be fair to claim that there is nothing in this data to suggest that the Industrial Engel Curves are *not* cumulative lognormal. This, in turn, offers some support for the hypothesis that S_{ct} and ϵ_t are lognormally distributed. As this assumption is so central to all of the predictions of the model, this result is comforting, if not conclusive.

Thirdly, for the data reasons already mentioned, little can be said about the constancy or otherwise of the b_j^1 over time. For three innovations only, is sufficient data available to permit estimation at different points in time. In each case, $\hat{b}^1$, i.e. $\widehat{\sigma/\beta}$, does not vary much between years.[5] This limited evidence does suggest that the assumption of roughly constant σ^2 may be reasonable (and this is indirectly confirmed by the relatively convincing performance of the basic time series predictions of the model which assume constant σ^2, in the previous chapter). Nevertheless, a more thorough test of this assumption would have been desirable.

6.4 The explanatory power of firm size

Turning to the magnitudes of the $\hat{b}_j^1$, an interesting perspective on the role of firm size in the model, as a whole, is possible. Reconsider now the equation which, in some senses, lay at the core of the analysis in chapter 4:

$$R_i^*/ER_{it} = \theta_t S_{it}^\beta \epsilon_{it} \qquad (4.10 \text{ repeated})$$

All of the empirical analysis of this study is based on various hypotheses concerning the manner in which this ratio of expected to target profitability varies over time and across firms. But one important question which so far remains unanswered is just how much of the inter-firm variance within each sample industry in this ratio can be explained by firm size.

In the hypothetical case in which R^*/ER could be *observed* for all firms, this question could be answered relatively easily by regressing the logarithm of this ratio against log firm size for all firms within a given industry at a fixed point in time. Now consider the R^2 which would be obtained from this hypothetical regression. As usual, R^2 may be defined as:

$$R^2 = \sum \hat{y}_i^2 / \sum y_i^2 \qquad (6.8)$$

where, in this case, (and omitting the t subscript):

$$y_i = \log{(R^*/ER)_i} - \overline{\log{(R^*/ER)}}$$

$$= \hat{\beta}(\log S_i - \overline{\log S}) + (\log \hat{\epsilon}_i - \overline{\log \epsilon}) \qquad (6.9)$$

and $\hat{y}_i = \hat{\beta}(\log S_i - \overline{\log S})$ $\qquad (6.10)$

(As usual, hats denote estimated values.)
Denoting the variance of log size and the estimated variance of the logged error term by, respectively, σ_{st}^2 and $\hat{\sigma}^2$, it follows that:

$$R_t^2 = \hat{\beta}^2 \sigma_{st}^2 / (\hat{\beta} \sigma_{st}^2 + \hat{\sigma}_t^2)$$

$$= [1 + (\widehat{\sigma_t/\beta})^2/\sigma_{st}^2]^{-1} \qquad (6.11)$$

Now of course, such a regression is impossible since observations are just not available for the dependent variable. On the other hand, the Industrial Engel Curves have provided estimates of (σ/β) for each innovation (namely, the reciprocals of $\hat{b}^1$). In addition, estimates of σ_{si}^2 are available for all sample industries. Therefore, from (6.11), this notional R^2 can easily be calculated for each of the innovations.[6] Intuitively, it is fairly obvious that the larger is the variance of βS_{it} relative to that of ϵ_{it} for a given innovation, then the more important is firm size as a determinant of firm behaviour in this context. The ratio in (6.11) merely formalizes the strength of association in a familiar way.

The third column in table 6.1 shows the R^2 estimated in this way. It would appear that firm size is, generally, a fairly powerful explanatory variable: for 7 of the 22 innovations, over half of the variance in $\log (R^*/ER)_{it}$ is 'explained' by log size, and for another 4, $R^2 > 0.4$. In fact, for only 4 innovations does R^2 drop below 0.2 and all 22 R^2s are significant using an F test.

Whilst the rough and ready nature of the estimates of the $(\sigma/\beta)_j$ suggests caution in interpreting these results, they do offer some justification for the central role attached to firm size in this model. (There is, after all, no reason why the $(\widehat{\sigma/\beta})_j$ should be biased downwards.)

6.5 Firm size and the speed of adoption

Finally, it is interesting to compare the present findings with those of previous research on inter-firm differences in the speed of adoption. Consider, in particular, Mansfield's work which has been imitated by most other studies. As reported in section 2.4.2, Mansfield tests the following relationship (abstracting from insignificant variables):

$$\log d_{ij} = \log A_j + B_j \log S_{ij} + \log U_{ij} \tag{6.12}$$

where d_{ij} is the number of years the ith firm waits before introducing the jth innovation (assuming $d = 0$ for the first adopter), A_j is a constant and U_{ij} a lognormally distributed error term. It will be recalled that Mansfield estimated (6.12) using grouped data on a number of different innovations, implying that $B_j = B$ for all j.[7] His results indicate $-0.03 > \hat{B} > -1.53$.

It is possible to generate similar equations to (6.12) from the present model. For instance, inserting the specific forms of θ, given by (4.22) into equation (4.10) it follows that firm i will adopt j at time t_{ij}[8] where:

$$\log t_{ij} = -(1/\psi)_j \log \alpha_j - (\beta/\psi)_j \log S_{it} - (1/\psi)_j \log \epsilon_{ijt}$$

for group A innovations (6.13a)

or $\quad t_{ij} = -(1/\psi)_j \log \alpha_j - (\beta/\psi)_j \log S_{it} - (1/\psi)_j \log \epsilon_{ijt}$

for group B (6.13b)

Given the conventions used in the present study, t_{ij} is equivalent to Mansfield's d_{ij} and, as ϵ_{ijt} is lognormally distributed (equation 4.14), it is clear that apart from different symbols (6.13a) is identical to Mansfield formulation. Whilst this is something of a coincidence, the interesting implication is that his model of inter-firm differences is not consistent with the epidemic diffusion model. Instead, and assuming a lognormal firm size distribution, it suggests a cumulative lognormal (group A) diffusion curve.[9]

However, to return to the present study, equations (6.13) have not been estimated because most of the sample innovations had not diffused 100% at the time of writing, consequently, d_{ij} is unknown for some i. Nevertheless, sufficient evidence is available to generate estimates of (β/ψ) which is clearly the key parameter in these equations.

From the time series implications of the model:

$$\sigma_{D1j}^2 = (\beta^2 \sigma_s^2 + \sigma^2)_j / (\beta\delta + \psi)_j^2 \qquad \text{(4.30 repeated)}$$

and rearranging,

$$\frac{\beta}{\psi_j} = \frac{\sigma_{D1j}}{(\sigma_s^2 + (\sigma/\beta)^2)_j^{1/2} - \delta_j \sigma_{D1j}} \qquad \text{(6.14)}$$

Since estimates of σ_{D1j} are available from table 5.1 and δ_j[10] from table 7.1, the above estimates of $(\sigma/\beta)_j^2$ and σ_{sj}^2 provide enough information to generate estimates of β/ψ for all the sample innovations. These are reproduced in table 6.1. The average estimate of $(\beta/\psi)_j$ for the group A innovations and the unclassified group (for which cumulative lognormal diffusion has been assumed) is 0.811. For the seven group B innovations, the mean value is 3.078. However, bearing in mind the difference in functional form in (6.13), these two figures are not comparable.

6.6 Conclusions

In this chapter, it has been shown that the model of chapter 4 provides a prediction of inter-firm differences in the behaviour of firms which is conceptually analogous to the Quasi-Engel curve in previous models of the diffusion of consumer durables. Although it has proved difficult to collect sufficient evidence to test this prediction rigorously, a number of tentative conclusions have emerged. *First*, it appears that in practice β typically assumes positive values. In other words, at any point in time, the probability that a firm will have adopted is larger, the bigger is the firm. As shown in the previous section, this is equivalent to the statement that, other things equal, larger firms will adopt innovations more rapidly than small firms. A useful measure in this context is the elasticity of adoption lag with respect to firm size, $(\delta d/\delta S)/(S/d)$. Results in section 5 suggest that the average value for this elasticity in the present sample is about -0.8, which compares with Mansfield's earlier estimates of between -0.03 and -1.53. The policy implications of this finding will be explored in the final chapter of the book.

Second, there is no evidence to suggest that the earlier assumption of a lognormal distribution for critical firm size is unjustified. As this is an important assumption of the model this result is encouraging.

Third, it has been shown that firm size is an important determinant of firm behaviour in the present context, which is also comforting given the central role attributed to firm size in the model as a whole.

7

An explanation of inter-innovation/industry differences in the speed of diffusion

7.1 Introduction

This chapter completes the empirical analysis of the study by attempting to answer the most interesting question of all: 'why do some innovations diffuse faster than others?' As reported in chapter 2, the only strong conclusion to emerge from past research is that more profitable innovations tend to diffuse more quickly, ceteris paribus. Partly because of the limited data base of past work, we know little about the role of the characteristics of the adopting industry in this context. The present study, being based on 13 different industries, presents a real empirical opportunity to fill in this gap in our knowledge. Specifically, it would be interesting to know whether the competitive structure and growth performance of the adopting industries have had any significant influence on diffusion speed of the sample innovations. A further test of the importance of the profitability of adoption variable would also be worth while, to see whether a similar strong significance emerges in the U.K. as has been found for the U.S.

In the next section, an operational measure of diffusion speed is derived and it is shown that the model suggests that there are two constituent parts to this measure. Section 3 hypothesizes about the determinants of these two constituents. In section 4, estimating equations are derived and measurement of explanatory variables is discussed. Sections 5 and 6 report the findings of cross-section regression analysis of the diffusion speeds of the sample innovations.

7.2 A measure of diffusion speed

The first task of this chapter must be to provide an empirically manageable measure of the speed of diffusion which can be used in the following cross-section comparisons of the sample innovations.

Fortunately, for both of the growth curves employed in this study, there is a fairly obvious summary measure of the pace of diffusion. In section 5,7, it was shown that once an initial level of diffusion (corresponding to the first introduction into the industry of the innovation) is specified, it is σ_D^2 alone which determines the diffusion time path for both the cumulative lognormal and normal curves. Indeed figures 5.2 and 5.3 show how the variations in this parameter affect the shape of the diffusion curve. In this section, the case for σ_D^2 as a measure of diffusion speed is merely formalized.

Consider, as a measure of the pace at which a given innovation spreads within a given industry, the time lapse between diffusion attaining any two levels: (m_1/n) and (m_2/n) where, as usual, m denotes the number of firms having adopted and n the total number of potential adopters. (For instance, these two levels might be 20% and 80% respectively.)

If the innovation concerned is of the group B type, then the model suggests *cumulative normal diffusion*, which may be written as:

$$Q_t = (m_t/n) = N(t \,|\, \mu_D, \sigma_D^2) \qquad (7.1)$$

$$\text{(4.26b repeated)}$$

Using the normal deviate transformation:

$$(m_t/n) = N(z_t \,|\, 0, 1) \qquad (7.2)$$

$$\text{(5.2 repeated)}$$

This may be rewritten:

$$z_t = a + bt \qquad (7.3)$$

$$\text{(5.4b repeated)}$$

where

$$a = -\mu_D/\sigma_D, \; b = \sigma_D^{-1} \qquad (7.4)$$

$$\text{(5.5 repeated)}$$

Equation (7.3) is, of course, the form in which the cumulative normal prediction was tested in chapter 5. Therefore, estimates of b, and thus σ_D, are available for all group B innovations.

From (7.3), the time lapse between (m_1/n) and (m_2/n) follows as:

$$t_2 - t_1 = \left(\frac{z_2 - a}{b}\right) - \left(\frac{z_1 - a}{b}\right) = \left(\frac{z_2 - z_1}{b}\right)$$

where z_2 and z_1 are the normal equivalent deviates of (m_2/n) and (m_1/n). Thus, the time taken for diffusion to grow, for instance, from 20% to 80% is $1.68b^{-1} = 1.68\sigma_D$ (the normal deviates of 0.20 and 0.80 being -0.84 and

+0.84 respectively). Quite clearly, the larger is b (that is, the smaller is σ_D) the shorter is the time lapse and the faster is diffusion. More generally, it is σ_D^{-1} which alone determines the time elapsing between *any* two non-zero levels of diffusion. As such it does appear to be a powerful summary measure of the entire diffusion process.[1]

Whilst things are not so clear cut for *cumulative lognormal diffusion*, the slope parameter is again a fairly useful summary measure.

Let $m_t/n = N(\log t \,|\, \mu_D, \sigma_D)$ (7.5)

(4.26a repeated)

then $z_t = a + b \log t$ (7.6)

(5.4a repeated)

where z, a and b are defined as above

In this case,

$$\log t_2 - \log t_1 = \frac{z_2 - z_1}{b}$$

and the time lapse is

$$t_2 - t_1 = \left[\exp \{(z_2 - z_1)/b\} - 1 \right] t_1$$

Here, one needs to know t_1 (i.e. the date at which (m_1/n) is attained), as well as b, before $t_2 - t_1$ can be computed. Nevertheless, in comparing different lognormal diffusion curves, so long as (m_1/n) is a small number, say less than 0.05, differences between innovations in t_1 are unlikely to be substantial (remembering that t_1 measures the number of years after the first appearance of the innovation). Thus, whilst not a complete measure of diffusion speed, b, and thus σ_D^{-1}, should represent most inter-innovation differences in $t_2 - t_1$ fairly comprehensively.

In the remainder of this chapter, therefore, b will be used as a summary measure of diffusion speed for both curves. It is, of course, merely the reciprocal of the theoretical parameter, σ_D, which from the above is inversely related to diffusion speed.

It is perhaps unnecessary to explain that this is a particularly convenient measure for present purposes, since the time series curve fitting in chapter 5 provides estimates of b for all of the sample innovations. It is these estimates which will form the dependent variable(s) of the present chapter.

As a first step towards an explanation of inter-innovation differences in this parameter, it should be noted that, according to the present model:

$$b_j = \frac{1}{\sigma_{Dj}} = \frac{\psi_j}{(\beta^2\sigma_s^2 + \sigma^2)_j^{1/2}} \text{ for the } j\text{th innovation}$$

(7.7)

(4.24 repeated)

This definition applies in the absence of growth in the adopting industry. Allowing, more generally, for a constant growth rate in industry size of δ

$$b_j = \frac{1}{\sigma_{Dj}} = \frac{(\psi + \beta\delta)_j}{(\beta^2\sigma_s^2 + \sigma^2)_j^{1/2}} \text{ for the } j\text{th innovation}$$

(7.8)

(4.30 repeated)

These definitions apply whether diffusion is cumulative normal or lognormal (although the ψ_j and δ_j are not comparable for the two curves).

7.3 Determinants of diffusion speed

The next task is to identify the likely determinants of the speed of diffusion. In this respect, equation (7.8) provides a potentially fruitful framework. According to the present model, there are two broad groups of determinants of diffusion speed: the *dynamic influences on the adoption decision* and *inter-firm differences* (the numerator and denominator respectively in 7.8). More precisely, from the specifications in chapter 4, the former can be interpreted as the growth rate over time in the mean value of R^*/ER, whilst the latter represents the standard deviation of the logarithm of this ratio (across firms in the adopting industry).[2]

Thus in broad terms, *diffusion of innovation j should be faster*:

(i) The larger is δ_j, the rate of growth of the adopting industry (assuming $\beta_j > 0$).
(ii) The larger is ψ_j, which is the growth rate of θ_t; this, in turn, will be larger, (a) the more substantial are the post-invention improvements to the technology made by the innovation manufacturers, (b) the more productive is information search by potential adopters and (c) the greater are competitive pressures on non-adopters,[3]
(iii) The smaller are firm size inequalities, σ_{sj}^2 (more specifically, σ_{ij}^2 is the variance of log firm size) and
(iv) The smaller is σ_j^2; this reflects the extent of inter-firm differences in expected profitability from adoption and in target investment rates (after allowing for differences due to firm size).

These four factors are interesting in a number of respects. First, and broadly speaking, only (ii) ties in with intuitive notions of what makes for rapid diffusion. Indeed a brief reading of chapter 2 will suggest that most previous research into the determinants of diffusion speed has concentrated on variables which would come under the broad heading of dynamic influences on the adoption decision (e.g. competitive pressures, relaxation in risk premiums). Yet a moment's reflection will confirm that this could not be the whole story: diffusion is only non-instantaneous because of differences between potential adopters in the way in which they react to a given innovation. It follows quite obviously that diffusion will be faster the less pronounced are these inter-firm differences (as reflected by (iii) and (iv) above). Second, the presence of δ_j and σ_{ij}^2 within the above list has interesting policy implications; the latter, for instance, is an important dimension of industrial structure and should be positively related to the level of industrial concentration.

Thus on one level, the model widens the discussion to include factors which have been previously largely ignored in the literature. On the other hand, the above list does not complete the picture: whilst δ_j and σ_{ij}^2 may be directly observable and treated as largely exogenous to the diffusion process, neither ψ_j or σ_j^2 is directly observable and, in any event, some further discussion of the determinants of these two parameters is undoubtedly necessary, prior to empirical testing.

The determinants of ψ_j To repeat, ψ_j reflects the rate of increase over time in the expected profitability of adoption and the rate at which the investment yardsticks used to assess adoption are relaxed (reflected respectively and, in both cases inversely, by ER_{ij} and R_{ij}^* for the ith firm with respect to the jth innovation).

From the analysis of chapter 4, three groups of explanatory variables may be important here. The *characteristics of the innovation* itself may determine the extent of learning by doing, the returns from information search and the competitive pressures on non-adopters. Specifically, more expensive and complex innovations may be subject to greater learning by manufacturers; if so, later vintages may be substantially superior to early vintages. Similarly, information search may yield greater returns the more complex is the innovation, if only because of greater scope for initial misunderstanding and uncertainty. For the same reasons, the risk premiums attached to adoption may be substantially reduced over the diffusion period. Furthermore, the inherent profitability of the innovation is likely to be important in a number of respects: competitive pressures on non-adopters and the speed at which information circulates within the industry are both likely to be directly related to the typical profitability of adoption.[4].

Second, the *economic environment facing the adopting industry* may determine potential adopters' readiness to search for information and to relax investment yardsticks. For instance, in rapidly growing industries, where pressures on capacity are typically high, and in which firms attach much importance to growth goals, information search may be a continuous activity and attitudes to risk may be far more favourable than in industries with a larger margin of spare capacity, and where market shares are established and stable. Similarly, opportunities to adopt may be more substantial in fast growing industries in which net investment is relatively more important. Having said this, there are counter arguments. For instance, where demand is static or falling, profits may have to be earned 'the hard-way' and, consequently, firms may be more amenable to cost-saving innovations.

Third, and particularly interesting, is the impact of the *competitive structure of the adopting industry*. One might expect this to be important in three different respects. It seems probable that the pressures on non-adopters to adopt will be greater in competitive, rather than oligopolistic industries. In the appendix to this chapter it is argued that the non-adopter will tend to lose profits at a faster rate as his competitors adopt, the more responsive is his demand to changes in his competitors' prices. If it is assumed that under oligopoly firms are more successful at differentiating their product and/or price competition is non-existent (as in the kinked demand curve), this implies that non-adopters may be able to hold out much longer before adopting. (In terms of the present model, search is less likely and R^* will be much more 'sticky'.)

Turning to the incentives to adopt, it is argued in appendix A.7 that post-invention improvements in the process will increase the profitability of adoption whatever the industry structure. However, since the profitability of adoption will be greater the more elastic is demand with respect to the firm's own price, the *rate of increase* of profitability may also be greater in more competitive industries with only limited product differentiation.

One other intriguing possibility is that the extent of information flows within the consuming industry may also reflect the structure of that industry. For instance, Martilla's case studies (1971) (cited above in section 4.2 under Proposition 2) indicate that information exchange may be less common in competitive industries. This is not surprising, of course, since it is particularly irrational for adopters to encourage non-adopters in adopting any new cost-saving process in these circumstances. Another related possibility is that information may be more slowly diffused, the greater is the number of firms in the consuming industry. As Williamson (1965) has shown, it becomes increasingly difficult for a firm to keep up comprehensive contacts with the rest of the industry, the more firms there are in that industry. As N_j (the number of firms) increases, the volume of 'transmissions' necessary to keep each firm in touch with every other increases roughly in proportion to N_j^2. Similarly, the efficiency of information transmission by the innovation supplier will also probably decline with increasing N_j. For instance, a market of 10 consumers, each with a potential purchase of 10 units of the innovation, can be more easily covered by salesmen than a market of 100 consumers, each with a potential purchase of 1 unit. If, in the early days of diffusion, the supplier only has a limited number of salesmen (often scientists or technologists) with an understanding of the process, this may also severely constrain the diffusion of effective information, where there are many potential adopters.

Overall then, the net influence of market structure on ψ_j is uncertain. On the one hand, the pressures on non-adopters to search for information and to relax yardsticks are likely to be greater in competitive industry, on the other hand, *returns* from search may be limited in competitive industries with many firms.

In the light of these arguments, the following general formulation is suggested for innovation j:

$$\psi_j = f_1(K_j, T_j, \pi_j, EA_j, IS_j, N_j) \qquad (7.9)$$
$$+ \ \ + \ \ + \ \ ? \ \ \ ? \ \ \ -$$

where K_j is the 'typical' capital outlay required to install the innovation; T_j is some index of the innovation's technical complexity; π_j measures the 'typical' profitability of adopting the innovation; EA_j is some index of the level of economic activity in the adopting industry; IS_j is some, as yet unspecified, measure of the competitive structure of the adopting industry and N_j is the number of potential adopters. The signs below each variable indicate the expected signs of the first order partial derivatives. The precise mathematical form of f_1 is not pursued at this point: there is no immediately obvious functional form.

The determinants of σ_j^2 Bearing in mind the basic definitions of the model, this parameter reflects those variations between firms in ER and R^* remaining after allowing for differences due to firm size (see equations (4.2), (4.4), (4.9) and (4.14)). A number of hypotheses seem plausible here. First, the variance in the profitability of adoption should be greater the more heterogeneity there is within the industry in the products sold, in the age of the capital stock and nature of other inputs employed. This follows from the argument of section 3.3.3. Thus, the *structure of the consuming industry* may be important: the extent of product differentiation will certainly influence the variability between firms in products and perhaps raw materials used, although Salter (1960, p. 91) has shown that the variability in the age of capital equipment employed should be no greater in more monopolistic industries. However, he goes on to argue that in industries in which new plant is typically capital intensive (and thus requires high investment outlays), existing capital equipment will have longer economic lives before being replaced. This derives, of course, from the assumption that machinery is only replaced when its operating costs exceed the total costs (including capital charges) of new equipment. Consequently: 'It follows, therefore, that a wide range between the labour requirements of co-existing techniques is likely in highly mechanized industries. This is as we should expect; adjustment is more costly when highly mechanized techniques requiring large amounts of investment are involved' (1960, p. 71). On this argument then, one might expect a *smaller variance in the age of existing machinery in more labour intensive industries*.

Moving on to the causes of inter-firm variance in information receptiveness and the yardsticks used in investment appraisal (as reflected by R^*) the hypotheses become, necessarily, more adhoc. Again, the *structure of the industry* may be important: in the extreme case of perfect competition there is no room for discretion in the goals and attitudes of firms, but as competition becomes less rigorous, one might expect to observe differences between firms in propensity to seek out information and in attitudes to risk.

Also important may be the *nature of the innovation itself*. For instance, the more complex and costly the innovation is, the more likely it is that firms will differ significantly in their understanding and in the risk they attach to adoption. On the other hand, smaller differences in knowledge might be expected for very profitable innovations: it seems likely that the more profitable is the innovation, the greater is the likelihood that it will be seen as a potential solution to non-fulfilment of goals and thus the subject of information search by most firms.

These hypotheses can be represented by the following simple specification for the variance of log ϵ_i for innovation j:

$$\sigma_j^2 = f_2 \, (IS_j, \; LI_j, \; K_j, \; T_j, \; \pi_j) \qquad (7.10)$$
$$\quad \; ?, \quad - \quad + \quad + \quad -$$

where IS_j, K_j, T_j and π_j are as defined above and LI_j is a measure of the adopting industry's labour intensity. As above, the expected signs of partial derivatives are shown under each variable.

Finally no definite hypotheses are suggested concerning the scale parameter, β_j, which also appears in (7.8). Apart from noting that larger firms may stand to gain most from the more costly and complex group B innovations (and thus β may be larger for such innovations), this parameter must remain largely unexplained without more detailed technological information than is available for the sample innovations.

7.4 Two alternative empirical methodologies and measurement of variables

Whilst there is an obvious case, on theoretical grounds, for 'decomposing' diffusion speed into these 'structural' parameters as above, the most appropriate empirical methodology with which to test the various hypotheses suggested is less obvious. Certainly the most straightforward method is to substitute these 'explanations' of ψ_j and σ_j^2 into (7.8), which can then be fitted to the estimates of b_j generated in chapter 5 using some computationally convenient specific functional form. Thus, from (7.8), (7.9) and (7.10):

$$b_j = f_3 (IS_j, K_j, T_j, \pi_j, N_j, EA_j, LI_j, \beta_j, \delta_j, \sigma_{sj}^2) \qquad (7.11)$$
$$\quad\; ? \quad ? \quad ? \quad + \quad - \quad ? \quad + \quad ? \quad + \quad -$$

where $f_3 = \left[f_{1j} + \beta_j \delta_j \right] \left[\beta_j^2 \sigma_{sj}^2 + f_{2j} \right]^{-1/2}$ \qquad (7.12)

A regression equation based on (7.11) would be quite easy to interpret, although the information content of such a regression would be limited. For instance, since π_j appears in both (7.9) and (7.10), only its *net* influence could be observed in a single regression 'explaining' b_j. This approach will be pursued in section 6.

A second more attractive approach would be to estimate (7.9) and (7.10) individually and directly. Again, the unknown mathematical forms, f_1 and f_2, would necessarily be approximated by some specific form, but a finer test of the various hypotheses embodied in these functions would still be possible. Once estimated, these equations could then be combined, acknowledging the precise nature of the relationship between ψ_j, σ_j^2 and b_j (as shown in (7.8)). In other words this approach would be slightly less arbitrary.

The obvious drawback of this second approach is that direct estimates of the ψ_j and σ_j^2 are just not available. However, a second best approach is still possible. From the cross-section regressions of the previous chapter, estimates of $(\sigma/\beta)_j$ are available for all sample innovations. Moreover, these can be used with ancillary information on σ_{sj}^2 and δ_j^2 to transform the time series estimates of b_j into estimates of $(\psi/\beta)_j$. Rearranging (7.8):

$$(\psi/\beta)_j = b_j \left[(\sigma/\beta)_j^2 + \sigma_{sj}^2 \right]^{1/2} - \delta_j \qquad (7.13)$$

Table 7.1 repeats the earlier estimates of $(\sigma/\beta)_j$ and reports the estimates of $(\psi/\beta)_j$, derived using (7.13). (The estimates of the σ_{sj}^2 and δ_j employed have been generated, respectively, from the observed firm size distributions for the sample industries and from time series data on the output of those industries, as explained above in section 5.3.3).

TABLE 7.1   *The constituent parts of diffusion speed*

Innovation j†	Inter-firm differences				The dynamic influences		
	$\hat{\sigma}^2_{sj}$	$\widehat{(\sigma/\beta)}_j$	$(\sigma^2_{sj} + (\sigma/\beta)^2_j)^{1/2}$	b_j	$((\psi/\beta)_j + \delta_j)$	$\hat{\delta}_j$‡	$\widehat{(\psi/\beta)}_j$
Group A(LN)							
1 SP	2.941	1.825	2.504	1.494	3.742	0.120	3.622
2 F	2.941	1.800	2.486	2.107	5.238	0.120	5.118
3 SF	2.941	1.425	2.230	1.231	2.745	0.120	2.625
4 WSB	2.941	2.900	3.369	0.441	1.486	0.215	1.271
5 GA	1.531	3.350	3.571	0.766	2.736	0.168	2.568
6 EH	1.605	0.860	1.531	0.667	1.021	0	1.021
7 ADH	1.605	1.150	1.711	0.311	0.532	0	0.532
8 ASB	1.605	2.450	2.758	0.339	0.935	0	0.935
Group B(N)							
9 BOP	1.145	0.960	1.437	0.151	0.217	0.009	0.208
10 VM	1.740	1.650	2.112	0.190	0.401	0.015	0.386
11 ATL	0.3645	2.810	2.874	0.179	0.514	0.050	0.464
12 TK	2.756	1.212	2.056	0.093	0.192	0	0.192
13 PCBC	2.941	2.625	3.136	0.140	0.439	0.011	0.428

Unclassified

	1	2	3	4	5	6	7
14 TC(LN)	3.842	2.375	3.080	0.238	0.733	0.280	0.453
(N)	3.842	2.375	3.080	0.046	0.142	0.028	0.114
15 CT(LN)	0.608	1.340	1.551	1.328	2.059	−0.055	2.114
(N)	0.608	1.340	1.551	0.186	0.288	−0.006	0.294
16 PE(LN)	0.701	0.645	1.057	0.561	0.593	−0.340	0.933
(N)	0.701	0.645	1.057	0.136	0.144	−0.017	0.161
17 SL(LN)	2.890	1.687	2.395	1.213	1.745	−0.310	2.055
(N)	2.890	1.687	2.395	0.148	0.278	−0.025	0.303
18 NCTB(LN)	1.960	2.234	2.637	0.890	2.346	0.200	2.146
(N)	1.960	2.234	2.637	0.161	0.424	0.016	0.408
19 NCTN(LN)	2.286	1.200	1.930	0.866	1.521	0.177	1.344
20 NCPP(LN)	3.063	2.250	2.851	0.509	1.451	0.280	1.171

† The abbreviations LN and N refer, respectively, to estimates derived from *lognormal* and *normal* diffusion curves.

‡ $\hat{\delta}_j$ for Electrical Hygrometers, Accelerated Drying Hoods and Automatic Size Boxes are unknown.

Sources: Column 1: firm size distributions reported in section 4.5 and Davies (1976).

Column 2: Industrial Engel Curves reported in table 6.1.

Column 3: derived from columns 1 and 2.

Column 4: time series diffusion curves reported in tables 5.1, 5.2, and 5.4.

Column 5: the product of columns 3 and 4.

Column 6: time series data on the output of the adopting industries, section 5.3.3.

Column 7: column 6 subtracted from column 5.

These estimates of $(\sigma/\beta)_j$ and $(\psi/\beta)_j$ are used in the following section to test the various hypotheses involved in the previous section. Quite clearly, the presence of the unknown parameter β in these ratios is undesirable, and probably limits the explanatory power of regressions with the ratios as dependent variables. But in the absence of information on the β_j this is unavoidable.

Measurement of the explanatory variables   The two functions f_1 and f_2 include seven explanatory variables which reflect various characteristics of the innovations and the industries in which they are diffusing. In addition three 'structural' parameters of the model, β_j, σ_{sj}^2 and δ_j, appear as determinants of b_j in (7.8). Thus measures are required for 10 explanatory variables in f_3. Unfortunately it has proved quite impossible to derive 'estimates' of the technical complexity of the innovations (T_j). Similarly, β_j (the scale parameter), as mentioned above cannot be observed and it is not obvious what proxy measure might be appropriate. Having said this, K_j, the capital cost of the innovations should serve as a useful proxy for T_j and it may 'pick up' some of the inter-innovation variance in β_j.[5] Even omitting T_j and β_j, however, there remain eight potential explanatory variables and, in an attempt to make the ensuing regressions more manageable, these have been reduced to six by using certain measures in a dual role. Problems of measurement of these variables are now discussed.

   (a) K_j: *the 'typical' capital outlay required for adoption of innovation j.*   Where possible, this is measured by the average capital outlay required for adoption; that is, the cost at approximately midway in the time series estimation period for an average sized firm in the industry concerned. More often than not, this ideal measure is unobtainable and, when a number of alternative estimates are available in the technical literature, the most typical (in the above sense) is used. No attempt has been made to normalize for the effects of inflation as no obvious price indices suggest themselves. Consequently, K_j is measured in thousands of pounds. In some of the regression experiments, this variable has been deflated by the average size of firm in the industry (size being measured by number of workers employed). Table 3.1 reports the observations on K_j.

   (b) π_j: *the typical pay off associated with adoption of innovation j.* Again, because π_j will vary over time and across firms, where possible an average estimate has been used. The pay off is defined simply as the number of years required for the extra revenues generated by adoption to pay back the initial investment oulay. *Thus π_j is inversely related to the profitability of adoption.* The data used is also presented in table 3.1, the main sources being various adopters of the innovations, the innovation suppliers and trade journals.

(c) LI_j: *the labour intensity of the adopting industry*. This is measured by the share of value added (net output) allocated to wages and salaries at the mid-point of the diffusion period: data has been obtained from various Census of Production reports at the M.L.H. level (in most cases, the 1958 or 1963 reports).

(d) EA_j: *the level of economic activity in the adopting industry*. This variable has been measured by $\hat{\delta}_j$ (reported in table 7.1). These have been estimated from time series industry data on output and are the $\hat{B}_j$ from equations 5.9. As $\hat{\delta}_j$ may be interpreted as the trend growth rate of output, over the diffusion period, this should reflect the intensity of economic activity in the adopting industry quite adequately. Unfortunately, for three of the innovations, it has proved impossible to derive estimates for this variable. The data on which the estimates are based are reported in table A.3 of the appendix at the end of the book.

(e) IS_j: *the industrial structure of the adopting industry*. Bearing in mind the arguments for the inclusion of this variable in f_1 and f_2, it is perhaps best measured by some index of industrial concentration. The index used here is the author's own U measure[6] defined as:

$$U_j = I_j^A N_j^{-1} \text{ where } A > 0 \tag{7.14}$$

where I_j reflects size inequalities and N_j firm numbers in the consuming industry. This is preferred to the conventional measures of concentration (such as concentration ratios, the Herfindahl and Entropy indices) because it explicitly reflects the two constituent parts of concentration, whilst not constraining the weights attached to them to take on pre-specified values. I_j is measured, in general, by $c^2 + 1$, where c is the coefficient of variation. In this particular case, because lognormal firm size distributions have been observed for the sample industries, it can be shown (Davies, 1978) that $I_j = \exp\{\sigma_{sj}^2\}$ where σ_{sj}^2 is, as usual, the variance of log size. In other words,

$$IS_j = U_j = \exp\{A\sigma_{sj}^2\} N^{-1} \tag{7.15}$$

where σ_{sj}^2 reflects size inequalities and N_j firm numbers. Since $A > 0$, this index increases with increasing size inequalities and with decreasing firm numbers.[7] U can easily be shown to be a general measure including, as special cases, the Herfindahl and Entropy indices. For instance $U_j = $ Herfindahl where $A = 1$ (Davies, 1978).

A major advantage of the index in the present context is that it introduces no additional measurement problems: N_j and σ_{sj}^2 both appear already quite independently of IS_j in f_3.

σ_{sj}, the variance of log size has been estimated for each industry in most cases from data collected on the sizes of all firms in the industry (but, in a few cases, from size class tables). The estimates are presented in table 7.1 and the data is described and discussed in more detail in Davies (1976, appendix 5).

The data used to estimate the N_j is also reported in the appendix at the end of the book. Both N_j and σ_{sj}^2 have been assumed constant over the diffusion periods.

The estimating equations   Equations (7.9)–(7.11) can now be re-expressed as estimating equations, where, in the light of the above, K_j is to act as a proxy for T_j (and perhaps β_j), IS_j is to be measured by N_j and σ_{sj}^2, as suggested by the U index, and π_j is an *inverse* measure of the profitability of adoption. (As before, expected signs of coefficients are shown below each explanatory variable.)

The unknown mathematical forms of f_1, f_2, f_3 are approximated, in each case, by the linear-in-logs form. Whilst this is convenient for regression analysis, it is of course largely arbitrary. However, for f_3 at least, it is reasonably appropriate in that this function is itself a multiplicative function of f_1 and f_2. Thus the estimating form of (7.11) is to be:

$$\log \hat{b}_j = a_{01} + \underset{(-)}{a_{11}} \sigma_{sj}^2 + \underset{-}{a_{21}} \log N_j + a_{31} \log K_j + \underset{-}{a_{41}} \log \pi_j + \underset{(+)}{a_{51}} \delta_j$$
$$+ \underset{+}{a_{61}} \log LI_j + u_j \tag{7.16}$$

The estimating form of (7.9), using the estimates shown in table 7.1 is to be:

$$\log (\widehat{\psi/\beta})_j = a_{02} + \underset{(-)}{a_{12}} \sigma_{sj}^2 + \underset{}{a_{22}} \log N_j + \underset{+}{a_{32}} \log K_j + \underset{-}{a_{42}} \log \pi_j + a_{32} \delta_j + v_j$$

$$\tag{7.17}$$

The estimating form of (7.10) is to be:

$$\log (\widehat{\sigma/\beta})_j = a_{03} + \underset{+}{a_{13}} \sigma_{sj}^2 + \underset{-}{a_{23}} \log N_j + \underset{+}{a_{33}} \log K_j + \underset{+}{a_{43}} \log \pi_j$$
$$+ \underset{-}{a_{63}} \log LI_j + w_j \tag{7.18}$$

u_j, v_j and w_j are disturbance terms.

7.5 Results: (a) an explanation of diffusion speed via its constituent parts

This section reports the results of fitting equations (7.17) and (7.18) to the observations on $(\hat{\psi}/\beta)_j$ and $(\hat{\sigma}/\beta)_j$ reported in table 7.1. From the argument of section 3, these 'variables' can be interpreted as reflecting parts of the two constituents to diffusion speed, namely, the 'dynamic influences' and 'inter-firm differences'. It must be acknowledged at the outset that both equations suffer from drawbacks: the dependent variables are, themselves, estimates and the problems involved by the unavoidable inclusion of β_j in the denominators have already been mentioned. However, so long as β_j varies across j according to an approximately log-linear relationship with one or more of the explanatory variables in these equations, this may not reduce the explanatory power of the equations too much.[8] Moreover, similar problems have faced previous attempts to explain diffusion speed (see chapter 2) and provided results are treated with caution, these equations are well worth investigating.

Taking first equation (7.17), the explanation of $(\hat{\psi}/\beta)_j$, this must be estimated separately for the estimates derived from cumulative normal and lognormal diffusion curves, because the ψ_j are not directly comparable (as is clear from the definition of ψ in equations (4.22)). 14 innovations have been included in the *cumulative lognormal group*, being the seven group A innovations and the seven unclassified innovations for which the cumulative lognormal yielded an acceptable description of diffusion (i.e. for which autocorrelation could be rejected).[9] Whilst it is unavoidable that the sample size is reduced in this way, the low number of degrees of freedom severely limits the scope for experimentation.[10]

Equation 1 in table 7.2(a) shows the result of including all five explanatory variables[11] and although the R^2 is surprisingly high, the low number of degrees of freedom leads to serious multicollinearity and it is difficult to disentangle the separate influences of the variables. The remaining equations in the table report the results of rerunning the regression excluding various of the weaker explanatory variables in an attempt to reduce the collinearity. As can be seen, both N_j and particularly π_j are generally significant at the 95% level: when only these two variables are included, an $\bar{R}^2$ of 0.55 is achieved and nothing appears to have been lost by excluding the other three variables. There is nothing in these results to suggest that σ_{sj}^2, K_j or δ_j have any influence on $(\psi/\beta)_j$. In other words, these results support the two hypotheses that ψ_j will be larger the fewer adopting firms there are (rationalized earlier in terms of information flows) and the more profitable is the innovation (because of higher competitive pressures and more active information search).

Interestingly, the picture is almost identical when (7.17) is fitted to the estimates of $(\psi/\beta)_j$ derived from the *cumulative normal diffusion curves*. In this case, only 10 innovations are included in the sample, namely the 5 group B innovations and the 5 unclassified innovations for which table 5.1 shows no conclusive evidence of autocorrelation when fitting the cumulative normal. As can be seen from table 7.2(b), again, the two variables N_j and π_j account for much of the inter-innovation variation in $(\psi/\beta)_j$: equation 4, for in-

TABLE 7.2   *Regression analysis of the $(\widehat{\psi/\beta})_j$: the dynamic constituent to diffusion speed (based on equation 7.17)*

Explanatory variables

	σ_s^2 $\hat{a}_{12}$	$\log N$ $\hat{a}_{22}$	$\log K$ $\hat{a}_{32}$	$\log \pi$ $\hat{a}_{42}$	δ $\hat{a}_{52}$	F	R^2	$\overline{R}^2$
(a) *The cumulative lognormal sample†*								
(1)	0.106	−0.269	0.070	−0.455*	−0.358	3.08	0.658	0.445
	(0.212)	(0.246)	(0.150)	(0.198)	(0.942)			
(2)	0.056	−0.219	0.089	−0.456**		4.22	0.652	0.498
	(0.158)	(0.198)	(0.134)	(0.188)				
(3)	0.153	−0.359**		−0.387**	−0.504	4.16	0.649	0.493
	(0.178)	(0.145)		(0.129)	(0.848)			
(4)	0.094	−0.319**		−0.361**		5.81	0.635	0.526
	(0.144)	(0.124)		(0.117)				
(5)		−0.321**		−0.379**		8.96	0.620	0.550
		(0.121)		(0.111)				
(b) *The cumulative normal sample‡*								
(1)	0.021	−0.361*	−0.072	−0.806**	−5.869	7.91	0.908	0.793
	(0.110)	(0.137)	(0.047)	(0.177)	(5.637)			
(2)		−0.304***	−0.091*	−0.727***		14.44	0.878	0.818
		(0.075)	(0.041)	(0.148)				
(3)		−0.284**		−0.857***	−7.764	11.37	0.850	0.776
		(0.082)		(0.180)	(4.603)			
(4)		−0.201**		−0.735***		12.37	0.780	0.717
		(0.073)		(0.185)				
(5)		−0.208*		−0.833**		15.03	0.938	0.875
		(0.060)		(0.173)				

Notes: Estimated standard errors in parentheses
* denotes a coefficient significantly different from zero at the 90% level
** denotes a coefficient significantly different from zero at the 95% level
*** denotes a coefficient significantly different from zero at the 99% level

† Regressions computed using 14 observations (i.e. all innovations for which the cumulative lognormal diffusion curve was appropriate as shown in tables 5.1 and 5.2)

‡ Regressions 1–4 computed using 10 observations (i.e. those innovations shown in table 5.1 as recording no conclusive evidence of autocorrelation for the cumulative normal diffusion curve). Regression 5 computed using 5 observations (i.e. the five group B innovations for which autocorrelation could be discounted in table 5.1).

stance, shows that the two variables together alone record an $\bar{R}^2$ as high as 0.717. The other three explanatory variables never approach statistical significance and, apart from noting that π_j and N_j are both even more strongly significant than for the lognormal $(\psi/\beta)_j$, and that the coefficient on π_j is substantially higher in this case (indicating greater sensitivity of ψ_j to π_j), there is little to add to the previous discussion.[12]

Taken together these results are encouraging: $\bar{R}^2$ are surprisingly high, especially in the cumulative normal sample, and it is interesting to note that N_j and π_j appear as significant for both samples. The failure to observe other significant variables is not altogether surprising, given the low number of degrees of freedom, and a verdict on δ_j, σ_{sj}^2 and K_j must be postponed on this evidence.

Turning now to the results of fitting equation (7.18), using the estimates of $(\sigma/\beta)_j$ from the empirical Industrial Engel Curves of chapter 6, two innovations, Vacuum Degassing and Continuous Casting have been excluded from the sample. (This is because the evidence of chapter 5 suggests that σ_j^2 cannot be assumed to be constant over time for these innovations.)

As can be seen from table 7.3, the results are a little disappointing and largely inconclusive (given the nature of the dependent variable, however, they are hardly surprising). The strongest result to emerge is the robust significance of the LI_j variable, the labour intensity of the adopting industry. When all five explanatory variables are included in the equation, only LI_j is

TABLE 7.3   *Regression analysis of the $(\widehat{\sigma/\beta})_j$: the inter-firm differences constituent to diffusion speed (based on equation 7.18)*

Explanatory variables

	σ_s^2 $\hat{a}_{13}$	$\log N$ $\hat{a}_{23}$	$\log LI$ $\hat{a}_{63}$	$\log K$ $\hat{a}_{33}$	$\log \pi$ $\hat{a}_{43}$	F	R^2	$\bar{R}^2$
(1)	0.136 (0.102)	−0.111 (0.120)	−1.702** (0.770)	−0.054 (0.052)	0.213 (0.142)	2.61	0.482	0.298
(2)	0.127 (0.088)	−0.127 (0.088)	−1.681** (0.669)	−0.059 (0.043)	0.212 (0.137)	3.48	0.481	0.343
(3)	0.107 (0.091)		−1.806*** (0.599)		0.166 (0.116)	4.19	0.440	0.335
(4)			−1.858*** (0.604)		0.141 (0.115)	5.47	0.392	0.320
(5)			−1.352*** (0.446)			9.18	0.338	0.301
(6)	0.150* (0.075)	−0.150* (0.075)				3.97	0.181	0.135

Notes: All regressions computed using 20 observations (i.e. all innovations, excluding VD and CC). See table 7.1 for estimates of the $(\sigma/\beta)_j$. See, also, notes to table 7.2.

significant at the 95% level, but bearing in mind the relatively large R^2, one might argue that the low number of degrees of freedom has led to the possibility of serious multicollinearity (indeed, the correlation determinant is low at 0.2).

The remaining equations shown in the table again report attempts to reduce this collinearity by 'dropping' various insignificant variables from the estimating equation. In general, however, these experiments provide little new information and the conclusions which may be drawn are unfortunately limited. First, as argued in section 3 and following Salter, σ_j is inversely related to the labour intensity of the adopting industry; this is because high labour intensity should reflect low variance in the age of existing capital stock (and thus low variance in the profitability of adoption across firms). This variable is consistently significant, sometimes even at the 99% level, regardless of which other explanatory variables are included in the equation. In fact the $\overline{R}^2$ achieved when only LI_j is included is sufficiently high (equation 5) to suggest that LI_j accounts for a large portion of the variance in $(\widehat{\sigma/\beta})_j$. Secondly, the signs of the estimated coefficients on σ_{sj}^2 and N_j are consistent with the hypothesis that more concentrated industries will tend to have higher σ_j. However, except in equation (6), which omits all other variables and implies the Herfindahl measure of concentration, the coefficients are not significant.[13] Even in (6), only 90% significance is attained. Certainly this particular result suggests grounds for further research but it is not strong enough to permit any very positive statements. Thirdly, the sign of the estimated coefficient on π_j is consistent with the hypothesis forwarded earlier that more profitable innovations should be associated with lower σ_j (remembering the inverse nature of π_j) but again, t values of about 1.5 are hardly convincing. Fourthly, and most surprising, there is no evidence of a significant relationship between K_j and σ_j.

To investigate the overall implications for diffusion speed, these 'explanations' of $(\widehat{\phi/\beta})_j$ and $(\widehat{\sigma/\beta})_j$ can now be substituted back into (7.8). Using only those estimated equations from the above tables in which all explanatory variables have been found to be significant at the 95% level, the explanation of *cumulative lognormal diffusion* is:

$$\hat{b}_j = (e^{2.319} N_j^{-0.321} \pi_j^{-0.379} + \delta_j) (e^{-0.562} LI_j^{-2.704} + \sigma_{sj}^2)^{-1/2} \qquad (7.19)$$

and for *cumulative normal diffusion*:

$$\hat{b}_j = (e^{0.627} N_j^{-0.201} \pi_j^{-0.735} + \delta_j) (e^{-0.562} LI_j^{-2.704} + \sigma_{sj}^2)^{-1/2} \qquad (7.20)$$

(these expressions employ equation 5 from table 7.3 in both cases, and equation 5 from table 7.2a for cumulative lognormal diffusion and equation 4 from table 7.2b for cumulative normal diffusion).

Thus, including σ_{sj}^2 and δ_j (which appear in (7.8), by definition, from the specification of the model), there are five determinants of diffusion speed in both cumulative lognormal and normal diffusion curves. From these equations it is an easy matter to calculate the elasticity of estimated diffusion speed ($\hat{b}_j$) with respect to each of these five determinants. As table 7.4 shows, the numerical values of these elasticities vary between innovations (depending on the values of the structural coefficients). If they are evaluated at mean values for the two samples used, a number of interesting implications emerge.

First, diffusion is faster, the more profitable is the innovation (remembering that π_j is an inverse measure of the speed of diffusion), the faster growing is the consuming industry, the more labour intensive is the industry, the fewer firms and the smaller the size inequalities of those firms in the industry. Second, on inspection of the mean values of the elasticities, it can be seen that although industry growth is a positive determinant, its effect appears minimal; for cumulative lognormal diffusion, N_j, π_j and σ_{sj}^2

TABLE 7.4   *The implications for diffusion speed*

Explanatory variable i†	The elasticity of $\hat{b}$ with respect to i‡	The elasticity of $\hat{b}$ with respect to i evaluated at the mean§	Percentage change in i required to reduced time lapse by 1 year¶
N (lognormal)	$-0.321(1 + k_1)^{-1}$	-0.319	-27
(normal)	$-0.201(1 + k_1)^{-1}$	-0.198	-30
π (LN)	$-0.379(1 + k_1)^{-1}$	-0.377	-23
(N)	$-0.735(1 + k_1)^{-1}$	-0.725	-8
LI (LN)	$1.352(1 + k_2)^{-1}$	0.771	$+11$
(N)	$1.352(1 + k_2)^{-1}$	0.876	$+7$
σ_s^2 (LN)	$-0.5\,k_2(1 + k_2)^{-1}$	-0.215	-40
(N)	$-0.5\,k_2(1 + k_2)^{-1}$	-0.176	-34
δ (LN)	$k_1(1 + k_1)^{-1}$	0.006	$+1400$
(N)	$k_1(1 + k_1)^{-1}$	0.013	$+5000$

† The elasticities are based on: the estimated coefficients in equation 5, table 7.3; for the lognormal curve (LN), those in equation 5 of table 7.2a; and for the normal curve (N), those in equation 4 of table 7.2b.

‡ For convenience, $k_1 = \beta\delta/\psi$ and $k_2 = \beta^2\sigma_s^2/\sigma^2$. The expressions in this column have been derived using equations (7.19) and (7.20).

§ Using mean values of $(\widehat{\sigma/\beta})$, $\hat{\delta}$, $(\widehat{\psi/\beta})$ and $\hat{\sigma}_s^2$ derived from table 7.1.

¶ As explained in the text, the figures in this column show the percentage change required to reduce the time lapse between 1% and 50% diffusion by 1 year (for the 'average' sample innovation in each of the two groups.)

have similar elasticities and LI_j stands out as numerically most important. (This does not imply, of course, that LI_j is the most important determinant of $\hat{b}_j$ – it might be mentioned, for instance, that this variable has a small variance relative to the other 4 determinants.) Third, it is interesting to note that, for δ_j, σ_{yj}^2, LI_j and N_j, the elasticities are numerically close for both cumulative normal and lognormal diffusion speed and only π_j shows a substantial difference between the two samples: apparently, cumulative normal diffusion speed is much more sensitive to variations in profitability.

Finally, and to give these elasticities a rather more obvious meaning, it is interesting to examine what they imply about the ways in which diffusion can be speeded up. From the estimated diffusion curves of chapter 5 it can be shown that on average, the predicted time lapse between 1% and 50% diffusion was 31.9 years for the cumulative lognormal curves and 16.6 years for the cumulative normal curves.[14] It is an easy exercise[15] to calculate the changes required of each of the explanatory variables to reduce this time lag by one year. Column 3 of Table 7.4 reproduces the results of these calculations, from which it is clear that large proportionate changes would be required. Having said this, it should be noted that these changes are not particularly substantial when compared with the observed variability in the explanatory variables in the present sample. For instance, N_j varies between 7 and 580; π_j between 0.25 and 10.87; σ_{yj}^2 between 0.36 and 3.84 and LI_j between 31% and 73%. In other words, these 4 variables are responsible for major differences between innovations in diffusion speed. The one exception is δ_j : the changes required in this variable are quite outside of the range of values observed in the sample. As such, there are no grounds for claiming that the growth rate of adopting industries has a numerically important influence on diffusion speed.

7.6 Results: (b) a direct explanation of diffusion speed

As an alternative empirical approach to that of the previous section, equation (7.16) is now fitted directly to the time series estimates of the $\hat{b}_j$. Whilst this approach is more straightforward, as argued earlier, it is somewhat less satisfactory in that it fails to acknowledge the exact nature of the functional relation between diffusion speed and the structural parameters of the model. On the other hand, it does provide a check on the above results and, in addition, on the significance of σ_{yj}^2 and δ_j as determinants of diffusion speed, which is merely assumed in the approach above. Furthermore, it may be seen to be similar to Mansfield's second empirical stage in which he regresses $\hat{\beta}_j$, the estimated slope parameters of his logistic curves, against various explanatory variables using a functional form which is also largely arbitrary (linear in his case).[16]

For the estimates of *lognormal* b_j, three of the explanatory variables emerge as significant determinants: N_j, π_j and LI_j, each having an estimated coefficient with a sign consistent with those achieved above when explaining the two constituent parts of $\hat{b}_j$: $(\widehat{\psi/\beta})_j$ and $(\widehat{\sigma/\beta})_j$. On the other hand, K_j, σ_j and σ_{sj}^2 are each found to be insignificant. This is unsurprising for K_j since this variable had little explanatory power in the separate equations for $(\widehat{\psi/\beta})_j$ and $(\widehat{\sigma/\beta})_j$. For δ_j and σ_{sj}^2, however, this is a little surprising since the model suggests that these two parameters are both constituents of b_j by definition. In fact, (7.8) shows that b_j should increase with increases in δ_j and decreases in σ_{sj}^2. Whilst the estimated coefficient on σ_{sj}^2 when fitting (7.16) is indeed negative, that on δ_j is also negative, contrary to expectations. Having said this, (7.16) does not include either parameter in a mathematical form equivalent to the 'true form' (i.e. 7.8) and their insignificance may well derive from this mis-specification.

Equation (1) in table 7.5 shows the results of fitting (7.16) to the lognormal estimates of b_j and excluding δ_j, σ_{sj}^2 and K_j: π_j and N_j are both significant at the 95% level whilst LI_j is only significant at the 90% level in this formulation (but again this weak significance may derive from the mis-specification of form).

For the estimates of $\hat{b}_j$ for *normal diffusion curves*, (7.16) again largely confirms the earlier results: as can be seen, LI_j, π_j and σ_{sj}^2 are always significant with coefficients having the expected sign and N_j is strongly significant (with its coefficient having the expected sign) when σ_{sj}^2 is excluded from the equation (i.e. equation 4). This is a fairly strong result, given the multicol-

TABLE 7.5   *Regression analysis of the $\hat{b}_j$: diffusion speed (based on equation 7.16)*

Explanatory variables

	σ_s^2 $\hat{a}_{11}$	$\log N$ $\hat{a}_{21}$	$\log \pi$ $\hat{a}_{41}$	$\log LI$ $\hat{a}_{61}$	F	R^2	$\bar{R}^2$
(a) *cumulative lognormal sample*							
(1)		−0.383** (0.127)	−0.498** (0.155)	1.500* (0.840)	5.56	0.625	0.513
(b) *cumulative normal sample*							
(2)	−0.189** (0.071)	−0.104 (0.070)	−0.819*** (0.163)	2.390*** (0.586)	17.13	0.932	0.878
(3)	−0.271*** (0.061)		−0.834*** (0.200)	2.321** (0.940)	11.53	0.902	0.824
(4)		−0.245*** (0.064)	−0.794** (0.230)	2.909** (0.779)	10.30	0.837	0.756

Notes: Regression 1 computed using the 14 innovations outlined in table 7.2a. Regressions 2–4 computed using the 10 innovations outlined in table 7.2b. See also notes to table 7.2.

linearity which must exist in equations with 3 or 4 explanatory variables and only 10 observations. Moreover, the $\bar{R}^2$ are surprisingly large. Perhaps the most welcome finding is the significant negative influence of σ_{ij}^2 on $\hat{b}_j$ which is consistent with the model's prediction, as in (7.8).

Overall, the results here largely reinforce those of the previous section. For instance, the implied elasticities of diffusion speed with respect to each explanatory variable (which are, of course, the coefficient estimates in table 5, given the log-linear form) are generally quite close to those calculated using the previous approach and reported in table 7.4.

7.7 Conclusions

This chapter has attempted to provide a general theoretical explanation of the determinants of diffusion speed which can be tested for the innovations in the present sample.

It has been shown that the speed of diffusion for any innovation can be summarized by the slope parameter of its estimated diffusion curve (whether that curve be cumulative lognormal or normal). The theoretical model of chapter 4 suggests that this parameter may be decomposed into two constituent parts, these parts have been termed 'inter-firm differences within the adopting industry' and 'the dynamic influences on the adoption decision'. Specifically, diffusion should be more rapid (a) the more homogeneous are firms in the adopting industry and (b) the stronger are the factors which increase the chance of any one firm adopting over time. Within the framework of the model a number of hypotheses have been suggested and tested concerning the causes of inter-innovation and inter-industry variance in these two constituent parts of diffusion speed. Whilst any conclusions drawn must be viewed in the light of the relatively low number of observations, some light has been thrown on the questions posed at the beginning of this chapter.

First, the one strong result to emerge from previous studies in this field has been confirmed for the present sample. Diffusion speed appears to be more rapid, the more profitable the new innovation is for potential adopters. This can be explained in terms of innovation profitability being an important dynamic influence on the adoption decision: information flows should be more pronounced for highly profitable innovations and competitive pressures on non-adopters should also be more intensive. It was suggested that these effects are reinforced if, for the more profitable innovations, there is less variability between firms in the quality of information on which decisions are based; however, only weak, non-significant, evidence could be found to support *this* hypothesis.

Second, there is little to suggest that innovations will diffuse noticeably quicker in industries in which demand and aggregate industry size are grow-ing rapidly. Certainly, the model suggests that there should be a positive relationship, since increases in size should make adoption more profitable. In addition, perhaps more rapidly growing industries will tend to be more active in information search. No evidence could be found to support the latter hypothesis and, even accepting the former hypothesis, it has been shown to have a negligible influence on diffusion speed.

Third, the evidence on industry structure as a determinant of diffusion speed is more substantial, but also more complicated. Taking the 'inter-firm differences' component first, the model shows that these differences in expectations, target rates etc. will be greater and diffusion slower, the greater is the variance between firms in their sizes. This conclusion follows logically if, indeed, firm size is an important influence on the behaviour of individual firms, and the findings of the previous chapter tend to confirm this. Thus the model predicts that diffusion speed should be inversely related to σ_s^2 and thus concentration, ceteris paribus. In addition, it has been hypothesized that the residual differences in behaviour (after allowing for size differences) will be greater in more oligopolistic industries if such industries permit larger differences between firms in attitudes and goals. (This would be reflected by a large value for σ^2 in the model.) There is some weak, but usually insignificant, evidence for this hypothesis.

Turning to the other component of diffusion speed, 'the dynamic influences', it has been argued that these will be less pronounced in more concentrated industries because competitive pressures on non-adopters are likely to be less substantial. On the other hand, information exchange and contacts with innovation suppliers may be less frequent and effective in less concentrated industries with large numbers of firms. The results confirm the importance of the second hypothesis, dynamic influences being inversely related (nearly always strongly significantly so) to firm numbers in both cumulative normal and lognormal diffusion curves. Overall, this means that the influence of industrial concentration is by no means straight-forward: remembering that concentration itself reflects both size in-equalities and (inversely) firm numbers, it is not possible to say, directly, whether increases in concentration increase or decrease diffusion speed. Certainly, greater size inequalities tend to reduce diffusion speed but so too do greater firm numbers. The overall policy implications of this are explored in the following chapters.

Fourth, a number of other sundry hypotheses have been suggested, of which only one is substantiated by the results obtained. Apparently, industries which are labour intensive have been quicker to adopt the new innovations. This seemingly strange finding may be explained if one accepts Salter's hypothesis that the variance in age of existing capital stock will be lower in labour intensive industries, and thus so too will be the variance in the profitability of adoption between firms in the same industry (given that the age and type of existing equipment may be significant determinants of the profitability of introducing the new innovation). Thus, this influence operates through the 'inter-firm differences' component to diffusion speed.

Finally, taking an overview of the contribution of the present chapter to the study of the determinants of diffusion speed, two points are worthy of note. First, and most obviously, the regressions reported provide virtually the first statistical evidence on the role of various characteristics of the adopting industry in influencing the speed with which it adopts innovations. Second, an important change in methodology has been pursued. In all previous research, the common methodology has been to use the estimated slope parameter of the logistic curve, when fitted to time series diffusion data, as a measure of the speed of diffusion.[17] Here, because no single curve can satisfactorily describe the diffusion of all innovations, it has been necessary to break the sample of innovations into separate groups, each group having a common diffusion curve shape. Differences in diffusion speed are then studied *within* each group: in other words, only like is compared with like. In this way it is hoped that measurement errors in the dependent variable have been minimized. Furthermore, by splitting the dependent variable into two constituent parts, the 'dynamic influences' and 'inter-firm differences', perhaps more insight has been gained into the likely determinants of diffusion speed. Thus previous research, which has implicitly concentrated on the 'dynamic influences', has failed to recognize that the speed of diffusion is heavily dependent on 'variables' which determine the variability in behaviour of potential adopters. For instance, intuitive adhoc theorizing would not support the inclusion of variables such as LI_j and σ_{sj}^s in cross-industry analysis of diffusion speed. However the present model not only provides a rationalization for these variables but also indicates how empirics may be developed in order to test for their influence.

Having said all this, a final note of caution must be struck: the explanation of inter-innovation difference provided is by no means comprehensive and it goes almost without saying that further tests on different samples of innovations would be desirable.

Appendix A.7 Market structure and the incentives and pressures to adopt

In the main text of this chapter, it has been argued that the incentives to adopt a new innovation and the pressures on non-adopters may be sensitive to the competitive structure of the consuming (adopting) industry, In this appendix, the implications of three existing theoretical models of industrial structure are briefly reviewed.

(i) The vintage model: perfect competition versus monopoly   Salter (1960, p. 93) shows that there is 'no reason for a greater delay in the introduction of new techniques in monopolistic industry compared to competitive industry', so long as firms are profit-maximizers. This conclusion (which concerns the incentive to adopt or the profitability of adoption) follows from the equalization, in both cases, of the total costs of marginal new capacity with the operating costs of marginal existing capacity. But he goes on to add, 'the important difference is that the monopolist is under no external pressure (that is, other than his own self-interest) to scrap obsolete equipment; while the producer in a competitive industry is forced to do so by the price changes resulting from the actions of his competitors'. The appearance of a new technique with lower costs, then, presents the same *incentive* – extra profits – but differing *pressures*. This analysis was based upon the classic vintage assumptions, including indivisible plant, and whilst it becomes less clear cut when allowing for piecemeal changes in plant[18] the main conclusion still stands.

(ii) Oligopoly and the kinked demand curve   On an intuitive level, there is some disagreement as to whether oligopoly encourages rapid adoption of new techniques or not; Adams and Dirlam (1966) suspect that oligopolists may tend to refrain from pioneering for fear of upsetting the status quo, but say nothing about the reactions of other firms, once a new technique has been pioneered. Salter, on the other hand, suggests that the state of oligopoly places a premium on being one jump ahead with respect to new techniques, 'so as to ensure that the expansion of output, which these allow, is achieved by his new capacity rather than that of his competitors (thus avoiding direct aggression)'.

A useful theoretical construction, which distinguishes the pressures and incentives resulting from the advent of a new process innovation, is the *kinked demand curve*.

In the diagram, as usual $D'D'$ is the demand curve facing the firm and $D'ABMR$ its marginal revenue curve. If adoption of the new process reduces the marginal cost curve from MC_1 to MC_2, then there is no incentive to reduce price or increase output; if price were reduced by the extent of the cost savings, all competitors would reduce their prices accordingly and only a small increase in the firm's demand would take place. This does not mean that the firm has no *incentive* to adopt – quite obviously it does, profit increasing by an amount equal to the area of $CDEF$. But, adoption

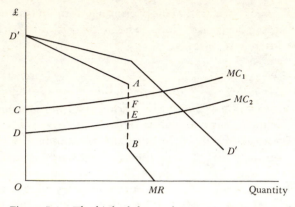

Figure 7.1   The kinked demand curve: incentives to adopt

does not affect the firm's competitors at all. They lose none of their market share and are under no *pressure* to adopt, no matter how many of their competitors have adopted. There are, however, two exceptional cases. If the cost savings are large enough to reduce MC_2 to such a level that it cuts the MR curve below the point B, then there is an incentive for a profit maximizer to reduce his price accordingly, thus putting pressure on non-adopters. Alternatively, if the new innovation improves the *quality* of the product, then non-adopters *would* be under pressure to follow suit, as they would be now offering an inferior quality, if not an inferior price.

(iii) Average cost pricing and product differentiation   Similar conclusions emerge if one assumes average cost pricing in an industry of downward sloping firm demand curves.

Suppose that in an industry of N firms, the demand curve facing firm i is given by:

$$q_i = f_i\,(p_i, p_j \quad \text{where } j = 1, \ldots, N, j \neq i) \tag{A.7.1}$$

and let η_i be i's price elasticity of demand and η_{ij} the elasticity of i's demand with respect to j's price. If firm i prices by adding a standard proportionate and constant mark-up, M_i, to average costs:

$$p_i = AC_i(1 + M_i) \tag{A.7.2}$$

then profits are:

$$\pi_i = q_i AC_i M_i \tag{A.7.3}$$

From which it may easily be shown that the proportionate increase in profit from adopting at time t is given by:

$$\frac{d\pi_i}{\pi_i} = (1 + \eta_i)\frac{dAC_i}{AC_i} \tag{A.7.4}$$

where dAC_i is the change in average costs resulting from introducing the new process. Abstracting from reactions by competitors, so long as $\eta_i < -1$, an increase in profits ensues which will be larger the higher is the firm's own price elasticity of demand. If, as seems likely, more concentrated and oligopolistic industries tend to exhibit low elasticities, this highly simplified model would tend to suggest *smaller* incentives under such market structures. If the model is widened to allow for the possibility of reactions by competitors to changes in i's price (i.e. $(dp_j/dp_i)(p_i/p_j) = R_{ij} > 0$), then the increase in profits is smaller, the larger are the R_{ij}. If the R_{ij} are higher in collusive industries, as is likely, then this strengthens the above finding.

Consider now the pressures on non-adopters as more of their competitors adopt. Making the following simplifying assumptions (to ease the algebra):

$$\eta_{ij} = \overline{\eta}_i \text{ for all } j$$

and $M_i = M$ for all i (A.7.5)

then from (A.7.1),

$$\frac{dq_i}{q_i} = \eta_i\frac{dp_i}{p_i} + \overline{\eta}_i \sum \frac{dp_j}{p_j} \tag{A.7.6}$$

Assuming constant returns to scale, suppose that D_t of i's competitors adopt the new process in a given period, and assume that for each of these adopters, costs and reduced proportionately by dAC/AC. The proportionate reduction in his profits in that period is:

$$\frac{d\pi_i}{\pi_i} = \frac{dq_i}{q_i} = D_t\frac{dAC}{AC}\overline{\eta}_i \tag{A.7.7}$$

Thus the proportionate reduction in i's profits from his competitor's adoption will be greater the bigger their cost savings and the higher the typical cross price elasticity of demand ($\overline{\eta}_i$). Assuming that oligopolists are more able to achieve low cross price elasticities of demand, (by differentiation through advertising), this suggests that pressures on non-adopters will be weakest under oligopolistic structures.

To summarize, in each of the models outlined in this appendix, there is no doubt that there are always incentives to adopt, although the last model suggests that these will be greatest in more competitive industries. Both the above model and the kinked demand analysis suggest that firms stand to lose more from their competitors adopting, the less oligopolistic is the industry concerned.

It might also be noted in passing that if dAC/AC increases over time (due to post-invention improvements in the technology) incentives and pressures increase as time elapses, other things being equal.

8

The influence of industry structure and firm size

Kennedy and Thirlwall conclude towards the end of their lengthy survey article on technical progress that:

> As it stands, the evidence appears to be heavily weighted against the hypothesis that a necessary condition for technological change and progressiveness is that firms should be large scale and dominate the market in which they operate. From the very origins of technical change, in the work that is put into research, to the commercial application of new knowledge, it does not appear that large firms or monopolistic industries are necessarily more dynamic or progressive, or produce more fundamental technical change. After a certain threshold size there is even evidence that R and D activity and the number of patents issued appear to increase less than proportionately with size [1972, p. 61].

This conclusion would seem to be a fair interpretation of the previous research findings surveyed in their article and there is little new evidence since the date of that survey which would cause one to revise this opinion.

In other words, the Schumpeter/Galbraith view that 'Bigness and Fewness' is conducive to rapid technical change has really not been confirmed by most empirical analysis to date of *invention* and *innovation*.

On the other hand, as argued in the introduction to this monograph, the role of industrial concentration, in particular, has not received very much attention in past empirical work on *diffusion*. Indeed, in the final sentence of their conclusions, Kennedy and Thirlwall point to the need for more research 'on the determinants of the speed of diffusion of innovations'. One of the major aims of the present study was to fill this gap.

In the event, some of the strongest findings of the previous chapters arose in just this area. For that reason the present chapter is devoted solely to a further discussion of the results on firm size and concentration.

8.1 'Technical progressiveness' and firm size

Taking the findings of chapter 6 first, the empirical Industrial Engel Curves do seem to establish, for each of the sample innovations, that the probability of a firm having adopted will be higher, at any point in time, the larger is that firm's size. As shown in section 6.5, this is equivalent to the finding, of Mansfield and others, that larger firms tend to wait less time, on average, than do small firms before adopting a given innovation.

But does this establish larger firms as 'more progressive' in this context? In view of the strong technological reasons (such as scale economies) which work in favour of earlier adoption of new processes by large firms, the answer is surely 'not necessarily so'. As Weiss argues, when discussing similar findings to the present ones in previous research: 'the more basic question [is] whether the larger firms were quicker to imitate than groups of smaller firms with about the same number of investment decisions to make' (1971, p. 396). In other words, in comparing large and small firms, one should acknowledge the inbuilt advantage of large scale in this context. At the very least, larger firms have more opportunities to adopt earlier. This is, of course, analogous to the view that, in comparing the research activity of large and small firms, one should be concerned with *relative* as opposed to *absolute* research and development expenditures. (That is, a fair comparison should be based on the R and D to total sales ratio, rather than absolute R and D.)

As it happens, the results in chapter 6 may be easily manipulated to provide an answer to Weiss's 'more basic question'.

Consider, for example, two adopters of innovation j (assumed for the moment to be of the group B type). Suppose firm 1, of size S_1, adopts t_{1j} years after the first appearance of the innovation, whilst firm 2, of *exactly half the size of 1*, adopts after t_{2j} years. The results of chapter 6 suggest that, on average, 1 will adopt earlier than 2: thus, it is to be expected that $t_{1j} < t_{2j}$.

More formally, using equation (6.13b):

$$t_{ij} = - (1/\psi)_j \{\log \alpha_j + \beta_j \log S_{ij} + \log \epsilon_{ij}\} \tag{8.1}$$
$$\text{(6.13b repeated)}$$

the probability that 1 adopts earlier than 2 can easily be derived as:

$$P\{t_{1j} < t_{2j}\} = P\{\beta_j \log 2 > \log \epsilon_{2j} - \log \epsilon_{1j}\} \tag{8.2}$$

Interestingly, exactly the same result applies if the innovation is of the group A type (i.e. using 6.13a instead).

Now retaining the assumption, which has been made throughout this study, that $\log \epsilon_{ij}$ is normally distributed with zero mean and variance σ_j^2, it follows, assuming independence, that $\log \epsilon_{2j} - \log \epsilon_{1j}$ will also exhibit a normal probability distribution, again with zero mean but with variance of $2\sigma_j^2$. In which case,

$$P\{t_{1j} < t_{2j}\} = N(\beta_j \log 2 \,|\, 0,\, 2\sigma_j^2)$$
$$= N\{\beta_j \log 2/\sqrt{2}\,\sigma_j \,|\, 0,\, 1\} \qquad (8.3)$$

Since estimates of $(\beta/\sigma)_j$ are already provided in chapter 6, it is a simple matter to compute this probability for all innovations. Since $\hat{\beta}_j > 0$ for all j, it should come as no surprise to learn that the estimated probability that a firm of given size will adopt earlier than a firm of exactly half its size exceeds 0.5 in all cases. The exact value of this probability is reported as an intermediate step of the calculations (column 2) shown in table 8.1.

Following Weiss, however, the more basic question concerns the pro-

TABLE 8.1   *The probability that a firm will adopt faster than two equally sized firms, each half its size.*

Innovation j[†]	Col. 1 $\left(\dfrac{\hat{\beta}}{\sigma}\right)_j \dfrac{\log 2}{\sqrt{2}}$[‡]	Col. 2 $P\{t_{1j} < t_{2j}\}$[§]	Col. 3 $\left[P\{t_{1j} < t_{2j}\}\right]^2$
SP	0.268	0.606	0.367
F	0.272	0.607	0.369
SF	0.343	0.634	0.402
GA	0.147	0.558	0.312
ADH	0.426	0.665	0.442
ASB	0.200	0.579	0.336
EH	0.570	0.716	0.512
WSB	0.169	0.567	0.322
BOP	0.511	0.695	0.483
VM	0.297	0.617	0.381
ATL	0.174	0.569	0.324
TK	0.404	0.656	0.430
PCBC	0.187	0.574	0.329
VD	0.157	0.563	0.317
CC	0.131	0.552	0.305
TC	0.206	0.582	0.339
CT	0.366	0.643	0.413
PE	0.759	0.776	0.602
SL	0.291	0.614	0.377
NCPP	0.218	0.586	0.343
NCTN	0.408	0.658	0.433
NCTB	0.220	0.587	0.345

[†] For full innovation names, see table 3.1
[‡] For estimates, $(\hat{\beta}/\sigma)_j$, see table 6.1.
[§] See text for definition of this term.

bability that a firm will adopt earlier than *both of two* firms, each exactly half its size. To investigate this, consider, in addition, a third hypothetical firm, adopting after t_{3j} years, also of size $S_1/2$. Using the Weiss approach, large size can only be associated with greater progressiveness if (assuming independence)

$$P\{t_{ij} < t_{2j} \text{ and } t_{1j} < t_{3j}\} = \left[P\{t_{1j} < t_{2j}\}\right]^2 > 0.5 \qquad (8.4)$$

(remembering $S_1 = 2S_2 = 2S_3$)

Now a very different picture emerges from the estimates of $(\beta/\sigma)_j$: for only two of the sample innovations does this probability exceed 0.5 (see column 3 in the table). In other words, for nearly all innovations, on average, a firm of any size will be *slower* to adopt than at least one of two equally sized firms, each exactly half the size of the first firm.

It should be noted that the probabilities in (8.3) and (8.4) are independent of the size of the first firm and, in that sense, this result is quite general.

On the basis of this finding then, one should be extremely wary of arguing the case for large scale in the diffusion context.

8.2 Industrial concentration and the speed of diffusion

In the present model, aggregate diffusion speed has been defined by the slope parameter of the diffusion growth curve, b, where

$$b = \left[(\psi/\beta) + \delta\right]\left[(\sigma/\beta)^2 + \sigma_s^2\right]^{-1/2} \qquad (8.5)$$

$$(7.8 \text{ repeated})$$

In chapter 7, three separate effects have been detected which suggest some sort of relationship between b and industrial concentration. First, as can be seen, by definition, b is inversely related to σ_s^2, the variance of log firm size in the adopting industry. This effect follows automatically given that the size of a firm is an important determinant of its speed of adoption. Thus, low values of σ_s^2 mean a relatively small variance between firms in the speed with which they adopt, and this, in turn, means that the diffusion period is condensed into a relatively short time period. In other words, low σ_s^2 implies high b, caeteris paribus. Second, a significant inverse relationship has been detected in the sample between (ψ/β) and firm numbers (N) in the adopting industry. This is consistent with the hypothesis that information flows (between innovation supplier and adopting firms, and between adopting firms) will be facilitated in low number, highly concentrated industries.

More precisely, the elasticity of (ψ/β) with respect to N has been estimated as -0.321 for group A innovations and -0.201 for group B innovations (see equations 7.19 and 7.20). Third, an only weakly significant and rather fragile relationship has been detected between $(\widehat{\sigma/\beta})$ and σ_s^2 (positively related) and N (inversely related). This is consistent with the hypothesis that firms in concentrated industries are more heterogeneous in a number of respects (e.g. in the investment yardsticks employed, in gathering information and in their operating conditions). More precisely the elasticity of (σ/β) with respect to N has been estimated as -0.150 and with respect to σ_s^2 as 0.150 (see table 7.3).

Abstracting for the moment from the third effect (because of its weak significance), a rather complicated overall relationship has therefore emerged between diffusion speed and concentration. On the one hand, the inverse relationship between b and σ_s^2 (the first effect) implies that lower concentration is conducive to faster diffusion, since low size inequalities, as measured by σ_s^2, imply low concentration ceteris paribus.[1] On the other hand, the inverse relationship between b and N (the second effect) implies that higher concentration is conducive to faster diffusion, since low N implies high concentration, ceteris paribus.

Now since most indices of concentration in common usage reflect both size inequalities (positively) and firm numbers (inversely), it is by no means certain that one would observe a monotonic, or even consistent, relationship between any one of these indices and diffusion speed.

Consider, as an illustration of this problem, the following hypothetical example using, H, the Herfindahl index (although similar arguments apply to most Entropy-based measures or Concentration Ratios). In general, the H index will increase with increasing size inequalities but decline with increasing firm numbers. Indeed, where lognormal firm size distributions can be assumed, Hart (1975) has shown that H depends *only* on σ_s^2 and N:

$$H = \exp(\sigma_s^2)N^{-1} \tag{8.6}$$

Now suppose three industries, I, II and III, identical in all respects except that $N_I = N_{II} > N_{III}$ and $\sigma_{sI}^2 > \sigma_{sII}^2 = \sigma_{sIII}^2$. As such, it is probable that $H_I > H_{II}$ and $H_{III} > H_{II}$; in other words, the Herfindahl index will record II as less concentrated than either I or III. From (8.6), this is certain if firm size is lognormally distributed in each industry. Suppose, further, that the same innovation is diffusing in all three industries; from the above findings, the speed of diffusion should be faster in II than in I, but slower in II than in III. In other words, there is no straightforward simple relationship between the Herfindahl index and diffusion speed in this example.

The Iso-concentration curve and the b curve   This problem can be formalized
and generalized quite easily within the following diagrammatic framework.

Assume, for analytical convenience, that firm size is lognormally distributed in all industries. Bearing in mind the findings reported in section 4.5,
this is not an unreasonable approximation for the present sample of industries. In which case it can be shown that most conventional indices of concentration can be defined in terms only of N and σ_s^2 (Hart, 1975), as has been
seen above for the Herfindahl index for instance. Therefore it follows that,
for any of these indices, one can construct a family of curves in N, σ_s^2 space,
each individual curve being the locus of all combinations of N and σ_s^2 yielding a given numerical value for the index. These curves have been elsewhere
labelled *Iso-concentration curves* (Davies, 1979). Thus, the equation of the
Iso-concentration curve for a fixed value H_0 of the Herfindahl is:

$$\sigma_s^2 = \log H_0 + \log N \qquad (8.7)$$

Movements along this curve indicate all those size distributions (as
described by N and σ_s^2) which the Herfindahl records as equally concentrated at value H_0. Quite obviously, as portrayed in figure 8.1, each Iso-
concentration curve for the Herfindahl will slope upwards from left to right
and, as concentration increases, the curves shift in a north-westerly direction.

It has been shown elsewhere (Davies, 1979) that a similar picture emerges
for other concentration indices – the major difference between different
indices being in the *slopes* of their associated Iso-concentration curves.
(Broadly speaking those indices which attach relatively more importance to
size inequalities will exhibit relatively flat Iso-concentration curves.)

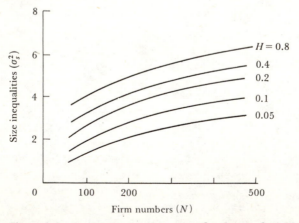

Figure 8.1   Iso-concentration curves for the Herfindahl index

Turning now to the results of the present study one can also conceive of a second set of curves in σ_s^2, N space. This time, each curve is the locus of all combinations of σ_s^2 and N yielding a given numerical value for the diffusion speed parameter b (assuming all other determinants of b unchanged). From (8.5) it follows that the equation of the curve for a value b_0 is:

$$\sigma_s^2 = b_0^{-2}\left\{\frac{\psi}{\beta}N + \delta\right\}^2 - \left(\frac{\sigma}{\beta}\right)^2 \qquad (8.8)$$

Remembering that the second effect identified above was a negative relationship between (ψ/β) and N, each 'b' curve will slope downwards from left to right, indicating that if N increases σ_s^2 must fall for b to remain unchanged. An expression for the slope can be derived by differentiating with respect to N, holding b, δ and (σ/β) constant and inserting the estimated elasticity (reported above) of ψ/β with respect to N. For a group B innovation, this results in:

$$\frac{d\sigma_s^2}{dN}\bigg|_{db=0} = -0.402\, N^{-1}\left[(\sigma/\beta)^2 + \sigma_s^2\right]\left[1 + (\delta\beta/\psi)\right]^{-1} \qquad (8.9)$$

Evaluated at mean sample values for (σ/β) of 3.56 and for $(\delta\beta/\psi)$ of 0.013,

$$\frac{d\sigma_s^2}{dN}\bigg|_{db=0} = -0.397\, N^{-1}\left[3.56 + \sigma_s^2\right] \qquad (8.10)$$

(An identical expression results for a group A innovation except that -0.397 is replaced by -0.638).

Thus the slope of the curve declines (absolutely) as N increases and as σ_s^2 decreases. As can be seen from (8.8), increasing values of b shift the curve towards the origin. Figure 8.2 shows a family of such b curves.

Now consider figure 8.3 which shows an hypothetical industry in which the Herfindahl index is H_0, there being N_0 firms and the variance of log size is σ_{s0}^2. Suppose a given innovation has diffused at speed b_0 in this industry. Thus the industry is located at point A on b_0 and H_0. In terms of the earlier example, let this be industry II; in which case it should be clear that industry I will be located vertically above A in the northerly segment of the diagram (i.e. in the area above A and bounded by b_0 and H_0). That is, I will lie on a higher Iso-concentration curve but on a numerically lower value b curve. Comparing I and II then, an inverse relationship emerges between b and H. Turning to industry III, this will be located directly to the left of point A in

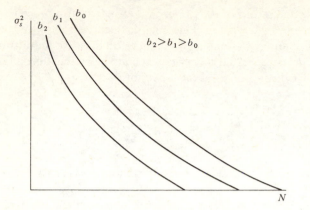

Figure 8.2   A family of b curves

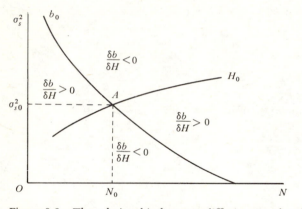

Figure 8.3   The relationship between diffusion speed and H

the westerly segment of the diagram; that is, on a higher Iso-concentration curve and a numerically higher value b curve. Comparing II and III a positive relationship therefore emerges between b and H.

Now of course this particular example has been selected specifically to indicate the potential indeterminacy of the relationship. In real world samples, it may be that industries will be so located in N, σ_s^2 space that, say, an inverse relationship predominates within the sample. Figure 8.3 provides some insight into the circumstances under which such a result might obtain.

The diagram shows that, in a straight two-industry comparison, there are four possible outcomes. If the first industry is located at A then an inverse relationship will be observed if the second industry is located in either the northerly or the southerly segment. As explained above, movements into the northerly segment imply higher concentration and lower diffusion speed; movements into the southerly segment imply lower concentration and higher diffusion speed (i.e. lower Iso-concentration curves but numerically higher value b curves). On the other hand, a positive relationship emerges if the second industry is located in either the westerly or easterly segment.

Within a sample of industries one would not expect to find a monotonic relationship between 'concentration' and b either way (and this is certainly not the case for the present sample). However, from the above, an inverse relationship is more likely *to predominate*, (a) the *flatter* are the Iso-concentration curves and the b curves (since flat curves will produce relatively small westerly and easterly segments) and (b) the more of inter-industry differences in concentration that are due to differences in σ_s^2, rather than N.

This finding provides at least two interesting implications. First, a simple correlation of b on H might give completely opposite answers for different samples of industries. For instance, within a group of industries with little variability in N but differing substantially in σ_s^2, an inverse relationship seems most likely, on average, whilst the reverse may be true if most differences in concentration within the sample are due to differences in N.[2]

Second, the concentration index employed may also be important. In the case of the Herfindahl, Iso-concentration curves *are* relatively flat: from (8.7) it follows that:

$$\frac{d\sigma_s^2}{dN}\bigg|_{dH=0} = \frac{1}{N} \tag{8.11}$$

On the other hand, the first-order Entropy (inverse) measure of concentration may be written, assuming lognormality (Hart, 1975), as:

$$E = \log N - \tfrac{1}{2}\sigma_s^2 \tag{8.12}$$

and thus,

$$\frac{d\sigma_s^2}{dN}\bigg|_{dE=0} = \frac{2}{N} \tag{8.13}$$

In other words, because, E is relatively more sensitive than H to firm numbers, it generates steeper Iso-concentration curves. In the present context this means that there is more chance of observing a generally positive relationship between diffusion speed and concentration when this index is employed.

The reverse is true, however, for the L, Lorenz index,[3] or any other measure derived from the Lorenz curve, L is insensitive to firm numbers and, indeed, where lognormal size distributions are assumed, it depends only on σ_s^2 (Hart, 1975):

$$L = 2 \phi (\sigma/\sqrt{2}\,|\,0,\,1) - 1 \qquad (8.14)$$

Where, here, the standard normal function is denoted by $\phi(.\,|\,0,\,1)$. Consequently, this index generates perfectly horizontal Iso-concentration curves:

$$\frac{d\sigma_s^2}{dN}\Big|_{dL=0} = 0 \qquad (8.15)$$

Therefore the use of this index should produce a strong inverse relationship to diffusion speed in most samples.

Finally it should be recalled that, throughout this discussion, the third effect mentioned at the start of this section has been ignored. If this is now introduced, and $(\sigma/\beta)^2$ is now assumed to be inversely related to N but positively related to σ_s^2, the slope of the b curves will obviously change. The overall negative influence of σ_s^2 on diffusion speed is reinforced whilst the overall negative influence of N on b is weakened, but not reversed (as can be shown by differentiating (8.5) with respect to N). Consequently, if this third effect is acknowledged, then the b curves are flatter, but still downward sloping. The potential indeterminancy of the relationship between b and 'concentration' therefore still remains.

8.3   Conclusions

Since the policy implications of the above findings are discussed in the final chapter, only a brief summary of the discussion is provided here. First, although the findings of chapter 6 suggested that larger firms will typically adopt new innovations more rapidly than small firms, this does not establish that larger firms are more 'progressive'. Once the inbuilt advantage of large scale is acknowledged, there is evidence within the present sample that, if anything, the reverse is true.

Second, there is no straightforward answer to the question of whether more concentrated industries diffuse innovations more or less quickly, other things being equal. This is not to say that elements of industry structure have no influence on diffusion speed: the present model and the results of the previous chapter suggest that they do. The problem arises because one constituent part to concentration (firm numbers) implies a positive relationship to diffusion speed whilst the other (size inequalities) implies a negative relationship. This leads to a number of cautionary conclusions. Perhaps most important, any exercise of correlating diffusion speed and a given concentration index may suppress more information than it uncovers. Further, the strength and the sign of the correlation may depend on the nature of the industries in the sample considered and on the concentration index employed. Having said this, some positive implications are still possible: it would appear, for example, that the optimal industry structure, given these results, is one of a few equally sized firms (i.e. low σ_z^2 and N). This implication is discussed in more detail in the next chapter.

9

Summary and implications

This final chapter provides a brief non-mathematical summary of the main arguments and findings of the study as a whole, followed by a development of some of the major implications.

9.1 A non-mathematical summary

The discussion in chapter 2 of previous theoretical contributions in this area suggested that no totally convincing economic model of diffusion of new processes exists in the literature. The Mansfield/Grilliches model, which rests on the epidemic analogy, was considered to be too mechanistic in that it has little to say about the nature of the adoption decision at the firm level, but concerns itself rather with the behaviour of firms in aggregate. Moreover, the implied technological assumptions of this and related models seem to be unrealistic. In chapter 3, an analysis of the 22 innovations in the present sample confirmed the unlikely nature of these technological assumptions and provided a number of interesting findings concerning the nature of the typical new process innovation. Some of these findings were incorporated in chapter 4 into a simple behavioural model of decision making in this context. Within this model two assumptions, in particular, are quite crucial and are reflected in the predictions generated.

First, partly because of the technological nature of process innovations and partly because of imperfect information, there may be major differences between firms in their expectations of how profitable adoption of any innovation will be. This, coupled with the likelihood that firms will differ in their attitudes to risk in general and new innovations in particular, leads to the obvious conclusion that different firms will react quite differently to the same innovation. More specifically, the lag before adopting the innovation will probably differ significantly between firms within the same industry. For technological and economic reasons, it was suggested that an important contributor to inter-firm differences will be differences in firm size. In chapter 6 this argument was formalized in the so-called Industrial Engel Curve which relates the probability of a firm having adopted the new innovation to the firm's size. When the Industrial Engel

Curve was fitted to data collected for each of the sample innovations, results were fairly encouraging. In no case did the data suggest that the shape of this curve is not as predicted by the model (i.e. cumulative lognormal) and it was possible to show that differences between firms in size explained a substantial portion of the variance in their behaviour (speed of adoption). Interestingly, in every case, the data pointed to a positive relationship between speed of adoption and firm size. Whilst it is true that a similar relationship has sometimes been detected in previous empirical work, doubts have already been expressed in chapter 2 (section 4) concerning the statistical underpinnings of some of this past work. As such, it is believed that the present finding offers an important confirmation. Some of the implications of this relationship are discussed in chapter 8 and the following section.

A second major assumption of the model in chapter 4 concerned the nature of the learning curve for the manufacturers of new innovations. It was suggested, again on the basis of findings in chapter 3 (section 3), that post-invention improvements in the specification of major, technically complex, processes are likely to occur over a long period, with little tendency for them to 'tail off' after the first few years of the innovation's life, as is likely for cheaper and more simple innovations. This gave rise to the group A/group B distinction – a distinction which has implications for the nature of information flows and competitive pressures on non-adopters. On the basis of this assumption it was shown in chapter 4 that the general shape of the diffusion growth curve (describing the growth in the cumulative number of adopters of the innovation) should differ between these two broad types of innovation. Specifically, the major, group B, type should exhibit symmetrical cumulative normal S shaped diffusion, as opposed to the positively skewed cumulative lognormal diffusion curve predicted for the, relatively minor, group A innovations. This constitutes a departure from the conventional wisdom, which assumes that all innovations will have the same shaped diffusion curve, namely logistic. These predictions were tested, in chapter 5, against time series data on the diffusion of the 22 innovations in the present sample. In all but one case, using a crude comparison of $\overline{R}^2$, the curves predicted by the model performed better (although sometimes only marginally) than the logistic, the latter often proving to be an apparent mis-specification. Moreover, for only four innovations was there any evidence of the model's basic predictions being inappropriate and, for three of these four, ancillary evidence suggested that the observed differences between actual and predicted diffusion could be explained within the framework of the model. On the other hand, another of the time series predictions – that cyclical patterns might be observed in diffusion curves – was only partially confirmed by the present sample. It was argued that cyclical fluctuations would occur if the expected profitability of adoption and risk attitudes vary over the business cycle. A significant cyclical pattern was only observed, however, for five of the sample innovations.

The third main area in which the model was used was the explanation of differences between innovations and industries in the aggregate speed of diffusion. Again, the model yields a new perspective. In chapter 7 it was shown that the speed with which any innovation will diffuse within an industry is determined not only by so-called dynamic factors, such as the extent of competitive pressures on non-adopters and the rate at which information improves and risk declines, but also by the extent of inter-firm differences in technological characteristics, information receptiveness and attitudes. Previous work had tended to concentrate only on the former set of factors. As a result of the econometric analysis of inter-innovation differences in diffusion speed, five explanatory variables were identified. Specifically, diffusion should be faster, (a) the more profitable is the innovation, (b) the fewer firms there are in the adopting industry (and because diffusion is a proportional concept this is not a trivial finding), (c) the smaller the size inequalities between firms, (d) the greater the labour intensity of the adopting industry, and (e) the faster the rate of growth of the adopting industry. However, the last mentioned variable was shown (in table 7.4) to be substantially less important than the other 4 as a determinant of inter-industry differences.

9.2 Some implications

The results of the four previous empirical chapters have a number of implications, particularly for policy, and at this stage they are well worth some further development.

9.2.1 The nature of the innovation

As a backcloth to the discussion, it can be confirmed from the time series data shown in the Appendix that diffusion is often a long drawn out process. Whilst four of the sample innovations had been adopted by about half, or more, of all potential adopters only six years after their first introduction, for another sixteen, 50% diffusion (measured in this way) had not been attained even eight years after their first introduction. Indeed, for seven of those, over half of all potential adopters had still not adopted even fourteen years after the first appearance of the innovation.

As already explained, present results suggest that the nature of the innovation itself appears to influence its diffusion path in at least two respects, both of which are of potential interest to firms marketing and supplying the innovations, and, to a lesser extent, government in formulating research policy.

First, the *shape*, or functional form, of the diffusion curve appears to differ between the two broad types of innovation (group A and group B).[1] The findings of section 5.7 suggest that, on average, the (technically simple and relatively cheap) group A innovations will tend to diffuse much more rapidly in the early years than the typical (more complex and expensive) group B innovations. Once the initial spurt has passed, however, it appears that group A diffusion slows down more noticeably than group B diffusion and, in the long run, 100% adoption appears to be more likely for the latter type of innovation. Having said this, however, one must point to the significant differences observed *within* the A group. It is clear, for instance, that the more rapidly diffusing group A innovation can attain 100% diffusion in a relatively short period (compared to the typical group B case) whilst it is fairly obvious that the slower diffusing group A innovation will never even approach total adoption. On the other hand, within the present sample at least, the variance in performance within the B group seems to be less pronounced.

If these findings are representative, it seems reasonable to conclude that, in most industries, almost all firms will eventually use the same major processes (albeit different vintages of those processes). But there may be large numbers of firms not using relatively minor (perhaps supplementary) processes, even many years after those processes first become available.

In terms of the present model, this has been explained, of course, by reference to two different broad types of learning curves and the effects they might have concerning information flows and competitive pressures. Thus competitive pressures and post-invention improvements in the major processes make their widespread adoption almost unavoidable. The competitive disadvantages of not adopting the more minor innovations are perhaps less significant and may be obscured by other inter-firm productivity differences.

Now, if this rationalization is correct, it constitutes an addition to the existing stock of knowledge concerning 'learning by doing' and may have implications beyond the present context. In addition, it suggests an important role, within the diffusion process, for information flows between suppliers and potential customers and between potential customers.

However, whatever the rationalization used to explain this difference between major and minor innovations, there are implications for the optimal marketing policy (in terms of advertising and pricing) by the innovation manufacturers. This is not the place to pursue this matter in much detail but Glaister's work (1974) on the optimal marketing strategies for the manufacturers of consumer durables (assuming a logistic diffusion curve) does point the direction in which it might be pursued.

The second major implication under this category concerns the *speed* of diffusion (as reflected in the parameter of the diffusion curve). The results of chapter 7 suggest that an innovation will diffuse faster, the more profitable it is to adopt. This unsurprising result confirms the previous findings in this field, notably those of Mansfield and Griliches, and really requires little further comment. It is certainly consistent with a number of fairly plausible hypotheses; for instance, highly profitable innovations should presumably impose greater competitive disadvantages on non-adopters and perhaps excite most interest and discussion (and thus information) within adopting industries. Both factors should make for more rapid diffusion. The implication of this result for the pricing policy of innovation manufacturers is obvious and Stoneman (1978) has indicated how it might illuminate studies of the determinants of aggregate investment behaviour.

Finally, one negative finding in this area should also be mentioned. It appears that within the two broad groups, there is no tendency for the more expensive innovations to diffuse more slowly. This contrasts with Mansfield's (1961) finding of an inverse relationship between speed of diffusion and the typical capital outlay required to install the innovation in question. He argues that this is to be expected if more costly innovations are viewed as inherently more risky and as presenting financing problems. It is possible that the failure to observe any such relationship here is due to the group A/group B break-down which means two separate sets of observations, neither set exhibiting substantial variance in the cost variable. But, as it stands, the present study differs from Mansfield's in that it suggests a significant role for the capital outlay in determining the functional form, but not the slope, of the innovation's diffusion curve.

9.2.2 The role of industry growth and cyclical factors

One of the major empirical objectives of this study, as outlined in the introduction, was to examine the influence of diffusion of the general economic environment in which the adopting industry is operating.

It is probably fair to identify as widely held, the view that steady, sustained growth in aggregate demand promotes greater technical progressiveness in general. It is sometimes argued, for instance, that stop–go and a generally low level of capacity usage reduce the opportunities and incentives for firms to invent or adopt new techniques. Certainly Schmookler's findings (1962 and 1966) do confirm that *inventive* activity (as measured by patents) responds positively to the level of aggregate demand measured in a number of ways. Moreover, as reported in section 2.3, Gold et al. (1970) have already presented some evidence to suggest that growth in the adopting industry may have an important influence on the diffusion of new processes.

The model developed in chapter 4 is not without implications on this score. First, if the size of a firm is an important positive influence on its speed of adoption, then it follows that aggregate diffusion should be faster, ceteris paribus, in industries of rapidly growing size. Second, and in addition to this size effect, it was argued that search activity, competitive pressures and the disruption costs involved in adoption may all vary across the business cycle and differ between fast and slow growing industries. If this is so, the model predicts that cyclical fluctuations may occur in the aggregate diffusion curves; and the speed of diffusion, as measured by the parameters of those curves, may be sensitive to the growth rate in output of the adopting industry.

However, as already reported, there is only partial evidence to support these predictions. Even *assuming* the size effect, the calculations of chapter 7 suggest that it results in only a very marginal positive influence on diffusion speed. Moreover, after allowing for this effect, there appears to be no relationship (either way) between diffusion speed and industry growth (see table 7.4).[2] There is *some* evidence of cyclical fluctuations in the diffusion curve, but only for about one quarter of the sample innovations.

Bearing in mind the unsatisfactory nature of the data with which these hypotheses were tested, it would be wrong to entirely discount the possibility of a significant influence of demand factors on diffusion. But on the basis of the present sample there is only limited support for Gold et al.'s findings.[3]

9.2.3 *The role of firm size and industry concentration*

As the results in this area have already been discussed in some detail in the previous chapter, only a few additional remarks concerning policy implications are necessary here.

It was suggested earlier that although large firms should be quicker to adopt, on the average, than smaller firms, this does not establish that larger firms are necessarily more progressive. More specifically, the results of table 8.1 suggest that a firm of size S will typically adopt earlier than one of, say, size $\frac{1}{2}S$. However, when compared with two firms, each of size $\frac{1}{2}S$, the larger firm will be slower, on average, than at least one of those firms. Following Weiss, the latter comparison may be more 'fair' if the larger firm has twice as many investment decisions to make (and thus twice the opportunity) than each small firm.

The policy implications of this finding are not straightforward but the following example, which is fairly typical of the present sample, provides some suggestive insights. It was found that in the brick industry, the probability that a firm of size S would adopt a Tunnel Kiln earlier than a firm of $\frac{1}{2}S$ is 0.656; but that the probability that the first firm would adopt earlier than both of two firms, each of size $\frac{1}{2}S$ is only 0.430 (see table 8.1). In the light of these numbers, consider the following hypothetical example. Suppose, prior to the appearance of the Tunnel Kiln, there are two equally sized brick firms contemplating a merger. Each firm owns one plant in which it is technologically feasible to use one Tunnel Kiln. Assuming it is considered socially desirable that the Tunnel Kiln should be adopted as widely as possible, as soon as possible, would the proposed merger be beneficial?

From the above figures, all else equal, it is (0.570) probable that the innovation will be first introduced into at least one plant earlier, if the merger does not take place. On the other hand, it is improbable that a large firm will be slower than *both* of the two small firms (the probability is $(0.344)^2 = 0.118$ in this case). Therefore the merger might still be justified if, once having adopted in one plant, the new larger firm would introduce the innovation into its other plant more quickly than would have been the case, had that plant been under separate management.

Thus the results reported in table 8.1 certainly do not provide an over-whelming case *against* large scale in the diffusion context. On the other hand neither is the case *in favour* of large scale established. In the present example, it would rest on the supposition that intra-firm diffusion is typically more rapid than inter-firm diffusion. Apart from Mansfield's work (1963b) little is known about intra-firm diffusion (perhaps for the data reasons cited in section 1.4), and certainly there is no known evidence as to whether it is typically more rapid than inter-firm diffusion.

Turning to the effects of industrial structure on aggregate diffusion speed, the two most relevant findings of chapter 7 are that innovations diffuse more rapidly in industries with fewer firms and where the inequalities in the sizes of those firms are small. As was seen in the previous chapter this makes it difficult to draw definitive conclusions about the relationship between diffusion speed and 'concentration', but some policy implications can still be suggested. Most obviously, on the face of it, the optimal industry structure would appear to be one of a few, but equally sized, firms. Having said this, it is always dangerous to extrapolate regression results to values of the explanatory variables beyond the ranges observed within the sample data. It is important to note, therefore, that for the sample industries, firm numbers (N) falls below 20 in only one case and size inequalities (σ_s^2) below 1.0 (implying small size inequalities) in only two cases. As such, it would be stretching things to argue that these results suggest, as optimal, a duo-poly of equal firms. Nevertheless, in general, it does seem reasonable to conclude that policies aimed at reducing firm numbers or size inequalities should have a beneficial effect in the diffusion context.

The main problem for the policy maker is to derive policies which can reduce firm numbers without, at the same time, increasing size inequalities. Perhaps the most obvious options are policies of rationalization (i.e.

encouraging mergers) and of discouraging entry (and relying on natural wastage to bring firm numbers down). But in both instances, changes in σ_s^2 would probably also occur. For instance, take-overs by the larger firms would certainly decrease firm numbers, but possibly only at the cost of increasing size inequalities. Similarly, the prevention of entry by potentially dynamic new firms might be counter-productive in the long run if it results in reduced competitive pressures on the larger firms (and an increase in their market share). On the other hand, mergers between small or medium sized firms might actually achieve the best of both worlds: reducing firm numbers and concentrating more of industry output in firms of roughly average size (thus reducing σ_s^2).

Policies aimed directly at reducing size inequalities might also be counter-productive if they can only be effected by increasing firm numbers. This is possible, for instance, where breaking up the large firms is envisaged. However, any increase in N entailed may be proportionately small when compared to the reductions in σ_s^2 achievable.

9.3 Directions for future research

One of the prime objectives of this study has been to provide more 'facts' on the diffusion of process innovations. As noted in the introduction, and in stark contrast to the related areas of inventive and innovative activity, there have been few past studies (in fact none for the U.K.) based on examination of the diffusion of relatively large numbers of different innovations. It is probably fair to claim some success in achieving this objective: on the basis of the technological and diffusion data collected, a number of generalizations have been possible and some of the stronger empirical findings, based on these generalizations, have been enumerated in the previous section. At this point it would be interesting to see whether these findings can be confirmed for other samples, both in the U.K. and abroad. In addition, some improvement on the explanation achieved here of inter-innovation differences in the speed of diffusion is desirable and, given adequate data, not unlikely. Similarly, whilst the importance of firm size as an indicator of individual firms' behaviour has been established, there is surely room for extending our understanding of this aspect, by introducing further explanatory variables as explicit determinants of the individual firm's adoption decision.

On a more theoretical level, the model which has been used is probably richer in the range of its predictions than existing models based on the epidemic analogy. It also derives some interest value from its affinity to previous models used to analyse the diffusion of consumer durables: perhaps the similarities between process and product innovations have been too readily ignored in the past. On the debit side, however, the role of innovation suppliers has been largely ignored,[4] as in previous research: unfortunately, it has proved singularly difficult to obtain much information about the behaviour of these firms and any hypotheses in this context would be speculative and difficult to test. Nevertheless, this is an aspect of the problem which deserves some attention in the future.

Taking a broader view, studies such as the present one will hopefully provide some assistance, both methodologically and factually, to future attempts to explain inter-industry and international productivity differences.

Appendix: Data sources and definitions

This appendix outlines the sources and definitions used in constructing the variables employed in the various regressions reported in chapters 5, 6 and 7.

A.1 The time series data used in chapter 5

A.1.1 The determination of the sets of feasible adopters (n_j) The model discussed in chapter 4 requires that diffusion be measured by the number of firms having adopted, as a proportion of the number who could feasibly adopt. Thus it is essential to identify for each innovation the number of feasible or potential adopters. For most of the sample innovations, the number of potential adopters has been calculated only for the final year for which diffusion data is available and so the implicit assumption made is that firm populations were constant over the period studied. This, is, of course, an unavoidable simplification since it would have proved virtually impossible to collect information for each year on the number of firms in each industry. (Very few of these industries conform to the minimum list headings of official statistics.) Casual empiricism would suggest that this may not be too unrealistic an assumption, especially given the relatively short periods considered in most cases.

It is apparent from the technical literature on some of the innovations that certain technical idiosyncracies of some sectors of the adopting industry effectively bar the firms concerned from ever adopting the innovation. Clearly, in measuring diffusion, one would want to exclude such firms from the feasible set. In past work this has led to concepts such as the 'technological ceiling' (Nabseth and Ray, 1974, p. 298) or the 'technically feasible maximum' (Davies, 1971, p. 64). Mansfield generally overcomes this problem by studying only the largest firms in each industry because (in certain cases) 'it seemed very unlikely that firms smaller than this would have been able to use them (the innovations)' (Mansfield, 1968, p. 135). However, here, firms are only excluded from the feasible set of adopters if there are strong technical reasons for doing so; size itself is not considered reason enough.

TABLE A.1   *Definitions of feasible sets of adopters*

Innovations	Industry definition and data sources
Special Presses; Foils; Synthetic Fabrics; Wet Suction Boxes; Computer Control of Paper Machines	All paper and board makers as defined by B.P.B.M.A. reference tables
Numerically Controlled Machine Tools (in three separate industries)	All manufacturers of Printing Presses Turning Machines and Turbines (in each case using N.I.E.S.R. sampling frames, *Kompass* and other trade directories).
Photo-electrically Controlled Cutting Machines	All Shipbuilding firms as identified by the Geddes Report (1966)
Gibberellic Acid	All firms carrying out malting (compiled from the *Brewers Almanack, Kompass* and N.I.E.S.R. sampling frames).
Shuttleless Looms	All weavers as defined by the Textile Council.
Computer Typesetting	All provincial evening newspapers (as defined by the Evening Newspaper Advertising Bureau).
Vacuum Melting[a]	All firms manufacturing 'permanent' magnet, tool and high speed steels (plus one or two other special steels) as defined by B.I.S.P.A.
Automatic Track Lines	The six independent car manufacturers existing before 1960 (the date by which all had adopted) with large enough capacities as defined by N.I.E.S.R.
Basic Oxygen Steelmaking Process[a]	All steel refiners with blast furnaces (i.e. using pig iron) as defined in the *Iron and Steel Board Annual Statistics*.
Continuous Casting[a]	All steel refiners, excluding solely special steelmakers (see Nabseth and Ray, 1974, p. 238 for justification of the exclusion of these firms). *Source: Iron and Steel Board Annual Statistics.*
Vacuum Degassing[a]	All firms using open hearth, basic oxygen and electric arc furnaces. *Source: Iron and Steel Board Annual Statistics.*
Tunnel Kilns[b]	All clay brickmakers, excluding those using clays which make the Tunnel Kiln inoperable due to its high carbon content. *Sources: N.I.E.S.R. sampling frame, trade directories.*
Tufted Carpet Machines[c]	All existing carpet manufacturers, as defined by Trade directories and T. Scott.

TABLE A.1 *Continued*

Innovations	Industry definition and data sources
Electrical Hygrometer, Accelerated Drying Hood and Automatic Size Box.[d]	All Lancashire weavers surviving throughout the diffusion period.

[a] The nationalization of the steel industry obviously substantially reduced the number of feasible adopters of these innovations (excluding Vacuum Melting which is applicable to that part of the industry which was not nationalized). Consequently, diffusion in these cases has been considered only up to the date when investment projects were those decided upon by the British Steel Corporation.

[b] When the carbon content of the clay used exceeds a certain proportion (usually about 3%) the Tunnel Kiln cannot be used, mainly because it does not permit sufficient flexibility in the application of heat. This flexibility is essential when large amounts of carbon are present since the carbon itself acts as a fuel. In such cases, brickmakers have little choice but to use the more flexible old technology kilns. As it happens, information on the carbon content of clay is only available for about eighty firms (from the N.I.E.S.R. sample). Consequently, it has been assumed that the incidence of high carbon content clay firms outside this sample is the same as for firms within the sample for each of five different size classes.

[c] In recent years, a number of new firms have entered the industry, in every case using Tufted Carpet Machines. Moreover, it is known (see Scott, 1975) that in 1963, at least, these new entrants each employed between 25 and 200 employees. Thus the feasible set of adopters has been taken as all firms reported in the 1963 Census table minus sixteen new entrants in the 25–199 size range. In other words, for reasons of comparability with other sample innovations, these entrants have been excluded.

[d] Metcalfe (1968), presents a time series for the number of Lancashire weavers since before the war from which it is obvious that there has been a very large decline in the population. Again for reasons of comparability, diffusion has been calculated for the set of firms surviving the diffusion period. Thus all firms which died during the period have been excluded from the set of potential adopters and those adopters who subsequently died are also excluded from the total set of adopters.

In the event, as reported in table A.1, special technical barriers to adoption can be identified for 10 of the innovations and in these cases the feasible sets of adopters exclude those firms for which these barriers seem to have been operative.

A.1.2 Numbers of adopters (m_{jt}) The time series data on numbers of adopters of each innovation has been collected from a number of different sources.

(i) *Trade and scientific publications.* Data for Basic Oxygen Process, Vacuum Melting and Vacuum Degassing has been collected from various editions of the *British Iron and Steel Board Annual Statistics* (supplemented for Vacuum Degassing by Flux (1965) and for Vaccum Melting by Barraclough (1969)); for Continuous Casting from a U.N.E.C.E. report (1968) and for Computer Typesetting and Computer Control of Paper Machines from various editions of *Computer Survey*.

(ii) *The National Institute of Economic and Social Research.* As their contribution to an international study of diffusion (Nabseth and Ray, 1974) N.I.E.S.R. collected data mainly by questionnaires on the following innovations: Special Presses, Gibberellic Acid, Tunnel

Kilns, Automatic Track Lines, Shuttleless Looms, Photo-electrically Controlled Cutting, Numerically Controlled Machine Tools.

(iii) *The National Institute of Economic And Social Research*, also collected data on three other innovations (Synthetic Fabrics, Foils, Wet Suction Boxes), which in the event was not used in the above study.

(iv) *Independent researchers*. Data on Tufted Carpet Machines has been provided by T. Scott in connection with his Ph.D. thesis at the University of Sussex and the data for Electrical Hygrometers, Accelerated Drying Hoods, Automatic Size Boxes is presented by J. Metcalfe (1970).

For all but one of the N.I.E.S.R. innovations (Automatic Track Lines), data was collected only for a sample of firms within the appropriate industries. In general, selection was made by stratified (by firm size) random sampling techniques. (On average, the sample proportion exceeded 50%.) In most cases the risk of non-response bias was substantially reduced by repeated approaches to non-respondents (usually with the result that such firms at least gave answers to the basic questions of whether or not they had

TABLE A.2   *Time series data for* m_{jt}/n_j †

Year‡	Innovation§										
	SP	F	SF	WSB	GA	ASB	ADH	EH	BOP	VD	VM
1	1.1	3.2	2.7	2.3	3.0	0.6	0.3	0.3	5.0	2.6	4.5
2	1.1	3.2	10.8	2.3	18.2	1.5	1.1	1.5	10.0	5.3	4.5
3	2.2	9.5	16.2	2.3	24.2	3.0	7.3	3.4	15.0	5.3	6.5
4	7.7	15.8	18.9	4.6	36.4	4.1	11.7	4.6	15.0	5.3	13.6
5	14.4	28.5	29.7	4.6	39.4	5.0	13.4	7.0	20.0	7.9	18.2
6	18.8	50.6	40.5	6.9	42.4	5.6	15.6	8.6	20.0	7.9	22.7
7	24.3	57.0	48.6	6.9	57.6	6.2	18.2	10.3	45.0	10.5	22.7
8	25.4	63.3	51.4	6.9	60.6	6.5	19.0	11.6	45.0	10.5	22.7
9	26.5	63.3	51.4	6.9	63.6	6.5	19.3	14.2	45.0	18.4	31.8
10				6.9		7.7	19.6	15.8	45.0	31.6	50.0
11				9.2		8.6	19.8	18.8	45.0	34.2	59.1
12				11.5		8.9	20.4	19.1		39.5	
13				16.1		9.8	20.7	20.8		42.1	
14				16.1		10.1	20.9	22.4		44.7	
15						10.1	20.9	23.1			
16							21.2	23.4			
17								23.9			
18								23.9			
19								23.9			
20								24.3			
21								24.5			

adopted and, if so, the date of that adoption; for the present purposes, this is sufficient information).

For eleven innovations concerned, the sample findings have been used to generate estimates of m_{jt} using the following standard formula:

$$m_{jt} = \sum_{k=1}^{r} M_{kjt} \frac{n_{kj}}{N_{kj}}$$

where M_{jkt} refers to the number of firms in the kth size class having adopted in the jth industry by year t, and N_{kj} and n_{kj} to the number of respondents and the population respectively in the kth size class. In other words, the absence of non-response bias has been assumed. (See Davies, 1976, appendix 2 for further discussion of the N.I.E.S.R. samples.)

A.1.3 S_{ljt}   Table A.3 shows the definitions and sources for S_{ljt}: output of the jth industry at time t. As can be seen, data series on demand, rather than output, have often been used because of the lack of reliable information on the latter. Probably more serious problems are caused, however, by the unavailability of *any* data for some of the more finely defined industries (e.g. printing press manufacture and output of provincial newspapers). In these cases, very unsatisfactorily, the outputs of more aggregate industries have been used as proxies.

TABLE A.2 *continued*

Year	CC	ATL	TK	PCBC	TC	CT	PE	SL	NCPP	NCTN	NCTB
1	4.2	16.6	1.2	1.0	2.1	1.8	2.9	0.7	6.8	3.6	9.6
2	4.2	16.6	1.2	1.0	9.4	1.8	8.8	0.7	13.5	3.6	9.6
3	4.2	16.6	2.4	2.0	10.2	1.8	8.8	0.7	20.3	3.6	19.2
4	12.5	33.3	2.4	4.1	10.4	10.7	14.6	0.7	27.0	3.6	19.2
5	20.8	50.0	2.4	5.1	11.4	14.3	20.4	1.4	27.0	3.6	19.2
6	25.0	50.0	4.8	5.1	11.6	17.9	23.4	2.9	33.8	3.6	19.2
7	25.0	50.0	4.8		12.4	23.2	23.4	3.6	33.8	3.6	19.2
8	25.0	66.7	7.2		12.4	25.0	23.4	5.0	40.5	7.2	38.5
9	25.0	66.7	7.2		12.4	26.8	23.4	6.5	40.5	21.8	57.7
10	25.0	66.7	10.8		14.0			8.6		29.1	57.7
11	29.2	83.3	10.8		15.0			10.8		32.7	67.3
12		83.3	13.3		19.0			12.9		36.4	67.3
13		83.3	14.5		19.4			13.6		40.0	67.3
14		100.0	16.9		18.7					40.0	76.9
15			20.5							43.6	
16			24.1								

† Diffusion figures presented in percentage form.
‡ Year 1 denotes the first year of introduction into the industry.
§ For the key to innovation abbreviations, see table 3.1.

TABLE A.3   Data series used to compute S_{Ijt}

Innovation(s)	Measure of 'output'
Special Presses, Foils, Synthetic Fabrics, Wet Suction Box, Computer Control of Paper Machine	Production of all Paper and Board (B.P.B.M.A. reference tables).
Basic Oxygen Process, Continuous Casting	Crude steel output (*Iron and Steel Board Annual Statistics*).
Vacuum Degassing	Total steel output (I.S.B.A.S.).
Vacuum Melting	Special steels output (I.S.B.A.S.).
Electrical Hygrometer, Accelerated Drying Hoods, Automatic Size Box	No series available.
Numerically Controlled Machine Tools	Deliveries of machine tools, turbines and presses (various *Business Monitors*).
Gibberellic Acid	Beer production (*Economic Trends*).
Shuttleless Loom	Woven cloth production (*Textile Council Quarterly Review*)
Tunnel Kiln	Production of clay bricks (*Housing Statistics*).
Photo-electrically Controlled Cutting	Index of production for shipbuilding (*Economic Trends*).
Computer Typesetting	Consumers' expenditure on newspapers (*Economic Trends*).
Tufted Carpet Machine	Deliveries of all carpets (*Textile Council Quarterly Review*
Automatic Track Line	Production of cars (*Economic Trends*).

A.2 Cross-section data used to compute the Industrial Engel Curves in chapter 6

The following tables show, for each innovation and industry, the number of firms in various employment size classes at a single date, T, during the diffusion period. For each size class, the average size of firm and proportion of firms having adopted at that date is also shown. For the N.I.E.S.R. innovations, this data refers to the *samples* mentioned above, but unless otherwise indicated, all other tables refer to all potential adopters.

As reported in chapter 6, there was generally little discretion in the choice of date T: for some innovations data on the size break-down of adopters was available for only one year, for others the date of adoption was known for each firm but time series figures on their size was not. Similarly the choice of size classes was dictated usually by the form in which data was available: in some cases, it was only available in grouped form, in others, individual firms' sizes were only known to lie within certain ranges. The sources of this information were as above for the time series data on m_{jt}. Information on firm sizes was also collected, in some instances, by direct approach to firms and from trade directories (see Davies, 1976, appendix 5.)

TABLE A.4   Cross-section data employed for Industrial Engel Curves

Innovation (j) (Sample as a proportion of population & year T shown in brackets).	Size class (k) (employees)	Average firm size S_{kjT} (employees)	Number of firms in class (N_{kj})	Proportion having adopted $(M/N)_{kjT}$
Special Presses	50 and above[a]	4195	14	0.786
(46%, 1970)	31–49	616	10	0.6
	21–30	424	8	0.5
	11–20	246	9	0.333
	1–10	64	4	0
Foils	50 and above[a]	4195	7	0.857
(25%, 1966)	21–49	531	10	0.500
	6–20	183	7	0.286
	1–5	38	0	–
Synthetic Fabrics	50 and above[a]	4195	7	0.857
(25%, 1966)	21–49	531	10	0.4
	6–20	183	7	0.143
	1–5	38	0	–
Wet Suction Boxes	50 and above[a]	4195	7	0.429
(25%, 1966)	21–49	531	10	0.300
	6–20	183	7	0.143
	1–5	38	0	–
Gibberellic Acid	70 and above	168	8	0.875
(56%, 1967)	25–69	59	10	0.7
	13–24	16	6	0.5
	1–12	6	7	0.571
Automatic Size Boxes	2000 and above[b]	1333	n.a.	0.19
(100%, 1956)	801–2000	634	n.a.	0.11
	401–800	272	n.a.	0.06
	1–400	71	n.a.	0
Accelerated	800 and above[b]	785	n.a.	0.598
Drying Hoods	401–800	272	n.a.	0.25
(100%, 1956)	201–400	136	n.a.	0.11
	1–200	45	n.a.	0.0035
Electrical Hygrometers	800 and above[b]	785	n.a.	0.82
(100%, 1956)	401–800	272	n.a.	0.29
	201–400	136	n.a.	0.09
	1–200	45	n.a.	0.007
Basic Oxygen Process	8500 and above	18300	6	0.833
(100%, 1968)	4000–8499	7247	6	0.5
	1–3999	2298	8	0.125
Vacuum Degassing	8400 and above	15780	8	0.625
(100%, 1968)	6000–8399	7007	7	0.571
	2000–5999	3272	8	0.500
	1250–1999	1635	7	0.429
	1–1249	529	8	0.125

TABLE A.4 *continued*

Innovation (j) (Sample as a proportion of population & year T shown in brackets).	Size class (k) (employees)	Average firm size S_{kjT} (employees)	Number of firms in class (N_{kj})	Proportion having adopted $(M/N)_{kjT}$
Vacuum Melting (100%, 1968)	1000 and above	3062	8	0.875
	350–999	496	7	0.571
	1–349	207	7	0.285
Continuous Casting (100%, 1969)	8100 and above	15800	8	0.375
	300–8099	5670	8	0.375
	1–2999	1375	8	0.125
Tunnel Kilns (41%, 1971)	200 and above	559	13	0.923
	50–199	119	14	0.286
	30–49	39	14	0.286
	1–29	21	15	0.067
Process Control by Computer (100%, 1970)	50 and above[a]	4195	14	0.214
	20–50	531	18	0.056
	0–20	106	66	0.015
Tufted Carpets (33%, 1966)	500 and above	1393	n.a.	0.8
	200–499	326	n.a.	0.71
	25–199	95	n.a.	0.4
	1–24	16	n.a.	0
Computer Typesetting (100%, 1972)	700 and above	1008	12	0.417
	400–699	493	10	0.400
	300–399	323	11	0.364
	240–299	266	12	0.085
	1–239	214	12	0.167
Photo-electrically Controlled Cutting (23%, 1961)	3000 and above	4850	5	0.8
	500–2999	1526	6	0.167
	1–499	265	3	0
Shuttleless Looms (14%, 1970)	2000 and above	2951	7	0.857
	500–1999	1199	8	0.75
	175–499	274	8	0.50
	125–174	136	8	0.25
	1–124	61	9	0.11
Numerical Control (printing presses) (56%, 1970)	500 and above	1338	9	0.667
	76–499	199	7	0.429
	1–75	39	8	0.125
Numerical Control (turning machines) (68%, 1970)	500 and above	1930	12	0.917
	200–499	293	13	0.461
	1–199	71	11	0.091
Numerical Control (turbines) (45%, 1970)	1000 and above	3786	7	0.857
	1–999	275	2	0.50

[a] For these innovations, the size classes (but *not* S_{kjT}) are measured in thousands of tons of paper produced.
[b] For these innovations, the size classes (but not $\overline{S}_{kjT}$) are measured by numbers of looms. There is no information on N_{kj}, see Metcalfe (1970, pp. 152–3).

Notes

CHAPTER 1

1 The term 'innovator' is not always unambiguous. Where a new process is invented and developed by a capital goods industry, the innovator may either be defined as the first firm to commercially produce the new process and offer it for sale, or as the first firm that decides to install and *use* the process in its factories.
2 It is probably fair to claim that the innovation and invention stages have, to date, attracted far more academic attention than diffusion. See, for instance, Weiss (1971) and Kennedy and Thirlwall (1972) for fairly comprehensive surveys.
3 Blaug (1963) has defined a process innovation as 'a novel way of making old goods' whilst a product innovation involves 'old ways of making novelties'. One might also add that the former usually involves a reduction in costs per unit of output in the absence of factor price changes. It should be noted, however, that one firm's product innovation may often be another's process innovation, for instance, a new type of steel furnace is produced by the furnace making industry but used by the steel industry. Moreover, the introduction of a new process may also involve a change in the product produced by the adopting firm: for example, the Tufted Carpet Machine led not only to major increases in the productivity of carpet making firms, but also to a significant change in the nature of the carpets produced. In this case, then, the distinction is fragile.
4 See the O.E.C.D. case study reports, 'Gaps in Technology' (1968) and Pavitt (1971) for documentation of the technology gap and Ray (1969) for some indications that the U.K. may be sluggish in diffusion but not in invention and innovation.
5 Interestingly, both Weiss (1971) and Kennedy and Thirlwall (1972) draw attention in their survey articles to this neglect.

CHAPTER 2

1 This exposition will follow loosely, and with amended notation, Bailey (1957) and Bartholomew (1970).
2 Similarly, zero infection is only approached asymptotically as t tends to minus infinity. Throughout, the population is defined so as to include only those individuals who are not immune. It should be stressed that this model assumes a fixed population in this sense.
3 For example, β is not the rate of growth of diffusion, $(\mathrm{d}m/\mathrm{d}t)/m_t$, which falls continuously over time.
4 Diffusion could have been measured, alternatively, by the proportion of industry output produced using the new process. See section 1.4.

5 Because π and S are assumed to be constant over time, this means that A must be zero at all times, and not only at the limit. This is unfortunate since there is no obvious reason why S and π should always assume values that ensure $A = 0$ for all innovations.

A milder, and possibly more realistic, assumption would be that A only tends to zero as t tends to minus infinity. But then this would require non-constant π and S, and thus variable β; in which case, as argued earlier, the logistic solution would not obtain.

6 Mansfield ranks the industries according to how competitive he thinks they are, and then estimates the rank correlation coefficient between this ordering and that of the intercept terms as 0.8. As he, himself, concedes, this is hardly a rigorous test.

7 Since it is not certain that all areas within states could be planted with hybrid corn, Griliches does not 'know' the saturation levels prior to estimation. (On the other hand, in general, all firms in Mansfield's samples have already adopted at the time of estimation, therefore n is known.)

In fitting (2.14), Griliches experiments with different values for n and selects, for each state, that value which maximizes the R^2. This means, of course, that he estimates three parameters for each curve, as opposed to only two for Mansfield.

8 In a recent case study of the diffusion of a single innovation, Numerically Controlled Machine Tools (NC), Romeo (1977) provides some much needed evidence on industry-level variables. He adopts Mansfield's model and methodology exactly and fits logistic curves to time series data on the diffusion of NC in ten separate U.S. engineering industries. However, in his equivalent to equation (2.8.), four extra determinants of λ are postulated, including F, the year in which NC was first adopted in the sector concerned and V, the variance of the logarithm of firm size in that sector. In the equivalent of Mansfield's second empirical stage, see equation (2.15.) above, both variables are found to be significant determinants of the β_j parameters estimated in the curve fitting (although none of the other four hypothesized determinants, including Mansfield's π_j and S_j, are significant at the 95% level). He finds that the β_j are positively related to F_j (rationalized on the grounds that late first introduction into the sector means more information is readily available on the reliability of the innovation) and inversely related to V_j (indicating that diffusion is more rapid in unconcentrated, low V industries). Whilst both results must be viewed in the light of the low number of degrees of freedom (four) available, the significance of V is particularly relevant to the present study, as will become clear in chapter 7. See also Romeo's earlier study (1975), on what he calls the 'displacement process', for similar findings.

9 Indeed, it is shown in section 6.5 below that (2.16) will predict a cumulative lognormal diffusion curve for innovation i, given fairly plausible assumptions about the distribution of S_{ij}. Since this curve differs noticeably in shape from the logistic, one could argue that (2.16) is not only independent of the epidemic model, but also inconsistent with it.

10 An almost identical set of results is provided by Romeo in his study (1977) on inter-firm differences in the speed of adoption of Numerical Control in U.S. engineering industries. He finds H_{ij} insignificant but S_{ij} significant at the 95% level with an elasticity of -0.673. But again, the effects of industry and firm size have not been disentangled.

11 On the other hand, it is by no means certain that Nabseth et al. would have been better advised in completely omitting the non-adopters from the sample. Given the 'bounded' nature of the dependent variable in that case, such an analysis might face the alternative problem of heteroscedastic errors.

An alternative approach, followed by Globerman (1975) and Romeo (1975), is to define the dependent variable as a binary variable, taking the value of 1 if the firm in question is an adopter at the date of research and 0 otherwise. Both authors use similar explanatory variables to those mentioned in the text. There are two main drawbacks to this approach (apart, again, from problems of heteroscedasticity). First, early and late adopters are not distinguished; so long as a firm has adopted by date d^* it records a value of 1, regardless of when exactly it adopted. Second, estimated regression coefficients are difficult to interpret: quite clearly they will depend crucially on the (arbitrary) date of research (i.e. d^*). In the long run, of course, the dependent variable will assume the same value, namely 1, for all firms. For the record, both authors find firm size and the age of the firm's president to be significant determinants, although Globerman employs a rather strange quadratic formulation for firm size. Globerman also reports a significant influence of the profitability of adoption. In both cases $\overline{R}^2$ are rather low.

In chapter 6 of the present study this problem is reconsidered and an alternative empirical methodology is suggested.

12 Unfortunately, one of the most important explanatory variables used in the cross-section stage is the date at which the innovation 'took-off' in the country concerned. Swan defines this as the date at which the fitted logistic predicts 10% diffusion. From equation (2.4) this is $-(2.2 + \hat{a})/\hat{\beta}$. It is unsurprising that this variable should be a highly significant determinant of the dependent variable, $\hat{\beta}$.

13 Yet these two types of decision will surely be influenced by different sets of variables. To give an obvious example, uncertainty will clearly have an important influence on any firm's initial adoption decision (and, thus, on inter-firm diffusion); on the other hand, the age distribution of a firm's existing capital stock and the growth of its output will probably be more important in determining how rapidly that firm adopts further computers (i.e. intra-firm diffusion). The stock adjustment approach loses much of its appeal if only inter-firm diffusion is to be considered because n_t is no longer the equilibrium stock but is, instead, the total number of potential adopters. If this is taken as constant (as in the Mansfield approach), there remains little to commend the stock adjustment approach.

14 Probit analysis has long been used in Biology and other sciences to analyse such things as the efficacies of different dosages of poisons in exterminating insect populations. See also Pyatt (1964) for an extentsion of the probit model which generates the stock adjustment model as a special case in the present context.

15 The formal intermediate steps are not presented here but they may be found in any of the works mentioned above, for example, Cramer (1969, pp. 36–7).

16 Having said this, an *explanation* of the parameters of the critical incomes distribution is still required, even if their role within the model is quite explicit.

CHAPTER 3

1 Of the 22 sample innovations, the time series data on diffusion was provided for 12 by N.I.E.S.R. For 3 more in the Lancashire textile industry, Metcalfe's study (1970) has proved an invaluable source and for one other, Tufted Carpet Machines, Tom Scott generously provided information from his own Ph.D. thesis. Data on the remaining 6 innovations has been collected from various trade and scientific publications.

2 The scarcity of readily available data on diffusion prevents the luxury of a random sample. The selection of industries and innovation for inclusion in this sample has been based on the accessibility of data, subject to the condition that no broad sector of manufacturing should be substantially over-represented.

3 But see Ray's discussion of Float Glass (chapter 7 in Nabseth and Ray, 1974), for an example of such an innovation.

4 See Davies (1976, chapter 3) for a fuller discussion.

5 But see a footnote mention in Mansfield (1968, p. 160), which Mansfield subsequently ignores. Furthermore, elsewhere he explicitly assumes the absence of scale economies (1963a, p. 292). See also Rosenborg, (1976, p. 526), for another brief (footnote) mention of this possibility. By far the most rigorous analysis of scale economies for a new process innovation is provided by Stoneman (1976, pp. 60–5) in his study of computers.

6 It is argued that this rule applies to most equipment which consists of cylinders, spheres, tanks, tubes etc. In such cases (mostly process equipment) production capacity is determined by volume, whilst capital costs depend more on the surface area of the vessels. Surface area, after all, dictates the quantities of materials and physical effort needed to construct the equipment. Basic mathematics show that to increase volume, surface area needs to be increased by only two thirds as much.

7 One implicit assumption of engineering data is that large installations do not take longer to construct. If in reality they do, then higher interest costs could reduce the extent of scale economies. Similarly, it is assumed that wage rates are insensitive to the scale of installation.

8 Hirsch (1956), Enos (1958) and Hartley (1965) have each established the quantitative importance of the learning effect over a wide range of industrial products, and Arrow (1962) has traced some of the implications for macro economic growth. It is interesting to note, further, that nineteenth-century economists, including Marx, were well aware of the significance of such learning effects (see Rosenborg, 1976, p. 525).

9 Both pieces of information were provided in communications from the innovation suppliers.

10 For a fuller discussion of this evidence see Davies (1976, appendix 1).

11 From the technical literature, the sample may be split into three roughly equal parts: eight innovations being obvious group A types and seven being obvious group B, the remaining seven innovations share some characteristics with both groups and are thus referred to below as 'unclassified'. See table 3.1 for the make-up of these groups.

12 This effect is also noted by Rosenborg (1976, p. 528).

13 In some senses the reverse occurred in the case of Continuous Casting: after a long period of experimentation and teething troubles, it became increasingly clear that the profitability of the process was particularly sensitive to many different technical characteristics of the potential adopter. Whilst this did not

rule out some firms from adopting, it certainly revised downwards expectations of profitability under certain operating conditions. See U.N.E.C.E. (1969).

14 This term derives from the improvements in sailing ships that followed the first introduction of steam ships. See Freeman (1975, p. 47) and Rosenborg (1976, p. 581).

15 For fuller technological description, see Davies (1976, appendix 1).

CHAPTER 4

1 The term potential adopter is used extensively throughout this study. In some industries certain firms are prevented from adopting new processes for purely technological reasons. For example, certain types of clay cannot be used in Tunnel Kilns because their high carbon content makes control of firing impossible. Such firms are quite clearly not potential adopters (see the appendix on data sources, section A.1.1).

2 For most process innovations there will be less than 100 potential adopters: this may be contrasted with the millions of potential adopters of most new consumer durables.

3 From questionnaires asking firms for the major sources of substantive information concerning a new innovation (Special Presses in papermaking), see Nabseth and Ray (1974, chapter 4).

4 See Rosenborg (1976) for a convincing discussion of the relevance of expectations of further technological improvements in the diffusion context.

5 In extreme cases, new innovations may actually be *resented* when they are seen as threatening the craft-base of the firm or industry concerned. For an interesting example of this phenomenon in the engineering industry see Mansfield et al. (1971, p. 201).

6 Mansfield (1968, p. 156) and Scherer (1971, chapter 15) provide comprehensive references and surveys of the literature on firm size and 'progressiveness'.

7 Although (4.1) is couched in terms of pay-offs, the specifications of ER and R^* below are sufficiently general to allow their reinterpretation as rates of return. However, it will be noted that since the pay-off interpretation is to be employed here, ER will be inversely related to the profitability of adoption and larger values for R^* imply *less* stringent yardsticks.

8 The multiplicative form of (4.2) is largely arbitrary but it does imply, realistically, that the effects on ER of any one characteristic will depend on the levels of all other characteristics in the firm.

9 It seems likely that most firms will initially underestimate the profitability of adoption especially as they have no way of knowing that the innovation will later prove to be a success. (This assumption clearly restricts the model to 'successful' innovations.)

It might be argued that ER could increase over time if early adoption produces super-normal profits, whilst late adoption merely transforms the firm in question from a position of loss-making into one of earning normal profits. However, even in the unlikely event of no vintage-to-vintage improvements, there is no reason why the increase in net revenue from adoption will not be the same ceteris paribus in both cases.

10 Clearly, the scrapping decision differs from the adoption decision, to the extent that capital outlays are not involved. Thus scrapping will only occur when the resale value of the equipment involved exceeds the expected net revenues over

the planning period plus any disruption costs involved. There is no certainty that this condition will be satisfied merely because readoption is considered insufficiently profitable.

11 Clearly (4.6) only misrepresents the condition for ownership if there exist firms (adopters) who are dissatisfied with the innovation, but who continue to employ the innovation given that the inital outlay is irretrievable (apart from any resale value). These firms may be dubbed 'regretters'. Undoubtedly one cannot be sure that such firms do not exist, even for successful innovations. On the other hand, the questionnaires, trade sources and journals used to construct the time series data on the diffusion of the sample innovations (as outlined in the appendix on data sources) have revealed no instances of such firms, even although in some cases firms were specifically questioned on this possibility.

12 It might be noted that this discussion has wider implications than for merely the present model and sample. This revised form of the ownership condition is analogous to that employed in previous probit models of the diffusion of new consumer durables (see, for instance, equation 2.25). In that context it is suggested that the probability that consumer i will own the durable at t is equal to the probability that his income is not less than some critical or tolerance income. Thus we are asked to assume that an adopter at time τ ($< t$) will only continue to own, say, a T.V. at t if his income continues to exceed his tolerance level. This clearly ignores the possibility that i may continue to use his T.V., purchased at τ, even when his income, or critical income, has changed subsequently so as to rule out adoption at t, if given the choice over again. As in the present context, this partial sacrifice of reality to analytical convenience may be unimportant so long as tastes continue to move strongly in favour of the durable (process), but where an alternative durable (process) emerges, or where income (firm size) changes significantly, there is a risk of disadoption which, as indicated above, is typically overstated by formulations such as (2.25) or (4.6).

13 It should be noted that, as usual when invoking the central limit theorem, one cannot be certain that all the (X and Y) variables are truly independent. For instance, it is probable that the educational attainment of managers will influence both information receptiveness and, perhaps, investment targets employed. It is believed, however, that there are a sufficiently large number of firm characteristics which are not common to both sets to justify the use of this theorem here.

As it happens, it is possible to test the lognormal hypothesis for ϵ_t and, as can be seen in chapter 6, there is no evidence for rejecting it for any of the sample innovations.

14 The theoretical case for the lognormal, in this context, rests on the assumption of Gibrat's 'law of proportionate effect' (Gibrat, 1931). This law has a number of implications which have been tested using various data by Hart (1962), among others. It is probably fair to claim that these implications are only broadly consistent with the observed facts. In more recent years, a number of authors have suggested various modifications to the law which increase its realism at the cost of generating more complex size distributions; for instance, Simon and Bonini (1958) and Saving (1963) show that the Yule and four parameter lognormal distributions, respectively, are perhaps more realistic. Under these circumstances, the case for assuming the simple two parameter lognormal must rest with its ability to approximate distributions observed in the real world.

On this count there is some controversy, largely arising from differences between researchers over what constitutes a 'reasonable' fit (see Hart and Prais (1956), Simon and Bonini (1958), Quandt (1966), Silbermann (1967) and Engwall (1974) for instance). In general, however, the following conclusions may be drawn from past empirical work. First, virtually all observed distributions are positively skewed and may be adequately described by one of the theoretical distributions generated by different versions of the law of proportionate effect. Second, of all the common skewed distributions, the lognormal offers the best overall fit for most industries (even the most exacting of statistical tests suggest it is appropriate for half of the industries analysed). Third, in those cases where the lognormal seems to be empirically inappropriate, it is nearly always the extreme upper tails of observed distributions which deviate from lognormality. However, for the purposes of aggregation (as advocated here), the upper tail has no special significance (unlike in the most common application of the lognormal assumption, i.e. in measuring industrial concentration). It seems unlikely, if $F_t(S)$ is approximated by the lognormal, that minor inaccuracies in $F_t(S)$ at high levels of S will lead to serious errors in Q_t. After all, $F_t(S)$ will, typically, be very small for large values of S.

15 See Davies (1976, appendix 5) for a fuller discussion and presentation of the data used in these tests. The estimates of σ_{st}^2 are presented in table 7.1 in the present study. Because of the immense amount of data collection involved, the assumption of lognormality was only tested for one year's data in each case.

16 Both the cumulative normal and the logistic curves are symmetrical with a point of inflexion at 50%. The main difference is in the relatively longer tails of the logistic. See Johnson and Kotz (1970, pp. 1–18) for a more detailed comparison of these two curves.

17 Industry size is, of course, the product of average firm size and firm numbers (n). In the case of a lognormal size distribution, average size is given by: exp $(\mu_{st} + \frac{1}{2}\sigma_{st}^2)$. Thus the logarithm of S_{It}/S_{I0} may be written as:

$$\log(n_t/n_0) + (\mu_{st} + \tfrac{1}{2}\sigma_{st}^2) - (\mu_{s0} + \tfrac{1}{2}\sigma_{s0}^2).$$

Equation (4.28) then follows, if firm numbers and size inequalities remain constant over time. As explained in the appendix (table A.1), for the only two sample industries in which significant entry or exit has occurred over the diffusion period, those firms exiting or entering have been excluded from the analysis. Thus industries have been defined so as to possess stable n.

18 The thrust of the following argument would be weakened if it could be shown that equations derived from a model based on (4.6) would tend to *over*-estimate $1/\beta(\log\theta_t - \log\theta_{t-1})$. However, to the extent that (4.6) will err, if at all, on the side of *under*-stating the true probability of adoption (i.e. diffusion level) at t, intuition would suggest that these estimates might tend to *under*-state $1/\beta(\log\theta_t - \log\theta_{t-1})$ which, crudely, reflects the pace of diffusion. Having said this, intuition is not always to be trusted and at any event, the use of point estimates in the ensuing analysis can provide little more than a rough feel for the magnitudes involved.

19 It should be noted that the value of θ_t will vary over the diffusion period for group A innovations and for the group B innovations for which a strong significant cyclical factor has been observed in θ_t (see table 5.3).

20 Indeed, without this rough stability of the ϵ_{it}, it would be difficult to sustain

another important assumption of the basic model, namely, constant variance for $\epsilon_{it}(\sigma^2)$ over time (see equation (4.21).

CHAPTER 5

1 Finney (1947) and Aitchison and Brown (1957, chapter 7) both advocate the use of maximum likelihood. Berkson (1955 and 1957) prefers the minimum normit χ^2 method. Both methods have been shown to yield asymptotically efficient estimates (Taylor, 1953, pp. 85–92) but there is some disagreement about their small sample properties. Berkson (1957), using a hypothetical small sample experiment, has found that both methods yield bias, which is quite small, but that the variances of the estimated coefficients are smaller for minimum normit χ^2. However, Finney (1947) reports some experiments of Cramer's which come out in favour of maximum likelihood. Mansfield (1968, p. 141) also prefers the minimum logit method which is equivalent to minimum normit χ^2 when estimating logistic curves.

The basis of the method lies in minimizing:

$$\Sigma n_t (z_t - \hat{z}_t)^2 W_t^2 \big[(m_t/n_t)(n_t - m_t)/n_t \big]^{-1}$$

where z_t is now to be defined as the normal equivalent deviate of (m_t/n), $\hat{z}_t$ is the predicted normal deviate and W_t is the ordinate of the standard normal curve at the point where its area is divided into (m_t/n) and $1 - (m_t/n)$. This may be achieved by using weighted least squares regression, each observation being weighted by $n_t W_t^2 \big[(m_t/n_t)(n_t - m_t)/n_t \big]^{-1}$. Conveniently, these weights have already been tabulated by Berkson (1957). For further discussion, see Berkson (1955), Finney (1947) or Davies (1976, pp. 6.2–6.5)

2 The ordinary least squares formula for $\hat{a}$ is: $\hat{a} = \bar{z} - \hat{b}\bar{t}$ in equation (5.4b) for instance. Thus, $\hat{a}$ does depend on t, and, therefore, also on the choice of origin for t. A similar problem is faced when fitting the logistic curve.

3 This implies that the time lag between the supplier's decision to commercially produce the innovation (at $t = 0$) and the first actual adoption does not exceed 5 years. This seems reasonable for all of the sample innovations although, as stated already, the exact date of the manufacturer's decision is rarely known.

4 Numerical control of machine tools is a good example of an 'unclassified' innovation: typically, it is technically complex but relatively inexpensive and can be built off-site; furthermore, it does not require a lengthy installation period on the adopter's site.

Interestingly, these three groups could have been predicted exactly by ranking the innovations according to cost and defining all those costing in excess of £100,000 as group B and all those costing less than £15,000 as group A. The remaining unclassified group each cost between £20,000 and £50,000 (assuming Shuttleless Looms to be installed in batches). These figures are only approximate and, in general, refer to late 1960s prices. See table 3.1 for more details.

5 The $\hat{a}_j$ are not reported as they are sensitive to the arbitrary choice of time origin (see section 3).

6 In fact, Theil has shown (1965, pp. 212–14) that comparison of $\bar{R}^2$ will lead 'on the average to the correct choice' (that is, an incorrect specification will record an $\bar{R}^2$ lower, or at least not higher, than the 'true' model on average). At first

sight this adds some support for the argument that this simple test establishes the model as superior to the logistic. But as Pesaren (1974, p. 154) points out, Theil's proof does require that the true model should satisfy all the characteristics of the classical regression model. This assumption may well not be justified here.

For the record, it may be noted that the lognormal and normal curves, when used for appropriate innovations, record higher $\bar{R}^2$ than when used for inappropriate innovations (columns 3 and 5 of the table). Again, in 13 of the 15 cases.

7 NC may be applied to many different types of machine tools used in most sectors of the engineering industry. The complexity of the technology in the early years was probably accentuated by the decision of British manufacturers to concentrate on perfecting contouring control – the most sophisticated type of application (Ray, 1969, p. 53).

8 See the earlier comments in section 3. It might be noted from the data sources given in the appendix on data sources that most of the innovations in table 5.3 are those for which reasonably adequate data on S_{Ijt} was available.

9 Initially, the main advantage of VD lay in its ability to remove hydrogen in the production of steel and, because this advantage is more crucial for certain types of steel than others, the process was much more desirable for some firms than others. As the technology developed, however, another major technical advantage emerged: more efficient deoxidization of steel. This property is highly desirable for virtually all steel makers. In terms of the model, this development should have produced not only a decline in mean (ER) but also in its variance. For CC, the reverse was true; after a long period of experimentation and teething troubles, it became increasingly clear that (ER) was particularly sensitive to many different technical characteristics of the potential adopter, and it is probable that the variance of (ER) increased significantly over the diffusion period. See Flux (1965) and Holden (1969) for relevant discussions for VD and Schenk (Ch. 9 in Nabseth and Ray (1974) and U.N.E.C.E. (1969) for CC. See also Davies (1976) for a summary of this evidence.

10 As a negatively skewed curve implies an acceleration over time for z and a positively skewed curve implies a deceleration, fitting the linear relationship (5.4b) to such data would generate the residuals actually observed for VD and CC.

11 Whilst reliable data on the output of the lancashire weaving industry is hard to come by, it is known that 'Total yarn sized' declined by 50% between 1948 and 1966 (Metcalfe, 1969).

CHAPTER 6

1 Unfortunately, even this finding is open to some question due to statistical problems in most previous research (see section 2.4.2).

2 In fact the model *could* be broadened to include other identified determinants of the expected and target pay-offs (ER and R^*.) Partly because of data problems and partly for reasons of analytical simplicity, this has not been pursued. If, however, say E, the educational attainment of managers was included as an explicit determinant of ER and R^* in equations (4.2) and (4.4), then similar predictions could be derived for the relationship between probability of ownership and E as have been for firm size.

3 The one innovation for which it is impracticable to estimate the curve is Automatic Track Lines. This is because of the low number of potential adopters. See note ¶ to table 6.1 for the alternative approach employed in this case.

4 Strictly, the choice of estimating technique should lie between maximum likelihood and the minimum normit χ^2 method (for reasons identical to those discussed in the previous chapter.) As a crude reflection of the weighting schemes employed by these estimators, in drawing the lines, more weight has been attached to central observations (for which $\bar{P}_{kt}$ is close to 0.5) than to observations with very low or high $\bar{P}_{kt}$ (see Aitchison and Brown, 1957).

5 For instance, for Special Presses, $(\widehat{\sigma/\beta}) = 1.7$ in 1966; 1.825 in 1968 and 1.825 in 1970.

6 Estimates of σ_{st}^2 are provided in table 7.1 of the following chapter. As these estimates have been computed for only one year in the diffusion period (which need not necessarily coincide with the years for which (σ/β) have been estimated), an assumption of rough constancy over time for *either* variance is required for the R^2s to be strictly applicable. Given the generally satisfactory performance of the basic model (which assumes constant σ_s and σ) in the time series empirics, this is probably not too bad an assumption.

7 This assumption has already been criticized in section (2.4.2).

8 This follows from the fact that i will have adopted j when $(R^*/ER)_{ijt} = 1$ (assuming this ratio increases monotonically with time, as is almost certain given earlier specifications).

9 This is presumably accidental on Mansfield's part: his work on inter-firm differences and the aggregate diffusion curve are quite separate, although the same innovations are considered.

   The result derived in the text may be obtained alternatively as follows. If, in (6.12), both S_{ij} and U_{ij} are lognormally distributed, then so too is d_{ij} (Aitchison and Brown, 1957, p. 11). Therefore, assume log d_{ij} to be normally distributed with mean M and variance V. Since the proportion of firms having adopted t years after the introduction of the innovation is equal to the probability that $d_j < t$, then the cumulative lognormal diffusion curve follows:

$$(m_{jt}/n_j) = P(d_j < t) = \Lambda(t\,|\,M, V) = N(\log t\,|\,M, V)$$

10 It is worth recalling the deficiencies of the data used to compute the δ_j (in fact, for EH, ASB and ADH no estimates are possible, see section 5.3.3). Fortunately δ_j are typically sufficiently low for errors to have little influence on $(\beta/\phi)_j$.

CHAPTER 7

1 Thus b assumes an analogous role to the slope parameter of the logistic curve in most previous research on diffusion, see section 2.2.

2 It should be recalled that for firm i, at time t, ER_{it} and R_{it}^* are, respectively, the expected pay-off from adopting and the target pay-off period against which potential adoption in assessed. Thus the ratio R^*/ER should grow more rapidly, the faster potential adopters revise *upwards* their expectations of profitability and revise *downwards* the targets which they require to be fulfilled if adoption is to occur. Similarly, the variance in this ratio will be greater, the larger are inter-firm differences in expectations and targets.
See chapter 4 for more detailed discussions.

3 Note that (*a*) and (*b*) will probably operate mainly so as to increase expected profitability (i.e. depress *ER*) over time, whilst (*c*) will govern the rates at which targets are relaxed (i.e. at which R^* increases over time.)

4 In terms of the behavioural theory, more profitable innovations are more likely to be seen as potential solutions to non-fulfilment of goals.

5 In fact the capital cost (that is the investment outlay required for adoption) is likely to be a reasonable proxy for technical complexity: certainly an intuitive ranking of the complexities of the sample innovations corresponds closely with their ranking by K_j. Rather more weakly, one might suspect some correlation between K_j and β_j to the extent that scale advantages are more pronounced on larger and more expensive processes.

6 Ideally, barriers to entry and the extent of product differentiation might also be included here. Unfortunately lack of reliable data rules out such measures for most of the sample industries. See Davies (1978) for a fuller discussion of the *U* index and its properties.

7 As is essential for any meaningful measure of concentration.

8 For instance, it has been suggested earlier that β_j may vary with K_j. If so, regression estimates of a_{32} and a_{33} in (7.17) and (7.18) will reflect the *net* influence of K_j.

9 See tables 5.1–5.4. For EH, the estimate of b_j from the 1935–47 sub-period is used, as are the sub-period (1962–70) estimates for NCTN and NCTB. Given the inapplicability of the cumulative lognormal to the group B innovations and one group A innovation, WSB, it would be quite incorrect to include these innovations in the cumulative lognormal group.

10 In fact, as estimates of δ_j are unavailable for three of the innovations, EH, ADH, ASB (for reasons given in section 5.3.3), estimates of $(\widehat{\psi/\beta})_j$ derived using (7.13) can only be calculated for 11 of these innovations. However, rather than discard these three innovations from the sample, regressions have been fitted using $\left[(\psi/\beta)_j + \delta_j \right]$ as the dependent variable. Fortunately $\hat{\delta}$ typically, takes on such small values for the other 11 innovations that there is little or no difference between the two variables. (Indeed for these 11 innovations, estimated coefficients and $\bar{R}^2$ are almost identical when fitting 7.17 to the two alternative dependent variables.)

11 For EH, ADH and ESB, δ is arbitrarily given the value of 0. However, when these innovations are excluded from the sample, the estimated coefficient on δ is virtually unchanged.

12 When equation 4 was re-estimated for the group B innovations only, there was little change in estimated coefficients (equation 5). This may be viewed as a crude sort of sensitivity analysis.

13 Equation 6 was estimated employing the restriction that the coefficients on $\log N_j$ and σ_{sj}^2 should be equal but of opposite signs. From the earlier discussion of the *U* index (see equations 7.14 and 7.15) this is the equivalent to the use of the Herfindahl index of concentration.

14 These surprisingly long periods are heavily influenced by a few very slow diffusing innovations in both cases.

15 Involving the calculation of the elasticity of the time lag with respect to b_j.

16 See Chapter 2, section 3. Surprisingly, when Mansfield's estimating equation (2.15) was fitted to the slope parameters of the logistic curves reported in table 5.1 of this study, neither explanatory variable was significant. This may be accounted for by the fact that dummy intercept terms could not be used here.

Either way, these results (Davies, 1976, chapter 8) cast further doubt on the applicability of the logistic curve.

17 Which therefore requires the assumption that *all* innovations have diffusion curves that can be approximated by the logistic.

18 Which means that it is impossible to allocate rent to any one part of the now divisible plant.

CHAPTER 8

1 The variance of log size has long been argued to be a good measure of size inequalities. See Gibrat (1931) and Hart and Prais (1956).

2 For the record, within the present sample, the simple correlation coefficient between H and b for the lognormal group of innovations is -0.013 and for the normal group -0.232. But if the present argument is accepted, these correlations have little meaning, being peculiar to this particular concentration measure and this particular sample. Moreover, the correlation coefficient measures only the strength of *linear* relationship. The present model suggests, of course, that neither N nor σ_s^2 is linearly related to b.

3 Defined to be the ratio of the area between the 45° line and the Lorenz curve to the area under the 45° line.

CHAPTER 9

1 In fact some further, indirect, support for this finding can be derived from Mansfield's (1961) and Metcalfe's (1970) apparently conflicting evidence already reported in section 2.3. Mansfield, studying the diffusion of 12 major innovations, has found that the symmetrical logistic curve (not unlike the cumulative normal in its shape) provides an adequate description of time series diffusion. Metcalfe, on the other hand, has found that the skewed logarithmic reciprocal transformation (quite similar to the cumulative lognormal) provides a fair fit for his three innovations. Quite clearly, the technical descriptions of these innovations provided by the authors establish that Mansfield's innovations are, with only one exception, group B and Metcalfe's, all group A.

2 This distinction between the size effect and any other influence of industry growth on diffusion speed can be best identified by recalling the definition of diffusion speed, b_j, in chapter 7. Because of the size effect, δ_j appears automatically in the numerator of b_j; any other influence of δ_j, the trend growth rate of industry output, must work through ϕ_j.

3 Unfortunately, lack of suitable data has ruled out the possibility of testing a number of other interesting hypotheses under this general heading. For example, the influence of changing relative factor prices remains unexplored, although the different hypotheses about manufacturers' learning by doing do acknowledge the possibility that the growth path of innovation price may differ between innovations. This general problem of data deficiencies arises mainly because of the narrow industry definitions used in this study.

4 The exception being, of course, the distinction drawn between the suppliers' learning curves for group A and group B innovations. However, pricing behaviour and the possibility of capacity shortages have been largely ignored, partly to retain the simplicity of the theoretical framework.

References

Adams, W. and Dirlam, J. (1966), 'Big Steel, Invention and Innovation', *Quarterly Journal of Economics*, May 1966.

Aitchison, J. and Brown, J. (1957), *The Lognormal Distribution*, Cambridge University Press, 1957.

Arrow, K. J. (1962) 'The Economic Implications of Learning by Doing', *Review of Economic Studies*, June 1962.

Bailey, N. (1957), *Mathemical Theory of Epidemics*, Griffin, London, 1957.

Bain, A. (1964), *The Growth of T.V. Ownership in the U.K. since the War*, Cambridge University Press, 1964.

Barnard, G. (1971), 'Foils, their Efficiency on a Slow Machine', *Paper Technology*, April 1971.

Barraclough, K. C. (1969), 'The Newer Specialist Steelmaking and Steel Refining Processes', *Journal of the Iron and Steel Institute*, June 1969.

Bartholomew, D. J. (1970), *Stochastic Models for Social Processes*, Wiley, London, 1970.

Berkson, J. (1955), 'Estimate of the Integrated Normal Curve by Minimum Normit Chi-Square', *Journal of the American Statistical Association*, June 1955.

(1957), 'Tables for Use in Estimating the Normal Distribution Function by Normit Analysis', *Biometrica*, 1957.

Blaug, M. (1963), 'A Survey of the Theory of Process Innovations', *Economica*, February 1963.

Bonus, H. (1973), 'Quasi-Engel Curves, Diffusion and the Ownership of Major Consumer Durables', *Journal of Political Economy*, May/June 1973.

Brisby, B. (1964), 'Process Selection in the Steel Industry', *Journal of the Iron and Steel Institute,* September 1964.

Bruni, L. (1964), 'Internal Economies of Scale with a Given Technique', *Journal of Industrial Economics*, June 1964.

Carter, C. and Williams, B. (1957), *Industry and Technical Progress*, Oxford University Press, 1957.

(1958), *Investment in Innovation*, Oxford University Press, 1958.

Chow, G. (1967), 'Technological Change and the Demand for Computers', *American Economic Review*, 1967.

Cramer, J. S. (1969), *Empirical Econometrics*, North Holland, Amsterdam, 1969.

Crookall, J. R. (1968), *Technical and Economic Aspects of Numerical Control*, Machine Tools Trader Association, June 1968.

Cruden, E. and Wild, C. (1971), 'Synthetic Forming Wires: Progress Design and Development', *The Paper Maker*, April 1971.

Cyert, R. and March, J. (1963), *A Behavioural Theory of the Firm*, Prentice Hall, New Jersey, 1963.

Czepiel, J. (1974), 'Word of Mouth Processes in the Diffusion of a Major Technological Innovation', *Journal of Marketing Research*, 1974.

Data Systems (1973), *Data Systems*, 'Composing Room Controller', April 1973.

David, P. A. (1975), *Technical Choice, Innovation and Economic Growth*, Cambridge University Press, 1975.

Davies, S. W. (1971), The Clay Brick Industry and the Tunnel Kiln', *National Institute Economic Review*, November 1971.

    (1976), 'The Diffusion of New Process Innovations in U.K. Manufacturing Industries', Ph.D. Thesis, University of Warwick, 1976.

    (1978), 'Measuring Industrial Concentration: An Alternative Approach', mimeograph, Sheffield University, 1978.

    (1979), 'Choosing between Concentration Indices: The Iso-concentration Curve', *Economica*, Feb. 1979.

Davies, S. W. Smith, R. J. and Lacci, L. (1974), 'Tunnel Kilns in Brickmaking' in Nabseth and Ray (1974).

Elliott Automation (1966), 'Paper Making', 1966.

Engwall, L. (1974), *Models of Industrial Structure*, Lexington Books, New York, 1974.

Enos, J. L. (1958), 'A Measure of the Rate of Technological Progress in the Petroleum Refining Industry', *Journal of Industrial Economics*, June 1958.

Finney, D. (1947), *Probit Analysis, a Statistical Treatment of the Sigmoid Response Curve*, Cambridge University Press, 1947.

Flux, J. (1965), 'Vacuum Degassing', *Journal of the Iron and Steel Institute*, December 1965.

Freeman, C. (1975), *The Economics of Industrial Innovation*, Penguin, London, 1975.

Gaddum, J. M. (1945), 'Lognormal Distributions', *Nature*, 1945.

Gebhardt, A. (1974), 'Numerically Controlled Machine Tools', in L. Nabseth and G. F. Ray, *The Diffusion of New Industrial Processes*, Cambridge University Press, 1974.

Gibrat, R. (1931), *Les Inégalités Economiques*, Paris, 1931.

Glaister, S. (1974), 'Advertising Policy and Returns to Scale in Markets where Information is Passed between Individuals', *Economica*, May 1974.

Globerman, S. (1975), 'Technological Diffusion in the Canadian Tool and Die Industry', *Review of Economics and Statistics*, 1975.

Gold, B., Pierce, W. and Rosseger, S. (1970), 'Diffusion of Major Technological Innovations in U.S. Iron and Steel', *Journal of Industrial Economics*, July 1970.

Griliches, Z. (1957), 'Hybrid Corn: An Exploration in the Economics of Technical Change', *Econometrica*, 1957.

Håkanson, S. (1974), 'Special Presses in Papermaking' in L. Nasbeth and G. Ray', *The Diffusion of New Industrial Processes,* Cambridge University Press, 1974.

Hampson, P. (1971), 'Wet Felt Economics', *The Paper Maker*, March 1971.

Hart, P. E. (1962), 'The Size and Growth of Firms', *Economica*, 1962.

    (1971), 'Entropy and Other Measures of Concentration', *Journal of the Royal Statistical Society, Series A*, 1971.

    (1975), 'Moment Distributions in Economics: an Exposition', *Journal of the Royal Statistical Society, Series A*, 1975.

Hart, P. E. and Prais, S. (1956), 'The Analysis of Business Concentration: A Statistical Approach', *Journal of the Royal Statistical Society, Series A*, 1956.

Hart, P. E., Utton and Walshe, S. (1973), *Mergers and Concentration in British Industry*, Cambridge University Press, 1973.

Hartley, K. (1965), 'The Learning Curve and its Application to the Aircraft Industry', *Journal of Industrial Economics*, March 1965.

Hirsch, W. Z. (1956), 'Firm Progress Ratios', *Econometrica*, April 1956.

Holden, C. (1969), 'Development in the Processing of Liquid Steel', *Journal of the Iron and Steel Institute*, June 1969.

Iron and Steel Board (1963), *Annual Report of the Iron and Steel Board*.

Johnson, N. and Kotz, S. (1970), *Continuous Univariate Distributions – 2*, Houghton Mifflin, Boston, 1970.

Kennedy, C. and Thirlwall, A. P. (1972), 'Technical Progress: A Survey', *Economic Journal*, March 1972.

Leckie, A. and Morris, A. (1968), 'The Effect of Plant and Works Scale on Costs in the Iron and Steel Industry', *Journal of the Iron and Steel Institute*, May 1968.

Lund, P. and Miner, D. (1972), 'The Investment Behaviour of Small Firms' in Research Report 11 to the *Boulton Committee of Inquiry into Small Firms*, 1972.

Manpower Research Unit (1970), *Report on Printing and Publishing*, Department of Employment, London, 1970.

Mansfield, E. (1961), 'Technical Change and the Rate of Imitation', *Econometrica*, 1961.

(1963a), 'The Speed of Response of Firms to New Techniques', *Quarterly Journal of Economics*, May 1963.

(1963b), 'Intrafirm Rates of Diffusion of an Innovation', *Review of Economics and Statistics*, November 1963.

(1968), *Industrial Research and Technological Innovation*, Norton, New York, 1968.

Mansfield, E., Rapaport, J., Schnee, J., Wagner S. and Hamburger M. *Research and Innovation in the Modern Corporation*, Norton, New York, 1971.

Martilla, J. (1971), 'Word of Mouth Communication in the Industrial Adoption Process', *Journal of Marketing Research*, May 1971.

Mellanby, W. R. (1959) in the *Journal of the North-East Coast Institution of Engineers and Shipbuilders*, 1958/9.

Metcalfe, J. S. (1968), 'Diffusion of Innovations in the Lancashire Textile Industry', M.Sc. thesis, University of Manchester, 1968.

(1970), 'Diffusion of Innovations in the Lancashire Textile Industry', *Manchester School*, June 1970.

Nabseth, L. (1973), 'The Diffusion of Innovations in Swedish Industry' in B. R. Williams, *Science and Technology in Economic Growth*, Macmillan, London, 1973.

Nabseth, L. and Ray, G. F. (1974), *The Diffusion of New Industrial Processes: An International Study*, Cambridge University Press, 1974.

Nissan, D. (1969), 'The Development of Special Presses', The Robert Gordon's Institute, Aberdeen, Department of Paper Technology, 1969.

Northam, P. C. (1962), Table VII, p. 302, in *Brewers Guild Journal*, June 1962.

O.E.C.D. (1968), *Gaps in Technology*, Paris 1968.

Ormerod, A. (1963), 'The Prospects of the British Cotton Industry', *Yorkshire Economic Bulletin*, 1963.

Ozanne, U. and Churchill, G. (1968), 'Adoption Research: Information Sources in the Industrial Purchasing Decision', *Proceedings, Fall Conference*, American Marketing Association, 1968.

Pavitt, K. (1971), *The Conditions for Success in Technological Innovation*, O.E.C.D., Paris, 1971.

Pratten, C. F. (1971), *Economies of Scale in Manufacturing Industry*, Cambridge University Press, 1971.

Pesaren, M. H. (1974), 'On the General Problem of Model Selection', *Review of Economic Studies*, 1974.

Pyatt, F. S. (1964), *Priority Patterns and the Demand for Household Durable Goods*, Cambridge University Press, 1964.

Quandt, R. (1966), 'On the Size Distribution of Firms', *American Economic Review*, June 1966.

Ray, G. F. (1969), 'The Diffusion of New Technology', *National Institute Economic Review*, May 1969.

Reynolds, W. A. (1968), *Innovation in the U.S. Carpet Industry, 1947–63*, 1968.

Rogers, E. (1962), *Diffusion of Innovations*, Free Press of Glencoe, New York, 1962.

Romeo, A. (1975), 'Inter-industry and Inter-firm Differences in the Rate of Diffusion', *Review of Economics and Statistics*, 1975.

(1977), 'The Rate of Imitation of a Capital-Embodied Process Innovation', *Economica*, February 1977.

Rosenborg, N. (1971), *The Economics of Technological Change*, Penguin, London, 1971.

(1976), 'On Technological Expectations', *Economic Journal*, September 1976.

Salter, W. (1960), *Productivity and Technical Change*, Cambridge University Press, 1960.

Saving T. (1965), 'The Four Parameter Lognormal, Diseconomies of Scale and the Size Distribution', *International Economic Review*, January 1965.

Scherer, F. (1971), *Industrial Market Structure and Economic Performance*, Rand McNally, Chicago, 1971.

Schmookler, J. (1962), 'Economic Sources of Inventive Activity', *Journal of Economic History*, March 1962.

(1966), *Invention and Economic Growth*, Harvard University Press, 1966.

Scott, T. W. (1975), 'Tufted Carpet Machines and the Carpet Industry', Ph.D. thesis, University of Sussex, 1975.

Silberman, I. (1967), 'On Lognormality as a Summary Measure of Concentration', *American Economic Review*, September 1967.

Simon, H. and Bonini, C. (1958), 'The Size Distribution of Business Firms', *American Economic Review*, September 1958.

Smith, R. J. (1974), 'Shuttleless Looms' in L. Nabseth and G. Ray, *The Diffusion of New Industrial Processes*, Cambridge University Press, 1974.

Stoneman, P. (1976), *Technological Diffusion and the Computer Revolution, The U.K. Experience*, Cambridge University Press, 1976.

(1978), 'Technological Progress, Investment and Diffusion', mimeographed, University of Warwick.

Swan, P. (1973), 'The International Diffusion of an Innovation', *Journal of Industrial Economics*, September 1973.

Taylor, W. F. (1953), 'Distance Functions and the Regular Best Asymptotically Normal Estimates', *Annals of Mathematical Statistics*, 1953.

Theil, M. (1965), *Economic Forecasts and Policy*, North Holland, Amsterdam, 1965.

U.N.E.C.E. (1969), *Economic Aspects of Continuous Casting of Steel*, New York, 1968.

Webster, F. (1970), 'Informal Communication in Industrial Markets', *Journal of Marketing Research*, May 1970.

Weiss, L. (1971), 'Quantitative Studies of Industrial Organisation' in M. D. Intriligator, *Frontiers of Quantitative Economics*, North Holland, Amsterdam, 1971.

Williamson, O. E. (1965), 'A Dynamic Theory of Inter-firm Behaviour', *Quarterly Journal of Economics*, May 1965.

Williams, B. R. (1973), *Science and Technology in Economic Growth*, Macmillan, London, 1973.

Wynn, R. F. and Holden, R. (1975), *An Introduction to Applied Econometric Analysis*, Macmillan, London, 1974.

Index